In 1992, there was an explosion of "stock f̦
moment I set foot in Shanghai until my last da̦ ......, ...
of life wanted to talk to me about the market," Ellen Hertz writes. Her study
sets the stock market and its players in the context of Shanghai society, and
it probes the dominant role played by the state, which has yielded a stock
market very different from those of the West. A trained anthropologist, she
explains the way in which investors and officials constructed a "moral storyline" to make sense of this great structural innovation, identifying a struggle
between three groups of actors – the big investors, the little investors, and
the state – to control the market.

Cambridge Studies in Social and Cultural Anthropology

108

THE TRADING CROWD

Cambridge Studies in Social and Cultural Anthropology

The monograph series Cambridge Studies in Social and Cultural Anthropology publishes analytical ethnographies, comparative works and contributions to theory. All combine an expert and critical command of ethnography and a sophisticated engagement with current theoretical debates.

A list of books in the series will be found at the end of the volume.

Founding Editors
Meyer Fortes, Edmund Leach, Jack Goody, Stanley Tambiah

THE TRADING CROWD

*An Ethnography of
the Shanghai Stock Market*

ELLEN HERTZ
University of Lausanne

CAMBRIDGE
UNIVERSITY PRESS

PUBLISHED BY THE PRESS SYNDICATE OF THE UNIVERSITY OF CAMBRIDGE
The Pitt Building, Trumpington Street, Cambridge, United Kingdom

CAMBRIDGE UNIVERSITY PRESS
The Edinburgh Building, Cambridge CB2 2RU, UK   http://www.cup.cam.ac.uk
40 West 20th Street, New York, NY 10011–4211, USA   http://www.cup.org
10 Stamford Road, Oakleigh, Melbourne 3166, Australia
Ruiz de Alarcón 13, 28014 Madrid, Spain

First published 1998
Reprinted 2000

Printed in the United Kingdom at the University Press, Cambridge

Typeset in Times NR 10/13   [SE]

A catalogue record for this book is available from the British Library

Library of Congress Cataloguing in Publication data
Hertz, Ellen
       The trading crowd: an ethnography of the Shanghai stock market/
Ellen Hertz.
       p.   cm. – (Cambridge studies in social and cultural
anthropology; 108)
       Includes bibliographical references and index.
       ISBN 0 521 56355 0. – ISBN 0 521 56497 2 (pbk.)
       1. Stock exchanges – China – Shanghai. I. Title   II. Series.
HG5790.S53H47   1998
332.64′251132 – dc21   97-23644 CIP

ISBN 0 521 56355 0 hardback
ISBN 0 521 56497 2 paperback

For my families

Contents

Illustrations

Preface

This book is about the Shanghai stock market. It describes the market as it appeared at its earliest stage of development in 1992, a stage which the Shanghainese themselves characterized as "immature." Since that time, significant changes have taken place in the size and complexity of this market. Some but not all of those changes have been documented in the final chapter to this book. If this account is centered on the market's first tentative steps, it is because the ethnographic material which I collected at that moment provides invaluable insights into the deep structure of this new institution and of the society in which it operates.

For Chinese government regulators and Western or Japanese securities firms with toeholds in this market, this is not the ideal public relations pamphlet. I cannot apologize for that fact, though I can say that a genuinely ethnographic account of the New York or Tokyo stock exchanges might not be more flattering. I do wish to emphasize, however, that none of the peculiarities or problems which I discuss can be laid at the doorstep of individuals or even of single institutions. Indeed, it is difficult to find a more savvy and interesting bunch of people than the Shanghainese – government officials and small-time investors alike – who gave so generously of their time to help me come to this understanding of their stock market. The Shanghai market's particular character stems not from its immaturity or from lack of experience on the part of its participants but from its insertion within a complex and quite particular political economic system. If this account conveys even a portion of that complexity, then I will have done what I set out to do.

Acknowledgments

The field research on which this study is based was funded by grants from the Committee for Scholarly Communications with China, the Fulbright-Hayes Doctoral Dissertation Research Fund, and the Committee for Legal Education Exchange with China (1992). I gratefully acknowledge this support. Bob Berring, Stanley Lubman and William Rowe have my special thanks for their encouragement at this early stage. Additional research in the spring of 1995 was funded by the Swiss National Scientific Research Foundation and the Société Académique Vaudoise.

Many friends and relatives have sent me unsolicited material, all of which was immensely helpful. I would like to thank Jean-Paul Bari, Jennifer Beer, Christian Bovet, Sarah Browning, Richard Buxbaum, Michel Chaouli, Chu Tzer-Ming, Don Clarke, David Cole, Dominique Dreyer, Claudia Dubuis, Jean-François Ducret, Selma Ebersman, Donna Goldstein, Louise Hertz, Neil Hertz, Tom Hertz, Mondher Kilani, Li Cheng, Nancy Miller-Randall, René Pahud de Mortanges, Laura Nader, Geneviève Perret, Nina Pillard, Christopher Reed, Anne-Sophie Rieben, Franz Schenker, Pierre Tercier and Jean-Baptiste Zufferey.

Some of the same people and others have kindly read, listened to and discussed with me parts of this book. My thanks go to Jean-Paul Bari, Jennifer Beer, Marie-Claire Bergère, Richard Buxbaum, Don Clarke, David Cole, Clayton Dube, Jonathan Elmer, Sabine Estier, Tom Hertz, Michael Herzfeld, Mondher Kilani, Michel Lackner, Alexandra Morphet, Frank Pieke, Jack Potter, Harro von Senger, Frederic Wakeman, Franz Werro, Susan Whiting and the readers at Cambridge University Press. And again and particularly, to Louise and Neil Hertz. Warm thanks also to Jessica Kuper and Virginia Catmur at Cambridge University Press for their professionalism and patience; and to Jun Zhang for his bold calligraphy.

If my fieldwork was a deeply rewarding experience, this was largely due to the support and friendship of my advisor in Shanghai, Zheng Shao, my research assistant, Zhang Zhongmin, and my friends Li Yihai, Rui Zhefei and Zhang Hongying. Likewise, if writing the thesis on which this book is based was at moments frankly pleasurable, much of the credit goes to the competition, my fine friend Michel Chaouli. The strength of mind and spirit I was faced with in the form of my graduate advisor, Laura Nader, have been a constant source of inspiration and insight. Further thanks go to Judith Aissen, Barbara Johnson and Marjorie Shultz for gracefully fulfilling the involuntary function of role model. And to Franz Werro, for showing me what it means to work. For even more intangible forms of inspiration, I thank Jonathan Elmer (again!), Donna Goldstein, Alexandra Morphet (again!) and Anna Werner. To all of them, I say, in the California idiom, thank you for being you.

Finally, my deepest gratitude goes to two key players: the Shanghainese for their unrelenting interest in the subject of this book, and my husband, Franz Werro, for his unrelenting confidence in its author.

Abbreviations

BS	*Baltimore Sun*
CCP	Chinese Communist Party
FEER	*Far Eastern Economic Review*
IHT	*International Herald Tribune*
KMT (GMD)	Kuomintang (Guomindang), the Chinese Nationalist Party
NYT	*New York Times*
PCMP	Petty capitalist mode of production
SASS	Shanghai Academy of Social Sciences
SHZQ	*Shanghai Zhengquan* (*Shanghai Securities News*)
SSE	Shanghai Securities Exchange
TMP	Tributary mode of production
TN	*The Nation*

Conversion rate

Chinese *yuan* (*renminbi*) to US dollars

Official rate: 5.50:$1.00 (February 1992)
                 5.65:$1.00 (December 1992)

Black market rate: 6.90:$1.00 (February 1992)
                   8.70:$1.00 (December 1992)

Introduction: Ways and means

Ways

This is an anthropological study of the Shanghai stock market based on ten months of ethnographic fieldwork in Shanghai, People's Republic of China, during the year 1992. It documents a particular moment in the history of China's experiments with economic reforms, the moment when this symbolically charged "capitalist mechanism" was first officially promoted on a large scale in one of China's most important cities. It tells the "moral" of the stock market as it evolved over the course of that year, the ways in which its main characters and important events were constructed into a political–moral storyline by Shanghainese investors and government regulators alike.

Comparing notes with colleagues, orally and in print (Golde 1986 [1970], Rabinow 1977, van Maanen 1988), it seems to me that this project has been both unusually easy and unusually difficult. What made it easy was the tremendous interest the Shanghainese themselves showed in my topic. The months of my fieldwork, from February to December of 1992, coincided with the Chinese government's first unambiguous signals in favor of popular participation in the stock market. The result was a movement of "stock fever" (*gupiao re*) of an intensity which China had not experienced since the Republican era. For the majority of people I talked with during that time, it seemed normal, and even desirable, that this historic moment be documented by foreign scholars. From the moment I set foot in Shanghai until my last day there, people from all walks of life wanted to talk to me about the market. They also wanted to talk to each other, and I spent most of my time listening to these conversations and recording the terms in which they took place.

My host institution, the Shanghai Academy of Social Sciences (SASS),

1

responding to this relatively relaxed political climate, encouraged my study and provided me with valuable contacts, including its own talented body of scholars and researchers.[1] Over the course of the year, I was able to interview officials at the principal government agencies responsible for the market in Shanghai – the Shanghai Branch of the People's Bank of China, the Shanghai Bureaux of Taxation and Finance, the Shanghai State Assets Administration Bureau, the Shanghai Structural Reform Commission and the Shanghai Securities Exchange.[2] I also interviewed managers at the four largest securities brokerages in Shanghai at the time (Shenyin, Shanghai International, Haitong and Caizheng), and carried out a month of participant observation in the managing offices of one of these brokerages.[3] I was able to visit a number of the companies listed on the Shanghai Exchange and talk with their officers. Finally, and without too much difficulty, I was also granted interviews with economists and managers involved in stock market regulatory work in Beijing (at the Chinese Academy of Social Sciences, the Stock Exchange Executive Council and the National State Assets Administration Bureau) and in Shenzhen, China's second official stock exchange (at the CDI Market System Institute and Futures and Options Center, and at the Shenzhen Securities Exchange). The difficulties I did encounter were rarely political in nature. Rather, officers and managers working in the new Chinese securities industry had begun to feel the time pressures associated with China's program of economic reforms.[4]

This openness was due to the Communist Party's shift in attitudes towards securities markets, a fact of enormous importance to my study. But, what made "stock fever" a historic moment – or, in the words of one

[1] Until very recently, all foreign researchers in China were required to work through an administrative "host," either a research academy or a university. While many have had their research redirected, delayed or completely blocked by this administrative system of control (see, e.g., descriptions in M. Wolf 1985, Friedman, Pickowicz and Selden 1991, Pieke 1996), my relations with SASS were entirely positive. SASS provided me with convenient living quarters in its guest house, introduced me to my Chinese advisor, research assistant and others, and then left me entirely to my own devices. I take this opportunity to thank the Academy for all that it did and, more importantly, for all that it did not do.

[2] These interviews were carried out in Mandarin Chinese which I speak and read fluently.

[3] In order to preserve anonymity, I have altered certain identifying characteristics of key personalities and institutions in the ethnographic descriptions which make up the body of this book.

[4] The frenzied rhythm of something resembling competitive capitalism – a factor that would make comparable study of a Western stock market a far more arduous affair – had just begun to make itself felt in the urban Chinese context. When I returned to Shanghai for a brief restudy in March–April of 1995, the busy-ness of business had overtaken virtually all of my friends and contacts, and I had a great deal more difficulty getting an hour's worth of conversation out of them.

investor, a "social movement" comparable in scope to the Cultural Revolution – was the remarkable outpouring of enthusiasm for stock trading at the popular level. Thus, the bulk of my time was spent in interviews, meetings and dinners with dozens of investors, rich and poor.[5] These investors were even easier to meet than officials and managers. Throughout the city and throughout the year, the streets in front of brokerage offices were crowded with people, waiting in line to place buy and sell orders, craning to see the small television screens in brokerage lobbies which posted current prices, discussing the market with other investors, gathering information, spreading rumors, selling copies of the multitude of small newspapers and fact-sheets that had cropped up to report on market movements, or just enjoying the "heat and noise" (*re'nao*), the Chinese term for a good time.

During the initial period of my fieldwork, I mulled with these crowds, talking to whomever would talk to me, which was frequently everybody. The problem with these encounters was that most often the crowd turned the tables on me; rather than respond to my questions about their stock market, they wanted to ask me about "mine," and I spent hours answering questions (with more or less accuracy) about how it is that people make money on the New York Stock Exchange. A short time into my stay, however, I had made enough friends and acquaintances to meet with individuals or groups of investors in other settings: at stock "*salons*" where stock market policies were discussed, at adult education classes on the stock market, and over dinners. To control for the representativeness of my data, I tried whenever possible to meet with people from different parts of the city, for though the class character of neighborhoods in Shanghai is not very marked, differences do exist. These meetings provided me with the occasion for the kind of prolonged discussion and observation which typifies the ethnographic method. To supplement interviews and discussion, I asked three of my friends to keep "connections diaries," in which they jotted down notes about all of the people whom they asked for help or who asked them for help with their investing. I also set myself up as an observer in one of the "VIP investors' rooms" that brokerages had opened throughout the city to provide special services to wealthy clients. I spent

[5] These discussions were most often carried out in Shanghainese, which I learned over the course of my fieldwork. By the end of that time, I could understand lectures and group discussions about the stock market, though I confess to difficulties when the conversation turned, for example, to vegetables. I could also begin, though rarely finish, a conversation in Shanghainese, but as virtually all Shanghainese also speak Mandarin, this was not a real hindrance to my research. Speaking Shanghainese was important mainly as a gesture of civility, a kind of deferential showing-off which helped to establish rapport.

four months in full-time conversation with the regulars there, and visited VIP rooms at a number of other brokerages.[6]

Over the course of my research, I carried out two informal surveys, one at the VIP room I visited regularly, another among participants in an adult-education course on stock market investing. Return rates on these surveys were 50 percent and 30 percent respectively, and my research assistant, a graduate student in finance, felt that higher returns would be virtually impossible, as most investors were reluctant to put down in writing answers to questions such as "how much money have you made on your investments in the past six months?". As with all qualitative research, however, the most reliable test of my impressions was saturation – the fact that after a certain amount of interviewing I began to be able to predict the tenor and direction our conversations would take.

What emerged from these conversations was a distinctly "native . . . point of view" (Malinowski 1961 [1922]:25), a set of observations, predictions and concerns that focused on the social and political implications of the new market in shares. Drawing on their analyses of the movements of the market and of the motives of its regulatory agencies and principal players, the Shanghainese – officials, investors and bystanders alike – elaborated interpretations of the nature of state and society, power and wealth, continuity and change, in Shanghai, China and abroad. In this study, I trace the development of one of these interpretations, one that I found central and compelling. I do not insist that only one such storyline exists, that the "native point of view" can be summed up as a single set of attitudes and beliefs. To the contrary, debates over the meaning of the market animated the conversations of literally millions of Shanghainese throughout the period of my fieldwork (see Gamble 1997). However, I do insist that interpreting the meaning of the stock market in socio-political terms was a distinctly Shanghainese preoccupation. It was my good fortune that this preoccupation coincided entirely with my own.

Unusually difficult has been the task of bringing what I observed and absorbed back to a Western audience. Since the beginnings of the discipline, anthropologists have been obliged to challenge Western preconceptions about the nature of social order to explain the societies they were observing. Malinowski (1926) showed that order is possible without law in

---

[6] I should note that the investors in the VIP room which I selected for long-term observation were relatively open to my presence there, as compared with investors in other VIP rooms I visited. This simply means that, as with most ethnography, the data I collected came from people willing to speak with me.

Trobriand society, while anthropologists working in Africa demonstrated that acephalous societies are governed though they possess no institutions that we in the West would recognize as government (Fortes and Evans-Pritchard 1940). However, these anthropologists were describing social structures that had no immediate counterparts at home. What about an object as quintessentially Western as the stock market? What other terms exist to describe a complex financial institution created over four centuries of Western capitalism than those used by Western capitalism itself?

I was faced, in short, with resistance, my own and that in the literature, to the notion that stock markets can be organized along lines other than those laid down by the evolution of Western markets. This was made all the more complicated by China's incomplete but real insertion in the global economy. The Shanghai stock market exists alongside, and in reaction to, financial markets in Tokyo, Hong Kong, London, and New York. The Chinese government's decision to create stock markets was guided by its comparative study of American, western European, and east Asian economic systems. Foreign experts from government (the Chairman of the US Securities and Exchange Commission), from private industry (executives from international banks and brokerages in the US, Taiwan and Switzerland), and from international organizations (such as the International Finance Corporation) were frequent visitors to Shanghai during my year of fieldwork. Furthermore, Chinese investors in Shanghai – who were by no means all Shanghainese – had none of the "stuck" qualities which, as Appadurai (1992) demonstrates, adhere to natives in traditional anthropological ideology: physically, they were frequently mobile, some of them internationally so; culturally, they moved easily between different, sometimes contradictory, social orders; and intellectually, they were well aware of their relative position in the world, that is, they had the self-consciousness necessary to imagine themselves in comparative perspective. I was thus forced to ask myself whether there was such an anthropological thing as a Shanghai stock market, whether this delimitation of my subject matter made any sense, or whether, to the contrary, it was not the creation of a nostalgic wish that some essence of Shanghai still existed for me to uncover. I had to ask myself, as Malinowski did not, what was "native" about the "native point of view"?[7]

---

[7] Following Appadurai's (1992) astute critique of the use of the term "native" in anthropological history, it might seem wrong-headed to rely on it here. If I do so nonetheless, it is because I am not convinced that the notion of the "local," with which "native" has been replaced, carries the weight necessary to counterbalance the often ethnocentric presumptions about imminent "globalization" which are the "local"'s flipside, and this is particularly true in an area such as financial markets (see e.g. Fardon's [1995] frenzied position). Nor, finally, does the term "local" eliminate the ideological tendency to attribute more

Cultural anthropology has traditionally addressed this concern by asserting that culture is not a collection of individual elements (beliefs, myths, behavior, mores) more or less traditional, but rather a coherent and self-sustaining system (Benedict 1934, Geertz 1973, 1983). What the anthropologist observes may be authentically native – in our case, part and parcel of the Shanghainese socio-cultural system of meaning and action – without being traditional, traditionally Shanghainese, traditionally Chinese, or even "Chinese." In the case of Shanghai, China's first modern, cosmopolitan city (Bergère 1986), traditional notions of tradition and Chineseness lose their clarity; in the context of the stock market, they become patently absurd. Obviously, many of the structures, concepts and practices found here are borrowed from the West; Shanghainese speak of bear markets (*xiong shi*) and bull markets (*niu shi*), of turnover rates (*chengjiaoliang*) and price–earnings ratios (*shiyinglu*). However, the argument runs, these structures, concepts and practices are immediately reconfigured to fit their new socio-cultural environment. Through nobody's fault and to nobody's credit, the result is completely and inevitably Shanghainese.

This set of assumptions provides only a partial solution to our problem, and a dangerous one at that, for it easily lends itself to the kind of orientalism which has dogged the discipline since its beginnings.[8] It finesses the question of cultural essence by simply shifting the debate to a higher level of abstraction. The distinctively native does not reside in particular customs or beliefs, we are told, but in the configuration of all customs and beliefs practiced or held within a determined territorial unit; the system secretes its own authenticity. But the question remains: how are we to fix the boundaries between borrowed and native, the boundaries of "the system," both in time and in space? At what moment in twentieth-century Chinese history, for example, did (a certain reading of) Marxism become so incorporated within Chinese culture that it ceased to represent

fixedness to local culture than it might desire or deserve. Ethnographers increasingly find themselves positioned between this particular rock and hard place. For a cushion, though not a solution, see Dakhlia (1995).

[8] A classic example of orientalism in Chinese studies which succinctly illustrates the processes first identified by Said (1978) under this name can be found in Etienne Balazs: "[T]he comparative sociology [of Chinese bureaucracy] has an outstanding virtue: it can be used as a mirror image in reverse of everything that is unique in the history of the West. . . . [A] glance at the social structure of bureaucratic China will be enough to bring to notice a curious reciprocity. Everything convex on one side is concave on the other. One is almost tempted to speak of a European *Yang* and a corresponding Chinese *Yin*" (1964 [1957]:21–22). One is driven to ask the author, "Why not a European *Yin* and a Chinese *Yang*?"

a foreign element and started to function as part of the native system which in turn was to incorporate future foreign elements such as free market economic theory? How much regional difference between cultural configurations is sufficient to qualify them as distinct "systems"; is the Shenzhen stock market, for example, governed by a different "culture," or can it be assimilated to the Shanghai market?[9] Finally, if cultural systems reconfigure all they encounter in native terms, how do we account for change in the overall function and tenor of a given system? In a carefully argued article, Barth raises a similar set of questions for the notion of society, concluding that "[w]hat we have called societies are disordered systems further characterized by an absence of closure" (1992:21).

Today, cultural anthropology can no longer maintain the comfortable assumption that there exists a "system" or, in George Marcus' words, a "Whole" (1990), to which the production of difference can be relegated. Rather, as Marcus suggests, attention has turned to the "ethnography of complex connections," ethnography which takes as its objects of analysis such untraditional matters as markets, social movements, the circulation of money and financial crises (1990:24). Clearly, my study is an offspring of this by now not-so-new movement in anthropology – indeed, I am studying markets, the circulation of money and financial crises under-stood as a social movement in contemporary Shanghai. However, in my view, if this new ethnography is to avoid a relationship to "complex connections" as reified and pernicious as that which traditional ethnography has entertained with "culture" and "society," it must be particularly careful – even more than its traditional counterpart – to take as its starting point "the native point of view." It is the native point of view which provides us with our only reliable entry into the question of how difference is produced and lived in an increasingly complex and connected world.

In short, we must avoid substituting one suspiciously mechanical vision – that of culture-as-system – for another – that of interconnectedness, as if "connections" exist objectively, independently of what "natives" think about and do with them. Alone, neither the culture-as-system nor the complex-connections paradigm helps us understand, for example, why the question of foreign influence in China seems to cause so much distress. A description of late Qing–early Republican China would hardly be complete without mention of the prolonged agony experienced by many of the period's leaders and intellectuals – perhaps, indeed, as Mao Zedong would have insisted, by "the Whole People" – over the question of Chinese

---

[9] For hints at a response, see Hertz (1996a).

culture and its place in the modern world. Neither the boundaries nor the essence of the Chinese "system" were apparent to these thinkers, who felt progressively overwhelmed by contact with Western institutions and ideas. One of the consequences of this distress, of course, was the Chinese Revolution itself, which seemed to provide a solution to the problem of boundaries by reasserting a new cultural system, a "New China," in the face of domination and humiliation by foreign powers. The thirty years of relative isolation which followed were in part structured by this quest for cultural purity. Today, with China's policy of "reform and opening" the question of China's cultural essence – is it "good" or "bad"? – and of her connections with the outside world – are they beneficial or dangerous? – is more than ever a site of confrontation and concern (see Nathan 1993 reviewing Fei 1992, Pye 1992, Schwartz 1985; Tu 1991, Wang 1991 and Wilson 1992; see also *FEER* 1996).

If the systems paradigm – "native" or "global" – produces a flawed description of the way in which people-in-culture live their own particularity, this is because it overlooks a phenomenon of primary sociological importance: power. When the Shanghainese cultural system encounters the capitalist world system, they do not meet on an equal playing field. Rather, capitalism of Euro-American origins is in a position of material and ideological dominance which puts pressures on the Chinese system. The power discrepancy between Chinese and Western-centered cultural systems is a fact of such fundamental importance that it seems to go without saying; indeed, to many Western observers (and Chinese heads of state) there is something indecorous about drawing attention to it.

This point was brought home to me during an encounter which bears retelling here. One of the most frequent (and no doubt silly) questions I asked in my interviews with investors was: "Why are Shanghainese so interested in the stock market?" Virtually everyone I talked with answered this question in the same way: "Because we're poor."[10] Few things irritated me more than this response. At first I simply ignored it. True, I thought, Shanghainese frequently live in crowded, inconvenient and tiring conditions, but they are not poor. By national standards, Shanghainese lead relatively well-to-do lifestyles, lifestyles that compare very favorably to the hardship and deprivation experienced by significant portions of the peasant

---

[10] If this response appears natural, contrast it with the reactions of European friends to whom I told this story. A first answer to the question "why do you invest in the stock market" in France, Switzerland or Germany might well be "Because we're rich." This is just a fleeting illustration of Roy Dilley's point that "representations of exchange are predicted on the recognition of particular forms of personhood and types of social agency" which vary across cultures (1992:2).

population. Neither are they especially poor by world standards. My dismay became more intense when I heard this line from some of my "big player" friends, men and women who had accumulated millions of *yuan* (that is, hundreds of thousands of dollars) on the stock market and elsewhere. I stubbornly set myself the task of explaining to them that they were richer than I was, that if I could not play the market, it was because I simply did not have the extra thousand dollars it took to make a minimum non-laughable investment. Of course, I never succeeded in convincing a single "big player" that, relatively speaking, it was I who was poor.[11] It took a heated argument with a Shanghai friend to make me wonder whether the Shanghainese were not right after all. While I did not have their cash, I had social and cultural capital simply because I came from the part of the world I did. By insisting they were poor, my friends and acquaintances were requiring me to take seriously the power discrepancies in our respective positions.

The question of power in the field is, of course, eminently difficult: it is the site where anthropologists' observations participate in creating the cultural imbalance which they seek to describe. (Indeed, this may be the strongest meaning of the anthropological oxymoron, "participant observation.") Furthermore, power relations in the field are in no sense stable. At the time of my fieldwork I could say without too much hesitation that a sense of Euro-American hegemony structured my encounters with mainland Chinese. A far more complicated situation prevailed in my encounters with Hong Kongese, Taiwanese and Singaporeans whose wealth, education and influence had long since been felt in the international business community. A short five years later, ethnic Chinese throughout the world appear growingly confident that China is on the verge of becoming, if not the center, at least a center of world wealth and power (see Berger 1996). This confidence alters the ethnographic relation significantly; that foreigners should visit China to observe this historic moment can be taken as a tribute to and further sign of China's rising international stature.[12]

---

[11] Indeed, a problem of credibility was posed by their conviction that I must have thousands of loose dollars at my disposal, for the question of why I did not invest them in their market became pressing. I finally realized that unless I offered them an alternative to my proposal that I was simply "poor," I would be seen as irreparably rude and/or stupid. I therefore told them that I was playing the real estate market in Switzerland, which was "hot" these days (indeed, my husband and I were buying an apartment). This straightened things out; yes, it seemed reasonable that real estate in Switzerland might be a better bet than stocks in Shanghai.

[12] Thus, the notion, implicit or explicit in some contemporary writing in anthropology, that the observer occupies a position of dominance, or worse, that observing is itself somehow an act of dominance, is belied by my field experience. If ethnographic observation has frequently smelled of domination in indirect form, this has more to do with the anthropological tradition of "studying down" (Nader 1969) than with the act of observing *per se*.

The question of power is present at every juncture of the ethnographic encounter; whether I liked it or not, framing my study in terms of "the native point of view" meant taking a position in a highly charged political debate. This is because, as Frederick Barth (1969) has demonstrated, issues of intercultural politics and boundaries precede and shape perceptions of intracultural traits and essences. The political contest over the Chineseness of China's experiments with stock markets was visible from the outset. The central government's first calls for experimentation were firmly placed under the banner of developing a "socialist commodity economy" using "stock markets with Chinese characteristics." These statements were instantly dismissed as a foolish exercise in nationalist bravado by the Western mass media. The West had its own parable to tell about China's experiment with financial markets, and with economic reform generally. Ideology must sooner or later give way to "practicality," idealism to individual self-interest. Mao, we were told, forced a billion Chinese to repress their latent money-making tendencies for thirty years, and that pent-up energy burst forth with Deng's "capitalist" reforms.

The Western press made frequent references to "capitalism" in China, with headlines such as "Stock market puts China under a capitalist spell" (*BS* 1992), "Coy capitalists" (*FEER* 1991b), "La Chine adopte le capitalisme rouge" (*Libération* 1992), "Deng's pattern takes shape: Hybrid 'capitalist totalitarianism' for China" (*IHT* 1992b) and "Capitalist leap: China plays the market" (*TN* 1992). (One notes a certain nuancing in more recent headlines such as "The great Shanghai shakedown: 'Capitalism with Chinese characteristics'" (*IHT* 1995u) or "Government edging towards capitalism" (*IHT* 1996c)). What "capitalism" meant in this context went entirely unexplained, signaling anything from the fact that rich individuals existed to the fact that Coca Cola was marketed, or that the pursuit of wealth had become an important social activity. This usage only made sense in the context of the on-going ideological struggle which mainstream Western ideology waged against "utopianism" and "Communism."[13] That the Chinese state never referred to the reforms as "capitalist," but rather as "socialist market reforms" which drew on certain "capitalist mechanisms," thus counted for little.[14] Economic "reality" had led the Communist government to adopt the world's only functional development model – that

---

[13] This was not new. Already in 1937, Thurman Arnold, in *The Folklore of Capitalism*, identified "capitalism" as an empty, though socially central, "polar word" (1937:167–184), that is, a word whose analytic relevance was held hostage to an ideological face-off.

[14] Chinese commentators often participated in, or appeared to participate in, this confused reading of the new "Chinese capitalism." See for example Lee's (1991) often complicit analysis of contemporary mainland economic journals.

of Western capitalism – but "politics" and "ideology" prevented these leaders from acknowledging what they were really doing.[15] As a corollary, it followed that it is impossible to organize a stock market along other than Western lines; the only real stock market is a Western stock market, and the Chinese will have succeeded in their experiment to the extent that they mimic this model.

The "special characteristics" (*teshuxing*) of Chinese markets were a frequent topic of discussion at the popular level as well, though popular discourse took pains to distance itself from self-serving government claims of Chineseness. Among investors, praise and criticism for this new institution often included explicit comparisons with Western markets, or with what they imagined Western markets to be. In the West, they would tell me, you no longer have the fabulous opportunities for making money that we have here, because your investors are already "mature" (*chengshu*). Or: In the West, the government does not intervene in the market, whereas here the state is always interfering (*ganshe*) and messing things up. The question then of what is native about the Shanghai stock market was not merely academic; it was a stake in the debates surrounding the existence and function of this market, at all levels of the social structure, both in China and abroad.

Clarifying the nature and degree of the Shanghai stock market's "Chinese characteristics" means assigning a weight to the "native point of view" in relation to the global discourse of capitalism. This study takes as its starting point the former while recognizing that it exists alongside the positionally dominant point of view of the latter. Furthermore, exercising the prerogatives of dominance, it is the point of view of global capitalism which holds itself out as universal. In other words, we must admit the political–economic force, though not ontological truth, of the claim that the only real stock market is a Western stock market. Quaint reconstructions of a uniquely Chinese approach to finance which fail to incorporate this fact miss the point of China's experiment with financial markets in the first place.

In this ethnography, I begin with the observation that the hegemonic pressures of global capitalism have helped to bring China to experiment

---

[15] What is striking about this parable is its Marxist structure: reality resides at the level of the economic base, which drives change, while secondary processes of explanation and justification are elaborated within the cultural superstructure. On closer analysis, one notes that it is Marx who reproduced, unconsciously and with nuances, the modern Western view of the relation of the economy to society (Sahlins 1976, Dumont 1977, 1983, Bloch and Parry 1989).

with one of its central institutions, markets in securities. Throughout this study, I will point out those moments when these pressures were brought to bear on particular people or institutions, and with what results. However, much more is needed to explain the particular form the Shanghai market took in 1992. This ethnography demonstrates how from its inception the market possessed a distinctive structure such that at the time of my study (and still today) it operated largely independent of and on a different basis from the capitalist world system.

The single most important aspect of China's stock market design which insulated it from international finance capitalism was the creation of two distinct markets for company shares, one for domestic investors ("A" shares) and another for foreigners. This second market, called the "B share market," was authorized in late 1991 as a means of attracting indirect foreign investment. The B share market competes with other markets internationally: with "H-shares" in Chinese companies listed on the Hong Kong Exchange, and with the handful of Chinese shares listed in New York. It also represents one of the markets targeted by the many China- or Asia-based mutual funds available throughout the world. By contrast, "A shares" constitute their own, very distinctive market, for it was and is illegal for non-mainlanders to play the domestic market, and virtually impossible for most mainland Chinese to invest in international markets from Shanghai.

Not only was the domestic market distinct from international markets, it operated along different lines, with different structures, different rules and a different ideological dynamic. This is not to say that the Shanghai stock market represented an example of "socialist market mechanisms with Chinese characteristics," as the current Party ideology would have it. Rather, the Shanghai stock market reflected most saliently the dual operations of what Hill Gates (1996) has labeled the "tributary" and the "petty capitalist" modes of production. It is within this political economic framework that we can identify a properly Shanghainese – and Chinese – stock market discourse and practice.

In her extraordinary study of one thousand years of Chinese economic history, Gates argues that "China, perhaps east Asia as a whole, constitutes an important exception" to the process by which capitalism originating in western Europe has reshaped the world since 1400 (1996:6). Late-imperial China maintained this degree of independence because it was structured by two distinct, though interdependent, logics of social organization of an extraordinary resilience. The first is the "tributary mode of production" (TMP), that political–economic system by which "a class of scholar–officials [. . .] transferred surpluses from the various pro-ducer classes (peasants, petty capitalists, laborers) to themselves by means of direct extraction as tribute, taxes, corvée, hereditary labor duties, and the like" (1996:7). The second, the "petty capitalist mode of production" (PCMP), is that set of regulations, norms and practices by which "free producers transferred any remaining surpluses *among* the commoner classes by means of wage labor and a hierarchical kinship/gender system" (*ibid.*, emphasis in the original). Petty capitalism, while the "motor of Chinese history" (1996:8), its driving force and defining characteristic, never evolved into capitalism proper because it remained

embedded in a dominant tributary mode managed by state officials who put their own requirements for reliable revenues, stable class relations, and continued hege-mony above any perceived need for economic expansion . . . The petty-capitalist mode remain[ed] subordinate, subsumed within the tributary mode, *because* the kinship/gender system crucial to petty capitalism [was] defined and maintained principally by the ruling class as an aspect of its hierarchical control of the entire social formation (1996:8, emphasis in the original).

The TMP/PCMP dialectic lent a particular form to China's class struc-ture and ideology. Corresponding with the dominance of the tributary mode, the primary class division in Chinese society was that between those within and those outside the state system of production and distribution. Reified by the Chinese themselves, this distinction was expressed in terms of a primary division between "the State" and "the People," or as Gates calls them, "the commoners." This picture was complicated by the very real discrepancies in power and wealth that the petty capitalist mode of production generated within the commoner class itself: between parents and children, between wealthy lineages and their poorer cousins, between masters and their indentured servants and slaves, and of course, between men and women at all levels of the social hierarchy. However, these differences were muted by the hegemonic workings of the TMP. By sanc-tioning the dual system of kin- and gender-based class exploitation, state ideology both naturalized the class differences between commoners and guaranteed that these proto-classes never grew beyond the limits of the "patricorporation" (1996:29–38).

For a brief moment in the early part of this century, petty capitalism combined with foreign-imported capitalism proper to produce a genuine threat to this thousand-year-old order. But the Communist Revolution of 1949, far from eradicating the dual TMP/PCMP system of production and distribution, reinforced it in certain crucial ways. In the countryside, Communist cadres quickly abandoned their program of apportioning productive assets equally to each rural adult; rather, they reinstituted the household as the lowest level accounting unit for the distribution of the means of production and its rewards (Stacey 1983). As a result, women and children continued to be subjected to the patriarchal system of exploitation and deprivation which had characterized the TMP/PCMP dialectic of control for centuries, and lent it its special longevity (Potter and Potter 1990:251–269, Gates 1996:246–249).

In urban China, the persistence of a tributary mode of production in modern guise is equally apparent. The increased scale of industry after the Revolution, far from undermining the tradition of state control, provided new avenues for its expression and expansion, reaching an ever greater proportion of the population. Drawing on Andrew Walder's analysis of "Communist neo-traditionalism" (1986) in state-owned industries, Gates argues that key features of these enterprises functioned to reproduce the traditional relations of loyalty and subservience emphasized by the TMP: the absence of a market for labor in the state sector, the fact that "employment [was] a value in itself, with many social services delivered at the state workplace"; and the resulting dependence of workers on the enterprise, on the party and especially on personalistic ties with supervisors (Gates 1996:252). These characteristics apply with equal accuracy to other state-run institutions such as "research institutes, post offices, hospitals, government bureaus, and the military" (*ibid.*:253). Like their late-imperial counterparts, cadres in these state-run institutions subordinate the goal of efficient production to the goals of control, stability and self-promotion. The result has been the increasingly apparent economic stagnation of the state sector, and a growing resentment on the part of those vast proportions of the populations who see state employees as "eating out of the common pot."

China's economic reforms, launched in the countryside in 1981 and in urban areas in 1984, were undertaken largely in response to the internal pressures on the system generated by the TMP/PCMP dialectic. As so many emperors had done before them, Communist reformers faced with declining revenues and popular dissatisfaction (Perry and Wong 1985a) loosed the forces of petty capitalism to produce the surpluses necessary to support the peasantry and the vast tributary state apparatus.[16] Under this analysis China's decision to experiment with the stock market, a mecha-

---

[16] Gates is the only student of Chinese political economy to write in terms of the coexistence of a "tributary" and "petty capitalist" "mode of production," but most commentators recognize that two competing "lines" existed in post-revolutionary China, one emphasizing central planning, the other socialist market mechanisms (see Solinger [1984b]).

nism by which the enormous savings of individual producers could be tapped for investment that was to remain largely under state control, represents a similar, and similarly ambivalent, appeal to the powers of petty capitalism.

There are quarrels one could pick with Gates' scheme, the most important, perhaps, that it is excessively schematic. However, it has the enormous merit of providing a positive description – in the analytical not moral sense – of state power in traditional and contemporary China, and thereby tackling head-on the question of its otherwise inexplicable persistence as the central institution of Chinese society. In this study, I lean heavily on Gates' model to set up the economic and ideological framework in which the new Chinese stock market operated. I stop short, however, of applying it directly to the market itself, for the ethnographic reality is just too complicated, and the analyst too close to its historical significance, to attain this degree of abstraction. While the stock market may well serve to tap the individual savings of petty capitalist producers, it is simultaneously a mass economic institution, bringing with it its own economic and ideological dynamic which rapidly extended beyond the terms Shanghai regulators had set for it. Furthermore, financial market reforms have occurred in the context of the increasing triumphalism of global capitalism, placing indirect but enormous pressure on the tributary mode both as distributive practice and as legitimating ideology. What is distinctive about the Shanghai stock market results from a combination of these internal and external pressures, and from the contradictions they generate. Read anthropologically, this market provides a particularly rich terrain for exploring how Shanghainese, both commoners and state officials, make sense of the contradictory circumstances in which they negotiate their livelihoods.

But this brings me to my second set of difficulties. Stock markets are not a standard topic in anthropology, and the anthropological method is not the standard approach to studying stock markets. Anthropology has not traditionally analyzed complex modern economic institutions such as financial markets because, generally speaking, these institutions did not exist in the communities anthropologists went to study.[17] Furthermore, it was assumed that the methods of ethnography – micro-analyses of small-scale communities – were not suited to grasping large-scale statistical

---

[17] To my knowledge, there are no published ethnographies of financial markets in the West or elsewhere. Anthropologist Jocelyn Gamble (1997) provides rich ethnographic detail on the Shanghai stock market from late 1992 to 1994. Anthropological theory and sociological studies touching on financial markets will be discussed below.

realities. However, whether by design or omission, in ignoring modern economic systems traditional anthropological studies have reinforced the
belief that culture is relevant to the study of economics only in exotic societies; in the West, economic institutions are merely economic. How then
does one read the stock market anthropologically? On what body of literature does one rely for insights and methods?

Means

Stock markets are economic institutions, one of a number of mechanisms
that capitalism has devised for pooling funds for large-scale productive
investment. With this unproblematic assertion comes a problematic corollary: that the study of stock markets should be left to economists. While
many would agree that stock markets function symbolically as well as
economically, their political, social, cultural and ideological effects have
occasioned little serious attention. Popular culture entertains a certain
romance with the image of the stock market, as evidenced by best-sellers
such as *Liar's Poker* (Lewis 1989). History books too participate in this
myth-making: it has been argued that the infamous 1929 stock market
crash was not an immediate or important cause of the Great Depression,
and yet it continues to stand for that generalized economic and social collapse as bank closings and bread lines cannot. As for the Shanghai
market, the West's investment is at least as much symbolic as it is financial.
Indeed, the contrast between the two registers is striking: given how little
money US investors have placed in this market thus far, news about it
occupies a disproportionate amount of space in the American mass
media. It seems that once the economics of stock markets have been
explained, we are left with a residual fascination which it is anthropology's
task to explore. How is this passage from economics to anthropology best
negotiated?

The economic study of stock markets in capitalist systems poses certain
well-defined questions. At the level of the primary market,[18] economists
ask whether the market efficiently allocates equity capital to productive
investments, comparing stock markets to other mechanisms of capital
allocation such as the market for debt or planned regimes (Phelps

---

[18] The primary market is "the first market into which an issue of securities is sold by the
underwriter, before trading begins" (Mayer 1988:289). It is contrasted to the secondary
market where subsequent buying and selling of shares takes place. From the corporation's
point of view, the secondary market serves the function of making the primary market
attractive to investors, as "securities are very difficult to sell to their initial buyer unless he
has good reason to believe there will be a secondary market into which he can resell if he
needs the money" (*ibid.*).

1985:437–468). When analyzing the secondary market, economists study the factors determining stock prices (the supply and demand for stock), asking to what extent these factors reflect the efficient processing of information by the market (Tarascio 1984). But economics is singularly reserved on the two questions that most interest stock market observers and participants: how can one best predict stock price movements, and how do we explain the spectacular mass movements of frenzy and panic which cause stock market booms and crashes (but see Cancelliere 1996)? The first question is generally left to financial analysts, the prevailing view among the scholarly economic community being that the market efficiently factors all information relevant to stock values into their price; out-predicting the market is therefore impossible (*ibid.*). The second question, if acknowledged at all, is left to crowd psychologists, as the behavior of investors in these moments is considered too irrational to be dealt with under the economic paradigm (Adler and Adler 1984b; Kindleberger 1989 [1978]).

Economics, then, relegates the money-making issues to financial analysis, that "applied science" which works to sustain a flourishing industry of brokers and consultants. Traditionally, financial analysts come in two schools, those who practice "fundamental analysis" and those who believe in "technical analysis." Fundamental analysis focuses on "the intrinsic value of the company as evidenced by a review of [its] balance sheet, income statement, cash flow, operating performance, etc." (Maturi 1993:201); its basic assumption is that the movement of stock prices will follow (more or less closely) the present earnings and future prospects of the underlying company. Technical analysis bases its predictions on market and stock price patterns, irrespective of the financial health of the companies or industries they represent (*ibid.*:204); it is technical analysis which produces stock brokers' impressive array of graphs and charts, based on the premise that past price patterns can be used to predict future movement.

From our point of view, the interesting thing about financial analysis is that despite the impressive mobilization of fact-gathering forces and statistical modeling procedures, neither fundamental nor technical analysis, nor any of their many combinations and variants, has succeeded in attaining the scientific validity which they systematically invoke. And, indeed, it is a good thing for the stock market that they have not, for were it actually possible to predict stock price movements with any degree of accuracy then all investors would follow the same course of action and the entire game would come to a halt. Even more interesting for the anthropologist, this realization – the open secret of financial analysis' fraudulent claims to scientificity – in no way diminishes its appeal.[19] Hundreds of books continue to be published and hundreds of thousands of analysts employed to vaunt the merits of this or that technique, suggesting that for investors, both expert and lay, action is not possible without this proxy of rationality separating them from their decisions.[20]

Clearly, financial analysts, as salesmen for the enormous investment industry, lack that distance from their object of study necessary to produce valuable sociological descriptions. Rather, financial analysis should itself be analyzed as contributing to the simulacrum of rationality on which stock markets feed. In peddling the merits of their various prophetic techniques, analysts must work with an image of a market governed by rules and regularities which utterly fails to reflect reality. Crowd psychologists, on the other hand, err in the opposite direction, describing investors in such irrational terms that no recognizable human or social patterns are discernible (Adler and Adler 1984b:4). The most extreme forms of mass behavior – the stampedes occasioned by booms and crashes – are taken as evidence of the primitive instincts lurking beneath the surface of any crowd.[21] The problem with this view is that it fails to explain investor behavior when no stampeding is going on, which is, after all, most of the time. This vision of the hysterical crowd – also an important part of stock market mythology – is the flip-side of the hyper-rationalism of financial analysis. In both perspectives, the groups and structures which make up society disappear, leaving us with homogenized actors without social position or cultural background.

In their pioneering edited volume on the "social dynamics of financial markets," sociologists Patricia and Peter Adler (1984a, 1984b) attempt to correct for these deficiencies by analyzing the market as a social arena. Their starting point – one that I share – is that economic and psychological models fail to understand the actual functioning of these institutions

---

[19] The same point could be made for economics generally. At an international conference on futures and options which I attended in the fall of 1994, the key-note speaker, Chancellor of the Exchequer under Britain's former labor government, waxed quite eloquent on the subject of economics' complete bankruptcy as a science, to the amusement and applause of an audience of financial analysts, investors and regulators. One might conclude that periodic denouncing of economics' pretensions to scientificity is part of an unexplored dialectic which keeps the economic hegemony intact. Or perhaps this is taking cause for effect; rather, as Dilley suggests (1992:1), free-market economics' recent triumph on the world political scene has spawned increasing discomfort with its status as a science, even amongst the community of believers.

[20] This is only to say that financial analysis functions as a modern form of that universal human behavior anthropologists call divination (see Bastide 1968).

[21] The classic example of this hysterical view of hysteria is LeBon's *The Crowd* (1895).

because they begin with reductive premises. In the case of economics, the more powerful of the two discourses, these premises include the individual (or worse yet, the firm) as rational maximizer endowed with complete and instantaneous market information, operating in an arena of pure competition. By contrast, recent sociological studies start with more complex assumptions about individual and group behavior. They ask how beliefs about value are formed and what is the role of "non-economic factors" such as rumor in these beliefs (Rose 1951, 1966); how group opinions and informal dynamics help reassure traders in an environment of constant uncertainty (Glick 1957); what role group dynamics, influence and charisma, professional identity and face maintenance play in the everyday movements of these markets (Klausner 1984); and how law influences professional behavior (Lejeune 1984).

These studies demonstrate that while markets are not necessarily rational from an economic point of view, they do make social sense. By bringing such forces as prestige, group-think, charisma and face into their descriptions, they more tightly approximate the language of those actually involved in trading securities, professionally or as amateurs (see Lewis 1989). However, in many ways their perspective remains circumscribed by the economic paradigm they criticize. While economics is taken to task for its single-minded focus on rational profit maximizing, these sociologists tend simply to view a wider range of individual human motivators – prestige, face, cognitive dissonance, peer-pressure – as positively (or negatively) charged commodities that individuals seek to maximize (or minimize) in their dealings with the social totality. The individual – unanalyzed in his or her relation to culture, power and history – remains the only conceivable starting point for the analysis. The assumption is still that financial markets are distinct economic institutions with distinct economic functions, functions that are distorted but not fundamentally altered by "the human factor." In sum, these studies take for granted the existence and historical inevitability of financial markets in human society, and seek merely to demonstrate, a little defensively, that sociology is a useful tool for explaining them.

A fully sociological – or anthropological – perspective, one which has not been coopted by the ideology it purports to explore, reverses this end; it asks not what social science can tell us about financial markets but what financial markets tell us about society. It is not that economics is irrelevant in this perspective. To the contrary, it is economics as a mode of thought and the economy as a mode of social action which must be explained. The "human factor" cannot be merely added on as a complement to gain fuller understanding of pre-existing economic institutions. Rather, we must ask how it came about that the economy took on a life of its own in modern Western society. As Polanyi has demonstrated, over the course of human history we have witnessed an evolution of the market from concrete form – the market as a site of exchange and encounter – to abstraction – the market as ideology (Polanyi 1944, 1957). In this evolution, financial markets have been both cause and effect.

The groundwork for a fully anthropological approach to economic phenomena can be sought in two traditions: first, the earliest sociologists, Marx, Weber and Simmel, who viewed the development of modern capitalism in Western Europe as a social, cultural, political and historical event requiring explanation. The most forceful articulation of an uncowed approach to economic phenomena can be found in Simmel's *Philosophy of Money*:

> Not a single line of these investigations is meant to be a statement about economics. That is to say, the phenomena of valuation and purchase, of exchange and the means of exchange, of the forms of production and the values of possession, which economics views from *one* standpoint, are here viewed from another. It is merely the fact that the aspect of these phenomena closest to economics is the most interesting in practical terms, is the most thoroughly investigated and can be represented in the most exact manner which gives rise to the apparent justification for regarding them simply as "economic facts." . . . Such a fact – that is one whose content would be exhausted in the image economics presents of it – does not exist
>
> (1990 [1907]:55, emphasis in the original).

For Marx, the ideological basis for the increased autonomy of the market under capitalism resulted from the power of capital to extract surplus value and then to fetishize the value produced under conditions of capitalist exploitation as value adhering in the commodity produced. For Weber, the calculative rationality which lies at the heart of Western capitalism had its source not in the economy but in a specific and contingent reworking of the Calvinist ethic of predestination, that is, in a moral/religious sphere subsequently defined in opposition to the economic. Simmel examines the development of capitalism within the broader context of what commentator David Frisby (1986) has called "fragments of modernity," more precisely the phenomena of "individualization," "transience" and "intellectualization" which modernity engenders. All three authors require us to look beyond "economic facts" to power, culture and history.

For a second source of inspiration, contemporary ethnographies of economic institutions can look to the general explanatory framework outlined in Marcel Mauss' famous essay, *The Gift* (1967 [1923–1924]). Drawing on ethnographies of non-market economics such as Malinowski's description of the Melanesian *kula*, Mauss examines complex systems of gift exchange to argue (in archaic terms) that in "archaic societies" economics, politics, aesthetics, morality and religion are institutionally united into rituals touching all members of society through all of its social registers. The practice of giving and counter-giving does much more than assure the circulation of goods; it expresses generosity and competitiveness, creates alliances and maintains boundaries between tribes, links man with the supernatural forces of growth and destruction, and brings members of society together to act out moments of collective belonging. The circulation of valuables is thus a social practice before it is a utilitarian one. It is by placing forms of production and exchange alongside forms of aesthetic, moral and political practice that we discover societies' latent and frequently contradictory logics of social order.

The holistic methodology[22] of Mauss and Malinowski was subsequently compromised by the development in the 1940s and 1950s of the specialized subdiscipline of economic anthropology as ethnographers – particularly of the Anglo-American school[23] – began to define their research paradigm within narrowly economistic terms. In a recent volume, Dilley argues that the "sub-discipline of economic anthropology grew as an offshoot of economics"; consequently "[s]ocial anthropologists have often taken the notion of the market as given from orthodox economic theory and adopted it uncritically into social analysis" (1992:14). The "formal-

---

[22] With the critique of the concepts of culture and society sketched out above comes a reworking of the notion of holism. If societies are characterized by "an absence of closure" (Barth 1992:21), then holism is impossible as it is impossible to take into account every aspect of an infinitely expanding object. However, as an (unattainable) goal, holism is invaluable; it is what grants anthropologists the license to range broadly over the socio-cultural landscape in constructing social theory.

    A less sanguine view of "the rhetoric of ethnographic holism" can be found in Thorton (1992). Thorton demonstrates how the wholeness of the ethnographic monograph substitutes for an imaginary wholeness of the ethnographic object – "society," "the field," or "the Balinese." This seems correct. However, he goes on to point out that sociological constructs such as "'rate of suicide' or a pig-to-yam ratio are conceptually distant and even irrelevant to the experience of a suicidal depression or feeding pigs" (1992:27). I, for one, can live with that. Is not ethnography's goal simply to identify discernible patterns in "society" or "culture" (or any other *ethnographically constructed* unit of analysis such as "the stock market"), rather than to replicate the experience of these patterns? The holistic imperative helps anthropology account for more than social sciences which start from less imaginative premises.

[23] In France, after thirty years of wrestling with Marxism, the Maussian tradition of economic sociology was resuscitated by the Mouvement Anti-Utilitariste dans les Sciences Sociales (MAUSS), which has published a scholarly journal, *La Revue du MAUSS*, since 1981.

ist–substantive controversy" that animated and finally exhausted the sub-discipline during the 1960s locked protagonists in a dispute over whether the theoretical construct of "the market" could be used as a modeling device to describe "a market," the localized site of exchange in non-capitalist economies (*ibid.*:12).[24] However, as a spate of recent publications in economic anthropology and related fields demonstrates,[25] the questions which anthropology now asks about economic phenomena have broadened once again, allowing us, for example, to examine the effects of gender ideology on the production and circulation of valuables (Strathern 1988); the symbolic logic of consumption and waste (Douglas and Isherwood 1979, Appadurai 1986); or the ideological uses of economic concepts such as "the informal economy" (Hart 1992).

Recent work on financial markets in economic anthropology – what little there is to date – has taken up this far-ranging comparative perspective. In *The Social Life of Things* (1986:48–51), Arjun Appadurai analyzes the Chicago grain exchange as a "speculative tournament" nourished by a "mythology of circulation." Building on Marx, Appadurai begins with the observation that the stock market represents

a kind of meta-fetishization, where not only does the commodity become a substitute for the social relations that lie behind it, but the movement of *prices* becomes an autonomous substitute for the flow of commodities themselves (1986:50, emphasis in the original).

The structural basis of this mythology of circulation lies in the fact that

it plays *indefinitely* with the fluctuation of prices; that it seeks to exhaust an inexhaustible series of variables that affect price; and that its concern with commodities is purely *informational* and *semiotic* and is divorced from consumption altogether. The irrational desire to corner the market in some commodity, the counterintuitive search for magical formulas to predict price changes, the controlled collective hysteria, all these are the product of this complete conversion of commodities to signs (Baudrillard 1981), which are themselves capable of yielding profit if manipulated properly. (Appadurai 1986:51, emphasis in the original).

Like the *kula* exchanges which form the basis for Mauss' theory of the gift, commodities markets are special arenas, separated from everyday economic practice, in which are exchanged "tokens of value that can be transformed into other media only by a complex set of steps and in unusual

---

[24] See, *inter alia*, Burling 1962, Cook 1969, 1966, Dalton 1961, LeClair 1962, Polanyi 1947 and Sahlins 1969.
[25] See Douglas and Isherwood 1979, Dumont 1977, 1986 [1983], Appadurai 1986, Gudeman 1986, Clammer 1987, Strathern 1988, Parry and Bloch 1989, Zukin and DiMaggio 1990, Gregory and Altman 1989, Dilley 1992.

circumstances" (*ibid.*: 50). More importantly, both build on a "romantic, individualistic, and gamelike ethos that stands in contrast to the ethos of everyday economic behavior" (*ibid.*). This analysis points to some of the same "social factors" examined in the studies collected in Adler and Adler (1984b) above – face, reputation, gamesmanship and cognitive dissonance – but places them in cultural, historical and political perspective. Most importantly, it provides us with a means of bridging the Great Divide between modern and non-modern economic institutions while neither ignoring the differences which mark them nor exaggerating the force of these differences.

Like its counterparts in London, Tokyo and Budapest, the Shanghai stock market is caught within this structure of meta-fetishization. Indeed, it is the double fetishization of commodities as signs accomplished through this mass institution that allows for stock markets' extraordinary degree of "interpretability." If stocks are signs, making money means reading the signs correctly, whether one is in New York or Jakarta. However, the precise terms of the interpretive framework one calls upon to read these signs vary tremendously across location. What distinguishes the Shanghai stock market from stock markets internationally – although this distinction is a matter of degree and not of kind – is the fact that the interpretive framework through which Shanghainese read their stock market is firstly political, and secondly, if at all, "economic." We might say that the Shanghai market is primarily subject to a third form of fetishization, the fetishization of the state.

As I have argued, a particular political–economic configuration – that defined principally by the dual workings of the tributary and petty capitalist modes of production – underpins the Shanghai market's "special characteristics." The reasons for Chinese leaders' decision to experiment with stock markets were, from the outset, both political and economic. The state sought to tap the large sums of individual savings, that is, to benefit from the petty capitalist activities of millions of individual investors, and thereby lessen the burden on strained state coffers. Share-holding reform policy was also guided by micro- and macro-economic theory imported directly from capitalist economies: transformation to the share-holding system, it was hoped, would bring increased micro-economic efficiency to management, and help control inflation by encouraging investment. However, in a society in which economic and political structures tend to coincide (Hsu 1991:xi), these economic motives quickly shaded into the political. Increased micro-economic efficiency was to come about by circumscribing the power granted to Party cadres who occupy important managerial positions in most state-owned and many collective enterprises. Through this complex and, as we shall see, often contradictory design, reformers sought to increase the efficiency of the state system of production and distribution while maintaining control over the overall course of state-sponsored industrial development. More specifically, they sought to make state cadres managing the vast state-owned enterprises system act like capitalist managers while ensuring that these same managers maintained a sufficient degree of dependence on the state tributary system to guarantee their loyalty and obedience.

At the level of ideology as well, the Shanghai stock market reflected the tensions inherent in the TMP/PCMP dialectic. Gates puzzles over the centuries-old "susceptibility of the Chinese to mass enthusiasm for alternating modes of right living" (1996:9). Popular enthusiasm for the stock market, after more than thirty years during which speculation was excoriated in political discourse and forbidden in practice, represents just such a sudden *en masse* about-face. Gates argues that the reasons for this "moral lability" (*ibid.*) lie in the TMP/PCMP complex: Chinese have for a thousand years been faced with two powerful and competing "behavioral/ideational systems" (7) and have learned to negotiate between them quickly and convincingly. "Tributary and petty-capitalist modes came complete with distinctive moral convictions, visions of the cosmos, kinship ideals and practices, contrasting patterns of production and exchange, and a millennial history of conflict and critique between them" (245). The establishment of the Shanghai stock market opened more than the possibilities for making a quick buck; it reactivated a particular form of the petty capitalist worldview, complete with social organizational forms and ideological/symbolic narratives.

Gates' explanation accounts for the instant enthusiasm with which the stock market was greeted at the popular level, but it does not fully account for its mass dimensions. What is it about Chinese social structure that gives rise to the startling moments of "mass movement" which have punctuated its history, from peasant revolts through the Taiping Rebellion, from the Great Leap Forward to the Cultural Revolution? As we have seen above, TMP hegemony instituted as the primary class divide in Chinese society the division between state bureaucrats and everybody else, overshadowing the many and fluctuating status differences between commoners themselves. Mao's perverse genius was to sharpen the use of the imperial notion of "the People" for modern ends of material and cultural control, thereby conferring on "the masses" a form of ritual reality. Thus, the age-old ideological construct of "the People" has, in imperial as in contemporary China, a distinct sociological base, a base which accounts for a rich tradition of mass egalitarian practice and discourse.

The mass egalitarian mode of action is visible throughout the contemporary Chinese social structure, from the "People's Movement" in Beijing during the spring of 1989 (Pieke 1996), to faddish trends in art and fashion (Link, Madsen and Pickowicz 1989), to a surge in interest in "traditional" Chinese medicine and the martial arts (Chen 1994, 1995). The stock market, with its premise of mass participation in the state–industrial economy, was promptly incorporated into this ideological structure. As such, it activated all of the state's techniques for mass ideological domination, and all of "the People's" techniques for counter-hegemonic deflection. The study of the Shanghai stock market thus involves the study of how "the masses" imagine themselves.

Put in these terms, one notices a remarkable lacuna in the social scientific literature on China to date. Through their analyses of family, kinship and village life,[26] ethnographers have learned an enormous amount about the forms which organize Chinese who know each other. Even in urban settings, ethnographers, sociologists and historians have concentrated on associations and particularistic networks.[27] The complex social dynamics of same-place associations, guilds and sects, and the idioms in which alliance, hierarchy and competition are articulated have been well documented. We know relatively little, however, about how Chinese organize themselves as strangers.[28] Granted, anthropology's preoccupation with kinship and networks is well justified in general, and imperative in the particular context of China studies. Anyone who has ever ridden a train with a group of Chinese meeting each other for the first time knows that Chinese are second to none in their ability to turn strangers into "connections." With an efficiency which puts to shame Dale Carnegie's best-selling *How to Win Friends and Influence People* (1981 [1936]), strangers in virtually any setting instantly begin sharing food and cigarettes, trading name cards, locating common interests, and generally establishing the basis for utilitarian exchanges which participate so powerfully in creating the bonds of sociality in China.

---

[26] See M. C. Yang 1945, Freedman 1958, 1966, 1970, Potter 1968, Cohen 1976, Ebrey and Watson 1986, R. Watson 1985, Siu 1989a and Potter and Potter 1990 to name just some of the book-length studies.

[27] See, e.g., Jones 1974, Baker 1977, Henderson and Cohen 1984, Bruun 1993, Yang 1994.

[28] But see Pieke's ethnography of the "People's Movement" at Tiananmen (1996); and Bennett (1976) and Cell (1977) for non-ethnographic work on mass mobilization campaigns. I thank Frank Pieke for articulating in these terms what it is that my book is about.

But my point remains. The stock market is a mass economic institution. As such, it mobilizes enormous numbers of people who do not know each other through reference to hegemonic and counter-hegemonic images of "the masses" propagated at both the official and popular levels. In this study, I explore what these images can tell us about urban Chinese social dynamics.

The above epistemological and methodological positioning is, of course, an *ex post facto* affair. I had set out for the field with a research question defined narrowly and naively within the economic paradigm. Thirty years of Communist rule, I reasoned, had accustomed the Chinese to an economic culture dominated by the Marxist concept of use value. With the economic reforms inaugurated in 1979, they were confronted with the concept of exchange value in the form of free markets for certain commodities and, to a lesser degree, for labor. Nowhere was this shift as radical as with the stock market; in studying it, I meant to study how its investors would adapt to the notion that stock has no utilitarian function and hence no "use value," only the value which the forces of supply and demand attribute to it and to the issuing company in the marketplace. My prediction was that the investing public would experience difficulty grasping this new reality.

The Shanghainese I talked with during the very first days of my fieldwork soon set me straight. Virtually the day I arrived, the market took off, drawing hundreds of thousands of citizens into the fray, citizens who had absolutely no difficulty imagining the profits to be made through the "meta-fetishization" of exchange on the bourse. Furthermore, they understood exactly what was wrong with my research question, and did not hesitate to tell me. All of the people I interviewed, from economists at state-run research institutes to street vendors, vigorously and insistently agreed on one point: "In China, you cannot look at economics without looking at politics." Or, more radically, "China has no economy." From the questions of value and return on investment with which I had set out to the field, I was obliged to move to questions of political organization, ideology and mass culture. It was only then that I began to look at what we in the West would call "the market" as what they in Shanghai might call a "social movement" (*shehui yundong*). The Shanghai stock market is the competing social entities of which it is made up.

These competing entities were thoroughly elaborated in and by Shanghai stock market discourse. Within the stock market, action and reaction were conceived of in terms of three categories of "player": "big players" (*dahu*), "dispersed players" (*sanhu*), and "the State" (*guojia*). Over the course of 1992, as the market undulated its way through a speculative cycle, its movements were ascribed to the activities of each of these players in turn, with an imaginary struggle for control dominating stock discourse. My study traces the evolution of this discourse, from the initial phase in which the state was locked in a game of carrot-and-stick with the big players to the moment when both the state and the big players were overwhelmed by the sheer mass of small investors, and a new politico-moral scenario was written.

Part I sets the scene for this social drama. In chapters 1 and 2, I outline the institutional structure of the market, focusing on the concept of state action. In chapters 3 and 4, I examine the other half of the tributary dialectic – popular reaction – as cultural construct and social practice, respectively. My portrait of Shanghai "stock people" (*gumin*) is a description of the cultural and social construction of community in contemporary Shanghai; I ask how collective actors are culturally configured and set into social motion.

In Part II, I examine each of the three collective actors operating on the stock market in turn – big players (chapter 5), dispersed players (chapter 6) and the state (chapter 7). Each is characterized by particular rules of social exchange, and each grows out of the evolution of Shanghai social structure in a different way. We will see how in the fall of 1992 the "dispersed players" "won" the battle for control over the stock market, which is merely to say that neither the "big players" nor "the State" proved powerful enough to manipulate the forces of supply and demand.

In the eighth chapter, I draw my conclusions from this ethnographic material. In 1992, the stock market's spectacular rise and equally spectacular fall was the occasion for the Shanghainese to discover how a large public market functions (or, as the case may be, fails to function). The changes of fortune which accompanied the market's rise and fall were the object of much commentary. As I have said, this commentary was rarely "economic"; it focused rather on the nature of power, particularly state power, as investors and observers discovered with a certain glee that the state was simply unable to control the stock market the way it controlled other institutions in Chinese society. The "victory" of the dispersed players represented the emergence of a new social actor, an actor I have labeled "the trading crowd."[29] The "trading crowd," like "the State" or

---

[29] The phrase "trading crowd" is used as a term of art on US stock markets to designate that group of buyers and sellers who determine the price of a given share at a given moment through competitive offerings. This reference acts as a reminder that the emergence of markets is linked with the emergence of a particular kind of crowd in the Western historical imagination as well.

"the People" – or, let us not forget, "the Individual" of Western liberal theory – is an imaginary entity. Borrowing Benedict Anderson's (1983) eloquent phrase, it is an "imagined community." Its particularity lies in the fact that, unlike "the State" or "the People", it is a community of effects and not of intention, that is to say, its actions cannot be attributed to the exercise of a collective will but must accommodate the accumulated effects resulting from the exercise of hundreds of thousands of individual wills.

Translated into Western ideological terms, the "trading crowd" is simply the market. Early on, however, the crowd-based nature of markets was thoroughly occulted in the West through the remarkable trope of "the invisible hand" (Smith 1980 [1776]); indeed, the success of Adam Smith's coinage[30] can be attributed to the fact that it lent a transcendence to the random and threatening activities of the crowds of traders gaining social prominence in eighteenth-century Britain. This teleological substitution is also evident in an earlier work of political economy, Mandeville's *Fable of the Bees* (1714), in which the random and self-centered operations of individual participants in a market are given a socially functional interpretation through the metaphor of the beehive. In Mandeville's metaphor, the element of a crowd, of the masses, is still present in the form of the hive, whereas in Smith's it has been erased. This study sets out to demonstrate that in China an equivalent de-massification – and hence de-politicization – of the concept of the market has not taken place.

---

[30] In a surprising and wonderful article, Lubasz (1992) demonstrates that the phrase "invisible hand of the market," everywhere attributed to Smith, in fact appears nowhere in Smith's writing. (That's some invisible hand!) While Smith wrote twice (once in *The Theory of Moral Sentiments* and once in *The Wealth of Nations*) of an "invisible hand," the context makes clear that the owner of that hand was Providence and not the self-regulating market. The ideological shift I am tracing should thus be attributed to Smith's commentators and not Smith himself.

PART I

"Above there is policy,
Below there is strategy."
(aphorism in circulation in urban China, c. 1990)

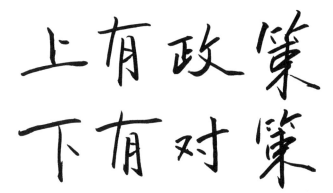

1

First contact

In September of 1992, a delegation of high-level Taiwanese experts in finance and securities came to Shanghai with the mission of establishing cooperative relations with the Shanghai Securities Exchange (SSE). Their visit was hosted by the Shanghai Academy of Social Sciences (SASS), also my host institution, and I was invited to tag along. There is no better way to begin exploring the "special characteristics" of Shanghai's experiments with the stock market than to describe the communication and mis-communication, the messages sent and not received, between the two parties to this encounter.

The day began with a visit to the Shanghai Exchange itself, symbolic center of China's vast securities markets, and site to which all visitors of any importance, foreign or domestic, are first led. The seven-person Taiwan delegation and I, along with a representative from SASS and another from the central Chinese Academy of Social Sciences in Beijing (CASS), piled into a van that was to take us from the old French Concessions district, where SASS had its offices, to the city's financial district. My place in the order of things was quickly established. It was discovered that the head of the Taiwanese delegation knew one of my professors from the University of California; as the student of teachers with whom the Taiwanese experts were friends, I was of the younger generation, and hence to be seen and not heard. My knowledge of Chinese and, more unusually, of Shanghainese made me an object of some interest, a possible partner in conversation, to whom both Taiwanese and mainlanders occasionally turned for complicity when amused or irritated by the attitudes of their "compatriots"[1] from

---

[1] The official mainland term for Taiwanese is "Taiwan compatriots" (*taiwan tongbao*), emphasizing the fact that the Chinese government, like its Taiwanese counterpart, still considers Taiwan a province of the mainland. The term is used with more or less irony by mainland speakers, but never sounds entirely natural.

across the Straits. But while my foreignness lent a luster of internationality to the encounter, the discussions that followed were, and were intended to be, fundamentally sino-centric.

As the van made its way through the crowded and narrow streets of Shanghai's French Concessions district, the representative from the Shanghai Academy, a slight note of apology in her voice, discussed the city's many and ambitious plans for infrastructural improvement: eight subway lines, highway overpasses, an enormous new bridge across the Huangpu River, reduction of bicycle traffic, etc., all to be accomplished in or around the year 2000. Arriving at the Bund, however, our SASS guide changed her tone. The Bund – a row of small but elegant skyscrapers constructed along the Huangpu River at the beginning of the century by foreign merchants, industrialists and financiers – is incontestably the best known symbol, in the Chinese-speaking world and beyond, of mainland China's economic influence and sophistication. It is here that imperialist capitalism established its foothold in pre-revolutionary Chinese trade and finance, and paraded its wealth and power most ostentatiously. After the Revolution, the Shanghai branch of the Chinese Communist Party and the Shanghai municipal government occupied most of these buildings, but city officials also maintain a certain symbolic continuity with the past, allowing the revamped Bureau of Maritime Trade and Customs, the People's Bank of China, and the renamed Peace Hotel to remain in their original locations. For the Chinese I spoke with, the colonial origins of these buildings posed no problems of national pride. Along with the similarly foreign main shopping street in Shanghai, Nanjing Road, these landmarks had long since been appropriated, by Chinese in general and by Shanghainese in particular, as signs of Chinese sophistication and modernity.[2]

The symbolism of place is legible to everyone even superficially familiar with Shanghai's pre-revolutionary history. Evidence of the Exchange's initially ambivalent position in reform politics can be found in the fact that SSE officials did not have the connections necessary to muscle their way onto the Bund proper. Rather, the Shanghai Securities Exchange is located in the Pujiang Hotel, a bulky but attractive building constructed by the Americans in 1910 as the Astor House Hotel, and situated just across Suzhou Creek from the Bund, facing the Russian Embassy. Its large neon sign is written in "complex characters," a gesture towards historical

---

[2] The landmark around which Chinese anti-colonial feelings officially coalesced was a public park situated between the Bund and the waterfront that had once posted the infamous sign "No Dogs or Chinese Allowed" on its front gate.

continuity with pre-revolutionary Shanghai and a tacit solicitation for investment directed at Chinese communities in Hong Kong, Taiwan and Singapore unfamiliar with China's simplified character system.[3] The east wing of the building still functioned as a state-run hotel, well known to foreign students for its cheap if austere dormitory rooms. The old ball-room on the west wing had been converted into the Exchange's main trading floor and at the time of our visit seated more than 200 representatives from securities brokerages around the country.

Like all visitors to the SSE, our delegation was first led to the enormous glass windows which allow the world to look in at the trading floor. What we saw, however, was disappointing, as "the action" on the market is located not at the Exchange but at brokerage houses throughout the city. No harried men in shirtsleeves rush about waving their hands, for no actual trading takes place at the SSE itself. Rather, row after row of women and men in red vests (in stock market parlance, the *hong majia*, or red jackets) sit at small desks entering buy and sell orders received from brokerages into the SSE's central computer, which matches these orders through its automated time/price priority system. Behind these busy seated people sit others, dressed in yellow vests (*huang majia*), SSE employees who facilitate the occasional institution-to-institution trade, and maintain order in the computer system. Above them, on the far wall, hangs the big board off which we could read the status of each order: the name of the stock or bond, the quantity offered or sought, the code number of the brokerage involved, and, when the trade is finalized, the transaction price. Except for the clack of computer keyboards and the ringing of phones, the floor was silent and dull.

Our delegation was next led upstairs where we were greeted by a middle-aged woman of formidable bearing from one of the SSE's subdivisions. No higher level officer of the Exchange appeared to welcome the Taiwanese delegation, a fact which could only have been intended by the Shanghainese and interpreted by the Taiwanese as a slight. Throughout the visit, the SSE representative maintained a stance of brash indifference to the expertise and good will of the exceedingly polite Taiwanese.

Our SSE guide launched into a brief and selective history of the Exchange to date. The Shanghai Securities Exchange, she explained, was officially opened for business on December 19, 1990, with eight traded

---

[3] After the Revolution, the Communist Party embarked on a program to simplify China's traditional ideograms, with the aim of making written Chinese more accessible to the general population. Ideograms written with the traditional number of brush strokes are called "complex characters."

stocks and a total market capitalization (principally in government bonds) of 240 million *yuan* (US $43 million under the official conversion rate of September 1992). As of August 1992, thirty stocks were traded with a market capitalization of 30 billion *yuan* ($5.4 billion), and another twenty to thirty companies were waiting for permission to trade on the Exchange. The trading floor had grown from an initial forty-five seats to 212 in August 1992, but the SSE, confident in its ascending star, was busy arranging for another 900 seats, and had already contracted for a new "Shanghai Securities Exchange Mansion" to be built in Pudong[4] that would house 2,000 traders, making it the biggest trading floor in all of Asia. Of the SSE's 138 members, 102 were brokerages from outside Shanghai. Our guide predicted that by the end of the year the Exchange would house representatives from every province in China. Furthermore, as Merrill Lynch had expressed a "strong desire" to set up offices to service foreign clients, the SSE might well include foreign members at a very near date. The Taiwanese delegation remained impassive before this display of municipal ambition, but our host from the Shanghai Academy of Social Sciences, clearly embarrassed, muttered to me that perhaps this Mme. So-and-so had become overbearing (*kuang*) because she held a doctorate in finance, a scarce commodity in China at the time.

Shanghai's projects for the future of its Exchange thus delineated, our guide turned to more technical topics. The market's operating procedures depended on four main attributes, all of which were as modern as contemporary financial technology would allow. The first was a fully automated computer matching system, which paired buy and sell orders by price/time priority. The second was centralized clearing and settlement by the SSE, a feature which distinguished the Shanghai Exchange from all other stock markets in the world where, by contrast, trading, clearing and settlement of shares are generally handled by the Exchanges, stock brokerages and clearance companies respectively. Thirdly, the market was entirely scriptless (*wuzhihua*); a few companies had printed stock certificates in the early phases of the share-holding reforms, but these paper certificates now had no economic value except as souvenirs and no paper certificates of share ownership circulated on the Shanghai market. Rather, and this brought us to the fourth feature of the Exchange, all transfer of stock ownership was centralized in the SSE computer. Individuals had a record of ownership in

---

[4] Pudong, a large piece of sparsely populated (by Shanghai standards) land east of the Huangpu River, was targeted in the spring of 1992 as a vast municipal development project, featuring preferential tax treatment for foreign and domestic investors. It will be discussed in more detail in chapter 3.

the booklet they were issued when they opened their registered "stock account" (*gupiao zhanghu*) through an authorized brokerage. This feature, our guide informed us, was obviously related to the "situation in the mainland": with automated stock transfer centralized at the Exchange, it has become impossible to carry out black market transactions. "Without a single arrest, the black market was entirely eliminated, and accounts registered with the Exchange have risen from 20,000 to 700,000," she said, smiling.

The SSE's progress in the area of regulation, according to our guide, also displayed the most modern of shifts toward a complete dependence on market mechanisms. From its opening in 1990 until the middle of 1992, the Exchange had employed a price control system, setting floors and ceilings for daily share price movement. As a result, the "market only rose and never fell, and investor risk consciousness was eliminated" (*fengxian yishi xiaomie le*).[5] In order to teach investors what risk is all about, on May 21, 1992, all price controls were lifted. On this topic, our guide became expansive: "The guiding ideology was clear: since we have put our faith in the market, we must let the market play its role." In any event, she continued, risk is not a concept that can be conveyed through propaganda; it must be experienced. Like the child whose father tells him to be careful with his balloon, Chinese investors would not believe that the market could fall until the balloon popped in their faces. Our guide concluded her introduction by reminding the Taiwanese delegation that, as in other countries, the responsibilities of the SSE were to provide efficient, fair and equal trading conditions for all investors on the market.

The floor was opened for questions. The first intervention, from the delegation leader, was a prepared speech setting the basis for what he hoped could be a successful cooperative agreement between the two Exchanges. He began with many compliments about the rapid advances the Shanghainese had made. He reiterated the common grounds which united their two enterprises: they were all Chinese, in feelings and in language there were no barriers between them, they could understand each other immediately. He had only "a few suggestions." Marx's critique of capitalism, he continued, was a reaction to the social injustices existing in England at the time he was writing. Marx did not oppose securities

---

[5] Unlike the New York Stock Exchange, but like Tokyo, the Shanghai Exchange does not have "market makers" or "specialists," those agents of the Exchange whose job it is to guarantee the liquidity of the market by buying (or selling) for their own accounts if no buyer (or seller) appears among the larger public. This feature, combined with the price floor/ceilings, meant that trading in a particular share frequently ceased altogether once its daily price movement limit had been reached.

markets. Rather, he worried about abnormalities. It is not enough to let the market govern the market, he urged; one needs laws and regulations. His humble suggestion, then, was that Shanghai control the market somewhat so as to regularize it (*guifanhua*).[6]

To this the representative of the Shanghai Exchange responded: "The market surpassed our expectations. The demand is out there, pressing us forward." The question of the proper speed for securities trading reforms had been studied by top economists in Beijing as well as by the local government. But they had concluded that "Shanghai cannot let the fact of existing imperfections keep it from marching forward." Personally, she added, her only worry, as opposed to Marx's, was that "conservative forces" (*baoshou shili*) were just waiting for a crash in order to close the whole market down.

A second representative from Taiwan took up the argument. He too began his comments with numerous compliments, but reiterated the concerns of the first speaker: a stock exchange cannot race forward by itself; it needs to keep step with the macro-economic climate. Recharacterizing the enemy not as "conservative forces" but as unspecified outsiders, he put the problem as follows: "We are all Chinese, in thinking and language we are alike, that is the particularity of the Chinese people. And, there are too many people out there who hope we will fail." The Shanghainese could look to the Taiwanese, he hoped, not as a model to follow but in order to learn from their mistakes; in this way "the Taiwan Stock Exchange could share just a tiny bit of its experience."

The SSE representative responded casually to these advances. "It is a joke about the Shanghai Stock Exchange," she said proudly, "that not a single one of us had ever seen a foreign exchange when we set up the SSE." She was well aware that many foreigners (*sic*!) had a strong desire to cooperate with them, including the Chairman of the US Securities Exchange Commission. "But the reason we have developed so quickly," she continued, "is not because of the subjective desires of a few people but rather because the market has forced us to do so. Market pressures lead to market results (*shichang de yali, shichang de jieguo*). Of course we should make

---

[6] The term *guifanhua* is particularly difficult to translate. To Western ears, the most accessible meaning is "to bring into conformity with regulations," and this translation can sometimes be employed. However, *guifanhua* – literally, to make normal or regular – is often used in the absence of legal regulations, to signify conformity to unspecified norms or rules. As applied to the Shanghai market, *guifanhua* often meant, in the words of one interviewee, "to bring the market closer to international standards," which was in turn taken to mean lack of corruption (or lack of reputation therefor), relatively moderate price fluctuations, price–earnings ratios resembling those found on Wall Street, and the presence of an operating framework of laws and regulations.

sure that the companies approved by the Exchange conform to regulations (*guifanhua*), but this is handled by mandatory government approval for share issuance, and by the requirement that firms show two years of profitable operations. These matters are decided by the structural reform departments."

As the question period went on it became clear that at least some members of the Taiwanese delegation were well aware that despite our guide's radical *laissez-faire* rhetoric the possibilities for state control – and manipulation – of this new institution were many. The proper question was not so much whether or not to regulate, but rather what kind of regulation, by whom and to what ends. Thus, one member of the delegation asked our guide whether the fact that stock clearance, settlement and transfer were all centralized under the Exchange did not give the government too much access to information about individuals' financial holdings, creating an incentive for investors to falsify their accounts. Another speaker hinted in this same direction when he pointed out that the Exchange's stated regulatory goals of "openness and fairness" required that there be no way for the government to intervene in the private affairs of investors. Furthermore, continued the first speaker, if the Exchange handled all settlement and clearing procedures, it would also be responsible for the entirety of the paperwork associated with share transfer and ownership, including the potentially enormous costs of sending out material for shareholders' meetings, for example.[7] The SSE guide responded partially to these concerns. As of October of that year, there was to be established a separate settlement center, as on other markets, but it would be under SSE "leadership."

In the view of our guide, all of the problems of institutional structure raised by the Taiwanese were offset by a single enormous benefit: the elimination of black-market trading. It is important to note that by "black market" transactions, our guide was referring to any private trading in security that did not take place through the Exchange. "Today," she boasted, "they [black marketeers] cannot even begin to get a market going." I wondered but did not ask what it was that seemed so threatening to Shanghai regulators about a "black market": what made it "black"; and

---

[7] The representative from the Shanghai Exchange did not chose to make clear at this point that no material is sent to shareholders; even dividends are distributed in person and not through the mails. Shareholders' meetings are announced in the principal national and local financial newspapers, but since there is no voting by proxy and only a very few individual shareholders meet the very high ownership requirements necessary for participation in these meetings under most corporate charters, the problem of adequate notification is not pressing from the regulators' point of view.

why, if the Exchange attained its goals of transparency, equality and fairness, would anyone want to trade outside the official market? Hints at an answer were evident in our guide's discussion: black marketeering was a "destabilizing" influence; its "destructive potential was enormous." At issue here was the notion not of state "regulation" but of the state's monopoly over the trading of shares in Shanghai.

The questions became more pointed and our SSE guide more vague. What role is played by accounting firms, asked another member of the delegation? We were told that they were entirely independent agencies, though their relations with government were relatively "intimate" (*miqie*). "And what about insider-trading," someone else asked. This was to be handled by a system of magnetized cards, like credit cards, with personal access codes which would store investors' account information on a central computer.[8] "But how would this eliminate insider-trading?," I asked, the only question I ventured to pose during the meeting. "What you don't understand," a Taiwanese scholar whispered to me in response, "is that there is no leveraging on this market, so the risks are smaller."[9] I received no other response, and the discussion moved on. "From the point of view of the investor," asked another member, "why would I invest when there are no regulations requiring public declarations of companies' financial situations? In such an environment, one could expect only speculation, no investment." Our guide responded that companies are required to print financial statements when their shares are granted permission to trade on the Exchange (*shangshi*), and thereafter they must publish bi-annual financial reports in the local newspaper. She also made it clear that the meeting was drawing to a close.

The head of the Taiwan delegation got the message and began his concluding remarks, reiterating his hopes that Shanghai and Taiwan could enter into mutually fruitful cooperative relations. Diving into his bag, he brought out the obligatory gifts in the form of two books, one a history of the Taiwan stock market, the other, an analysis of the current economic difficulties of the ex-Soviet Union ("with the hopes that China will not adopt this path of development"). As the Shanghainese had no gifts to offer in return, the official part of the visit was then over.

[8] These magnetized stock account cards were distributed in 1993.
[9] Contrary to international practice, neither margin trading nor selling "short" (selling shares borrowed from a broker with the expectation of replacing them with shares purchased when the market price goes down, and hence reaping the price difference in profits) is permitted on the Shanghai market. Financial derivatives such as share options and futures were introduced only in 1993. The futures market has been suspended or closed down repeatedly since then because of problems of insider trading. There were no mutual funds in Shanghai in 1992.

The afternoon was taken up by a meeting with economists and officials at the Shanghai Academy of Social Sciences. The discussion was lively, unencumbered by the displays of bravado to which the Taiwanese had been subjected that morning. As the leader of the delegation had gone off to meet with "his old friend" Wang Daohan (ex-mayor of Shanghai and still a powerful political figure on the municipal and national scene, as we shall see), the meeting was led by another member of the delegation. "My impressions of Shanghai on this trip are very strong," he began, in the complimentary mode. There were so many changes, so much progress had been made. In particular, he continued, he was glad to see how knowledge was being respected. He only hoped that China could avoid some of the painful experiences which they had undergone in Taiwan, and that their delegation might contribute to the continued progress of the reforms.

In that spirit – and animated, perhaps, by the condescending reception that they had gotten at the Exchange – the Taiwanese embarked on a frank critique of the Shanghai market. One speaker commented on the need for more "non-governmental organizations" (*minjian jigou*)[10] and "modern organizational forms." The advantage of the stock market, he pointed out, is that "it's the fastest way to spread economic knowledge among the people. With everybody investing in shares, everyone becomes an economic expert. In Taiwan today, anybody can pick up a newspaper and read the financial page." He then made a plug for an "intermediary agency" for advising on investment which SASS could help them establish here on the mainland. Meeting with no immediate response to this proposal, a second speaker discussed the need for more transparency in information, for an independent press and accounting system, and for "interest groups" (*liyi tuanti*) which could counter-balance the government. A third speaker raised the question of "how much, finally, the government should govern." A fourth speaker brought out the big guns: Shanghai needs "systemization" (*zhiduhua*), "internationalization" (*guoji-*

---

[10] The term *minjian jigou* raises interesting problems of translation. *Minjian* in isolation is translated in the Commercial Press' *Chinese–English Dictionary* as "among the people, popular, folk; non-governmental, people-to-people"; *jigou* as "organization." All of these alternatives, except for "non-governmental," are too folksy to capture the notion of a powerful social agent capable of counter-balancing government power. Clearly, what this Taiwanese economist had in mind was something like capitalist "private" (*siren*) organizations. It is likely that he chose to avoid the sensitive question of privatization, framing his point rather in terms of a type of organization which has its place in mainland political ideology. In the Chinese context, however, *minjian jigou* has a distinctly subordinate ring to it.

hua) and "marketization" (*shichanghua*) and this implies "liberalization" (*ziyouhua*).

The tone of the mainland scholars' response was set by an economist with SASS' Sectoral Economic Research Institute: "Marketization and internationalization," he said, "are goals, but we still have many problems, we don't have enough investors, and we desire your criticism and suggestions." It became clear that while transparency in information, independent private associations and "modern organizational forms" may have been laudable goals in the abstract, these were not the immediate concerns of mainland economists. "What you have said is very inspiring," continued another mainland economist, "but we face many contradictions [*maodun*]. What to produce can be decided according to the market, but there are other questions which cannot. For example, how much should the state interfere [*ganshe*] in the market, and what takes the place of government interference?"

To this, a fifth Taiwanese speaker came back with the same set of complaints. "Information is not an open market on the mainland, it needs to be made more transparent. Your accounting system needs revising. Currently there are six different accounting systems depending on the kind of enterprise being appraised. And the media need more freedom to express their opinions." He mentioned his disappointment with Chinese state-controlled television. "If there were more debate on television, a single sentence from a state official could not have the effect it has on the market."

Clearly, some pieces were missing in the discussion, for each side was busy repeating its concerns without addressing those of the other. The economist from Beijing stepped in, for he had had enough experience with "foreigners," he told me later, to see what it was they were not understanding about the mainland situation. "In the mainland, we have 'public shares' [*gonggu*]," he began. "Public shares come in two forms: 'state shares' [*guojiagu*] and 'legal person shares' [*farengu*, sometimes translated as 'institutional shares']." Here he was interrupted by another mainlander, eager for solutions: "The problem is, how do we put public shares into circulation? This is a particularly difficult question for us today. Before May 1992, enterprise shares circulated only among enterprises [and the state was not allowed to sell its shares]. Then, with the shortage of shares in May, the government suggested that legal person shares be allowed to trade on the Exchange, but the more these shares entered the market, the lower prices dropped until our investors began to lose confidence, they became scared. How should we solve this problem? There seem to be two possibilities. Either we let legal person shares and new issues come onto the market slowly, or we go back to the old system in which legal person shares are only traded among enterprises."

There followed a moment of quiet bafflement on the part of the Taiwanese. "State shares," "legal person shares," "separate markets for different kinds of shares"? These were new and, to Taiwanese ears, highly "irregular" (*bu guifan*) notions. It became clear to everyone present that, "the particularity of the Chinese people" notwithstanding, "in feelings and in language" there were "barriers between them." The Taiwanese shook their heads. "Don't worry that people won't buy," counseled one expert, a note of exasperation in his voice. "If there's money to be made, they'll buy." "In the future, you must unify the markets," said another. "It makes no sense to have three different markets."

"But what about the people's fearful state of mind [*laobaixing jupa de xinli*]?," retorted a mainlander, as unable to adopt the Taiwanese point of view as they were his. "The market has been very high because purchasing power has far outstripped supply. Now their hopes are great, too great. They expect fantastic returns." Another mainlander took up the argument. "The problem is their risk consciousness [*fengxian yishi*] is lacking. This is a central issue. The State Council wants things to go slower. First make state enterprises more efficient, this is the main goal, then the investors will follow. I fear that in this area, despite your polite talk, scholarship is not much respected on the mainland."

It is difficult to say where the discussion would have led had it continued in this vein, for we were interrupted by the return of the Taiwan delegation leader, clearly excited by his meeting with Mayor Wang. He launched into a general discussion of his impressions, of Mao, of Deng, of the new Shanghai International Airport, of knowledge and power. Formalities were exchanged and the meeting was drawn to a close. "They don't understand the mainland at all," said the Beijing economist to me in an aside, chuckling over the gift of a book on the ex-Soviet Union.[11]

As I will argue, and as this encounter suggests, "understanding the mainland" means accepting that the question of state action and popular reaction is the pivot around which all else turns. This is what the Shanghainese I interviewed had in mind when they stated that "China has no economy."

---

[11] After their visit to Shanghai, the Taiwanese delegation went on to Beijing where they met with central authorities in charge of securities experiments. When visiting Beijing a few weeks later, I asked the same economist how their stay in the capital had gone. "They understand the mainland now," was his cryptic response.

Put less parabolically, what mainlanders were pointing to were the ways in which questions of production, distribution and exchange in China are necessarily filtered through the prism of the state tributary mode of production. In the following chapter, I outline how this tributary logic shapes the form and function of the stock market, from the creation of new joint-share companies, to the issuing of shares to the public, to the regulation of the Exchange

But, before proceeding with the discussion, a caveat is in order. I have contrasted Taiwanese and mainland economic worldviews, but this contrast should not be overdrawn. Indeed, Gates has argued that far more commonality exists between the Taiwanese and mainland political economies than popular understanding of the "Taiwan miracle" would allow (Gates 1996:204–242). On the one hand, the Guomindang (Nationalist) Party instituted upon their arrival in Taiwan in 1945 the most powerful tributary state in the sino-centric world, employing a quarter of the island's population and monopolizing one seventh of its resources to maintain its position (207–208). On the other hand, Taiwan's large and powerful private firms remained "petty capitalist" to the extent that they were (and are to this day) constrained within this tributary framework (223). Thus, we might predict that commonality "in language and in feelings" that the Taiwanese delegation repeatedly invoked.

As with all encounters which the ethnographer observes or participates in, the rhetoric of each side to this exchange was determined situationally. A tacit competition to represent the future of Chinese finance set the tone of the meetings, with each side highlighting its advantages. The Taiwanese, who had just celebrated the thirtieth anniversary of the establishment of the Taiwan Securities Exchange, politely stressed their greater experience and more intimate association with the world capitalist system. The Shanghainese for their part displayed a remarkable confidence that history was theirs for the making, so evident was the symbolic significance of the "mainland," with Shanghai at its financial center. However, beyond this agonistic positioning, each side's discourse reflected internal histories, and seemed directed primarily at a domestic audience. On the mainland, the political battle for the mere existence of a stock market was barely won. Indeed, as our SSE guide made perfectly clear in her presentation, the use of market rhetoric – her characterization of the market, and behind the market, "the People," as an independent force to which Shanghai leaders could only yield – was in essence a tactical device directed at a domestic target, those "conservative forces" which lay waiting to seize upon the first major calamity in the Shanghai market as an excuse to cut short the entire experiment and, most likely, hold people such as our guide politically responsible. As those "conservative forces" were principally, though not exclusively, located in Beijing, this *laissez-faire* rhetoric was also a tool those active in the Shanghai experiments had picked up for staking their claim to independence from central control.

From the Taiwanese perspective, the problems facing Shanghai – of an independent press, of non-governmental interest groups, or of the proper degree of government "regulation" – were anything but foreign (Gates 1996:204–242). Indeed, the Taiwanese also attributed a "special nature" (*teshuxing*) to their stock market, characterized by a high degree of government intervention and oversight, the lack of a well developed private sector in the area of financial services, a marked reticence to allow foreign service providers into the domestic market, and most importantly, a degree of market volatility unmatched by anything experienced by stock markets in the West or in Japan (Huang 1989). From 1986 to 1988, Taiwan experienced one of the most spectacular stock market bubbles in world financial history. It was no accident, then, that the Taiwanese delegation spoke the language of "systemization" and "regulation"; more than descriptions of the Taiwan market, these were goals which Taiwanese regulators viewed with a certain urgency in the wake of their own recent experience with "stock fever."

Nonetheless, genuine miscommunication was in evidence at these meetings, miscommunication which centered around the role – political, symbolic, ideological and only lastly regulatory – which the mainlanders attributed to the state. If I have described these discussions at some length, it is to prompt my readers into the same state of befuddlement which I read in the eyes of the Taiwanese delegation. The concerns which mainland Chinese experts raised in discussing their stock market were frequently quite different from what "foreign experts" – Westerners, Japanese, Taiwanese – considered to be the real issue raised by stock markets: do they work to attribute capital to users on the basis of efficiency? As with all ethnography, if we are to understand what the Shanghai Exchange means and how it functions in mainland Chinese society, we must set aside our assumptions about the "real questions" and adopt the terms of the debate which the Chinese have set for us.

2

The Shanghai stock market and the tributary state

In 1992, the Chinese state was present in every aspect of the new market for shares in Shanghai, from the determination of which companies were to be transformed to the joint-share form of ownership, to the setting of prices for new share issues, to the regulation of the everyday workings of the Exchange. This fact of fundamental importance has been insufficiently acknowledged in studies of the Shanghai stock market (see Hertz 1996b). When it is acknowledged, the presence of the state is generally presented as a kink to be worked out, a problem to be resolved. Missing from this interpretive framework is a positive account of the role of state power in the market, that is, an account which explains why Chinese reformers designed their stock market they way they did. Such an account must link the structure and operation of the Shanghai market to the logic of the tributary state.

Regulating the primary market

Proposals for the use of a share-holding system to further industrial reform were circulated in China as early as 1980 (Bowles and White 1992:578). By the mid-1980s, faced with the sharp contrast between continued stagnation in state-run industry and growth in the reformed agricultural sector, the debate surrounding the use of joint-stock companies and financial markets took on a new urgency. After various attempts to "accomplish the key link" in structural economic reform (through profit retention, profit contracting, the factory director responsibility system, enterprise leasing, etc.),[1] share-holding reform was conceived as a further and more thorough-going effort, even the last hope, toward the "enlivening of enterprise" (Wu 1988:60).

[1] See Naughton 1985, Chamberlain 1987, Perry and Wong 1985b, Solinger 1993.

44

More concretely, through transformation to the share-holding system (*gufenhua*), a number of objectives were thought attainable: reducing government intervention in the everyday work of enterprise management and rationalizing managerial incentives; "activating worker enthusiasm" by allowing workers to invest in their own enterprise; providing investment funds where few were available from over-burdened state coffers; rerouting personal savings from consumption to investment, thereby lessening inflationary pressures; and, finally, providing a means for valuing and transferring ownership in enterprises which would in turn facilitate efficient restructuring of industries and industry sectors through firm mergers and acquisitions.[2]

As Bowles and White have pointed out (1992:576–577), given the political–economic context in which share-holding was to operate, some of these goals were inconsistent with others. Furthermore, not all proponents of the share-holding system advocated all of these goals. Hesitations were principally focused on the ideological question of the role of "ownership by the whole people" in a socialist economy (Xia, Lin and Grub 1992:93–94, Hu 1993, Hertz 1994). A distinct but related question was the degree and nature of state control over industry in the new joint-share enterprises. In the "whatever-cat-catches-the-mouse" Dengist spirit, share-holding reforms moved ahead before reformers had resolved either of these problems. They remained and remain, however, part of the background of the reforms, susceptible to reactivation by "conservative forces" should the need or opportunity arise.

The vast majority of "shares" issued during these early years were actually a kind of bond: these non-negotiable securities, called "enterprise" or "employee internal shares" (*qiye/zhigong neibu gupiao*), were issued frequently on a non-voluntary or quota basis and/or in lieu of regular bonuses, and amounted to certificates guaranteeing workers in the "joint-stock company" an unspecified percentage of enterprise profits, paid either periodically or upon retirement. These shares were later categorized as "irregular" (*bu guifan*), and thus reliable data on these early experiments is hard to come by. One survey found that sixty out of the seventy firms responding had sold shares to their employees, with interest and dividends maintained at approximately 15 percent per annum (Xia, Lin and Grub

---

[2] See, for a more detailed discussion of these goals, Bowles and White (1992:576–577), Y. Li (1986), Rong (1986), Tang and Gu (1989), Wu and Jin (1985), Xu (1987), Zuo (1986), Xia, Lin and Grub (1992).

1992:93–101).[3] These "internal shares" represent a particularly pure example of the state tributary logic operating in the share-holding context. In an inspired reworking of experiments in employee ownership carried out in advanced welfare state economies such as Scandinavia, these "enterprise internal shares" were designed to increase state workers' dependency on and loyalty towards their enterprise while extracting revenue previously destined as bonus payments. To avoid provoking worker resentment, factory managers tended to pay the highest possible dividends on these certificates, so much so that the government soon found it necessary to set an upper limit of 15 percent as the highest dividend enterprises could pay to "equity investors" (Xia, Lin and Grub 1992:97). Clearly, few of the goals behind share-holding reforms were attainable through this form of share: though inflationary pressures were perhaps decreased by this (frequently forced) investment mechanism, none of the other macro-economic goals of share reforms were touched by this measure. Within the enterprise, "worker enthusiasm" could not have been much activated by the obligatory purchase of a non-negotiable claim to "dividends," especially if these "shares" replaced bonuses previously distributed.

Shanghai was a forerunner in the enterprise–internal share experiments, with the Shanghai No. 17 Textile Mill issuing shares to its workers as early as 1980. However, it was forced to withdraw these shares after strong government criticism (Bowles and White 1992:591). This event no doubt accounts for the small percentage of "internal shares" in Shanghai today.[4] Undaunted, Shanghai enterprises were again pioneers in issuing shares to the general public in 1986.[5] Four collective enterprises were encouraged to apply to the public for funds rather than obtain budgetary appropriations from the local government or loans from the newly restructured banking system. Feile Yinxiang (Xiao Feile), Yanzhong Shiye and Aishi Dianzi, and Shenhua Diangong (later renamed Shenhua Shiye) were approved for

---

[3] Another source estimates the value of "irregular" shares in 1988 at 11 million *yuan* in Shanxi Province, 80 million in Liaoning, 164 million in Sichuan, 200 million in Heilongjiang, and 1.1 billion in Hunan, to cite only the most spectacular examples. Interestingly, this same source states that no "irregular" shares were issued in either Beijing or Shanghai (Jin, Xiao and Xu 1991:64).

[4] The *Shanghai Zhengquan Nianjian 1992* (*Shanghai Securities Year Book 1992*) reports that "enterprise internal shares" (*qiye neibu gupiao*) account for a mere 1.63% of all "valued securities" in Shanghai, as opposed to 5.55% in "enterprise shares" issued to the public (*qiye gupiao*). This ratio of approximately 1:4 can be compared to Guangzhou (24:1), Wuhan (12:1), or Beijing (8:1). The only other regions which have approved fewer "enterprise internal shares" than "enterprise shares" are Shenzhen (1:9), Hebei (1:1.5), Jiangsu (1:20), and Anhui (1:4) (Jin, Xiao and Xu 1991:65). Note that even these cryptic figures should be enough to demonstrate the enormous regional variation in the application of the reforms.

[5] Shenyang issued shares to the general public in 1984, but these early local experiments did not meet with encouragement at the central level (Solinger 1993:134).

transformation to the share-holding system (*gufenhua*) in 1984, 1985 and 1987, respectively, issuing seven million *yuan* worth of shares to the public. It is worth lingering for a moment over the initial motives for transformation to the share-holding system. In contrast to the many and complex theoretical justifications for experimenting with the share-holding system being debated in numerous publications at the time, the goal of these first experiments was simple: to tap the enormous savings reserves of Shanghai citizens.[6] Not surprisingly perhaps, the valuation and "stockification" of these collectives were performed in a rather *ad hoc* manner. Enterprise assets were assessed on the basis of book value. If the collectives had accumulated their own assets over the years, these were counted as their shares in the new company. However, at least two of these four collective enterprises were considering transformation to the share-holding system because, in the words of their vice-directors, they were on the verge of bankruptcy.[7] Some attempt was made to estimate the value of all loans which the local government and/or other enterprises had extended to the collectives, and this sum was converted into shares in the enterprise. Once the debts of the enterprises had thus been wiped from the accounts, these new companies were in a position to offer shares to the public, with minimal information available to investors.[8]

Experiments were extended to state-owned enterprises in 1987 with the

---

[6] Xia, Lin and Grub, in their survey of enterprises involved in share-holding reforms, found that 35% of enterprises responding had issued stock for the purpose of technological renovation, 28% to raise working capital, 16% to open new businesses, 18% to expand production, and 3% to enter into joint ventures with foreigners. This left 7% and 2% of enterprises who issued stock with the purpose of changing management or ownership structure respectively (1992:96). (The figures cited in Xia add up to 109.) I suspect that these figures, obtained in response to a formal, entirely voluntary questionnaire, overstate the "political correctness" of the reasons enterprises issue shares. In informal interviews with Shanghai officials, I was repeatedly told that many enterprises issued shares as an exercise in public relations, or simply because the opportunity presented itself; little previous consideration was given to the question of what to do with the money thus raised.

[7] When my interviewees claimed that their enterprises were "bankrupt," this was most likely not a technical determination, as the new Bankruptcy Law had not yet come into effect. (Note that no local bankruptcy regulations had been published for Shanghai at that time). Rather, they were faced with increasingly demanding creditors and no one willing to lend them more money. For an excellent introduction to the slippery notion of bankruptcy in Chinese industry, see Clarke (1991:51–55).

[8] Companies were held to no disclosure requirements under the 1984 "Temporary Measures of the People's Bank of China, Shanghai Branch, for the Administration of Share Issuance," July 1984, ("Zhongguo Renmin Yinhang Shanghai Fenhang Guanyu Faxing Gupiao de Zhanxing Guanli Banfa," reprinted in *Shanghai Securities Yearbook* (*Shanghai Zhengquan Nianjian*)) 1992. In 1987, new measures were issued, requiring that: "Any company which has issued stock must submit quarterly financial statements to the approving agency, and make its financial situation public to its share-holders" (Article 15, "Temporary Measures of the Shanghai Municipality for the Administration of Shares" ("Shanghai Shi Gupiao Guanli Zhanxing Banfa"), reprinted in *Shanghai Securities Yearbook* (*Shanghai Zhengquan Nianjian*) 1992. This article mandates some form of disclosure, but apparently not at the time of issuance.

approval of Feile Gufen (Da Feile) and Shanghai Dianzhenkong Qijian
Gufen Youxian Gongsi (Dianzhenkong, or Shanghai Vacuum), but there
were signs already that the central government was hesitant to proceed
without a more careful examination of the overall implications of share-
holding reforms.[9] For the next two years, no state-owned enterprises issued
stock to the public in Shanghai.[10] This gave central and local authorities
time to put in place an administrative system for governing share-holding
reforms, the centerpiece of which was "the new system of state assets management" (Jiang, Li and Li 1991).

In 1988, the State Council created the State Assets Administration Bureau
(Guojia Guoyou Zichan Guanli Ju, or Guoziju), with local bureaux
attached to the bureaux of finance at the provincial and municipal levels.
The responsibilities of this system are two:

first, to safeguard the rights and interests of the owner [the state], that is, to ensure
that state assets maintain their value and increase in value, to improve the efficient
management of state assets, and to make greater contributions to the increase of
social wealth and state revenue; furthermore, to work hard to make the state sector
full of vitality and vigor, to rationalize its structure and to improve its quality
incrementally so as better to bring into play its overall beneficial results and main
purpose and to stimulate the entire national economy towards a healthy development (Li and Li 1991:25).

As this text demonstrates, from the start the State Assets
Administration Bureau set itself goals which extended far beyond the
simple "safeguard[ing of] the rights and interests of the owner [the state]."
That is, rather than mimic the logic of capitalist management, as public
enterprises in capitalist systems tend to do, the State Assets Administration Bureau openly embraced a broadly formulated tributary logic in
which it was to represent the state in areas ranging from dividend policy to
rationalizing industry structure to, finally, stimulating the "entire national
economy." Probably because of this broad formulation the creation of the
state-owned assets management system allowed reformers to move
forward rapidly with the "stockification" of state-owned enterprises. In
Shanghai, three state enterprises were approved for transformation in
1991, with many more under consideration. However, it was not until
Deng's 1992 "Southern Tour" had clarified the direction of future reforms

---

[9] See the State Council's "Notice on Enhancing the Administration of Stocks and Bonds,"
Article 2 ("Guowuyuan guanyu Jiaqiang Gupiao Zhaiquan Guanli de Tongzhi"), March
1987, reprinted in *Shanghai Securities Yearbook* (*Shanghai Zhengquan Nianjian*) 1992.
[10] One Zhejiang enterprise that was later listed in Shanghai, Fenghuang Huagong Gufen
Youxian Gongsi, was "stockified" in 1989.

that transformation to the share-holding system really took off. Twenty-nine state-owned enterprises were approved in 1992, with a total market capitalization of 4.5 billion *yuan* (*SHZQ* 1993a).

The process by which state-owned enterprises were transformed into joint-stock companies was both more complicated and less improvised than that for the collectives examined above. In 1991, the State Council issued its "Administrative Measures for the Appraisal of State-Owned Assets," setting forth the main principles of state property appraisal.[11] Enterprises were required to apply to their local State Assets Administration Bureau for permission to undergo appraisal (*zichan pinggu*). If this permission was granted, the enterprise then chose a certified public assessor or accountant. It was the job of this office to calculate the value of the enterprise in shares (*zhejia rugu*). This was carried out with a combination of procedural rigidity and substantive flexibility which merits detailed examination.[12]

The main difficulty in this process was that there was no market for enterprises in China which could serve as an indicator of the value of the firm. Instead, the firm was broken down into its component parts, each of these was assessed separately, and a total was compiled. Of course, even at the level of component parts, there were often no markets by which to set price. Thus, the "market method" and the "estimated rate of return method," most frequently used in the West (according to my Chinese interviewees) were supplemented by a third method which estimated the cost of replacing individual components of the enterprise (*chongzhi chengben fa*). The appraisal of land use rights and intangible assets posed further difficulties. For ideological reasons, the conversion of these factors into valued assets was viewed with suspicion. Consequently, for most state-run enterprises converted to the share-holding form in 1992, the value of enterprise land and intangible property such as trademarks or customer good will was not included in the assessment of state share-holdings at this stage.[13]

---

[11] "Guoyou Zichan Pinggu Guanli Banfa," reprinted in *Compilation of Laws and Regulations Governing the Registration of Rights to State-Owned Property* (*Guoyou Zichan Chanquan Dengji Fagui Zhidu Huibian*) 1992. See also Jiang, Li and Li (1991).

[12] The material for this description comes from my readings and from interviews with the National State Assets Administration Bureau in Beijing, the Shanghai State Assets Administration Bureau, and the Shanghai Number One Certified Public Accountants' Office.

[13] This despite the fact that Article 6 of the "Administrative Measures for the Appraisal of State-Owned Assets" (1991) (see note 11 above) provides that intangible assets may be included among the state-owned assets in the possession of enterprises. One example of this practice, much discussed by investors and officials during 1992, was the share-holding conversion of Shanghai No. 1 Department Store. Though virtually all of its assets took the form of land use rights and customer good will, neither was included in the appraisal which served as the basis for quantifying state shares.

On the basis of this restricted inquiry, the certified public accountant or assessor estimated a net value for the company which was qualified as an "objective" determination. This value, however, merely served as a reference point for the State Assets Administration Bureau. Final value was determined through a discretionary analysis of the "health" of the company and its industry sector, and of the interests of the state. (Here, unquantified assets such as land or intangible property might be thrown back into the balance.) This value was then divided into "state shares" (*guojiagu*), which represent investment made by the state (at both the central and local levels) in the creation, expansion or upgrading of the enterprise up to the moment of its transformation to the share-holding form.[14] It is important to note that these shares, in principle, were entirely non-negotiable.

Once the value of past state investment had been quantified in terms of state shares, the new joint-stock company was in the position to raise new capital. Three kinds of share were "offered to the public" (*gongkai faxing*), with the Shanghai Branch of the People's Bank designating the proportions of each. "Legal person shares" (*farengu*) are partially negotiable, dividend-earning shares which are offered to institutions. In principle, this offering was open to any legal person interested in investing in the issuing company. In practice, these shares tended to go to other state-run enterprises with links to the issuing company, or to the legal-person arms of administrative organs, not infrequently the same organs which were responsible for the new joint-stock company before conversion. This is because joint-stock companies, who had discretion over whom they sold shares to, preferred agencies with which they had prior connections (and which therefore might be able to help them with administrative difficulties) over institutions with which they had no connections. Thus, the system of institutional ownership under share-holding recreated, wittingly or unwittingly, the network of administrative controls which it was designed to supersede. Furthermore, only a limited number of "legal person" shares were approved for trading amongst Chinese institutional investors on two computerized networks centered in Beijing, STAQS and NETS. Because institutions could not freely buy and sell "legal person shares" among themselves, this system could not – without further administrative mea-

---

14 Investment made by non- or quasi-state agencies (e.g. trust and investment companies, holding companies or groups) prior to "stockification" was labeled "initial investor shares" (*faqirengu*) and counted with state investment, to distinguish it from post-transformation institutional investment. These shares traded under the same conditions as those for "legal person shares" to be discussed below.

sures – promote the goals of enterprise rationalization and restructuring which figured prominently in the justifications offered by reformers for share-holding experiments.

A second kind of "publicly issued share" is "individual shares" (*gerengu*) offered, as their name indicates, to any individual who wishes to purchase them. Interesting questions of definition – central to the ideological justification for share-holding reforms – were posed by the distinction between "legal person" and "individual" shares. State shares and legal-person shares qualify as forms of public ownership of the means of production (*gonggu*, as the Beijing economist pointed out to the Taiwanese delegation). That state ownership is public ownership, because the state represents the interests of the Whole People, is a tenet of Chinese socialism and Western capitalism alike. That ownership by legal persons also represents public ownership is based on the fact that enterprises given the opportunity to invest in joint-stock companies are virtually always themselves state-owned. In fact, however, the "public" status of "legal person shares" is even more confusing that this account would have it. At the simplest level, legal person shares represent public ownerships because they cannot be purchased by individuals, nor even by small clearly private enterprises. However, shares offered to legal persons and individuals on the market are called "public" issuances (*gongkai faxing*). This classification makes reference to another notion of the public – that associated with the open market – and justifies classifying legal person shares as public ownership for very different reasons.

In contrast to the delicate political status of "legal person shares," "individual shares" appear relatively straightforward. These shares are dividend-earning and fully negotiable; indeed these are the only shares to trade on the Shanghai Securities Exchange, as the Taiwan delegation learned to its dismay.[15] In principle, it was the job of the brokerage or brokerages underwriting the issue to offer its quota of shares to the general public. In practice, however, because of the overwhelming demand for shares in 1992, municipal authorities instituted a lottery system of "share-purchase applications" (*rengouzheng*). In January and February 1992, these applications were sold for 30 *yuan* (approximately US $4.50) a piece, with the promise that draws would be held throughout the year.[16] If one's

---

[15] Shares issued to individuals by collectives are also called "individual shares" and trade under the same conditions on the Exchange.

[16] The black market price of these share-purchase applications rose as high as 2,000 *yuan* in Shanghai. A similar instrument, issued in Shenzhen, was at the origin of the riots in that city in August of 1992 in which a number of people reportedly lost their lives (Schell and Lappin 1992).

number came up, one then had the right to purchase a limited number of a specified share at the issue price.

The price of "publicly issued shares" (called "premium rate" [*yijia*]) was determined by the local branch of the People's Bank of China in a process which again followed the logic of tributary state control and not the mechanisms of finance capitalism. Contrary to practice on stock markets in the West and in Japan,[17] the People's Bank did not use prices on the secondary market – which throughout most of 1992 were viewed as excessively high – as an indicator for setting the price on the primary market. Rather, the bank made a preliminary calculation of the future earnings of the new joint-stock company, based on its estimates of the company's financial prospects but also on a re-examination of the company's worth assessed during the process of "stockification." (Here again, land use rights and intangible assets might filter back into the analysis.) It then set the issue price so as to produce a price–earnings ratio (*shiyinglu*) approximating international standards. (During the year of my fieldwork, the People's Bank attempted to keep this ratio at about 8:1.) Thus, the price–earnings ratio was used not as an indicator of value on the secondary market but proactively to determine value on the primary market.

In the eyes of officials at the People's Bank – who were well aware that their procedures differed from international practice – two reasons justified an administrative rather than market determination of issuing price. The first was their desire to downplay the speculative character of the Shanghai market; by artificially dampening prices at the issuing stage, the People's Bank was helping to establish Shanghai's reputation in the international financial community. Of course, this effort had limited effects, for the moment these shares were approved for trading on the secondary market they generally doubled, sometimes even quadrupled, in price, bringing price–earnings ratios back up to highly speculative levels.[18]

More fundamentally, however, Shanghai officials simply could not countenance setting issuing prices so much higher than their estimate of the share's "real" value. The attempt to control prices was based in an economic ideology which remained suspicious of the market – especially of

---

[17] On these markets, the price of a new share issue is determined through competitive bargaining between the issuing company, the lead underwriter and other investment houses interested in buying this issue for resale to the public. Price is ultimately constrained by the estimated price at which the new shares will trade in the secondary market. Although there is significant variation among individual stocks, among industry sectors, and among national markets, the average price–earnings ratios found on these markets are generally situated somewhere between 5:1 and 20:1.

[18] The price–earnings ratio of one particularly hot share reached 80:1 in the spring of 1992.

such speculative character – as a determiner of value. Officials could argue, as did many Shanghai citizens, that pricing primary issues at market prices would put these shares out of the reach of ordinary citizens.[19] Indeed, even at the artificially low prices at which these shares were issued, many investors found the entire process unjust; observing that the issuing price for legal persons and individuals was often five to nine times the "price" of shares held by the state (called "face value" or *mianjia*), many investors concluded that the state was getting its shares at a discount.[20] However, despite the distorted signals and incoherences inherent in this administrative determination of price, bank officials preferred the logic of state control (of reputation, of "real value," of access) to that of the market.

The administrative determination of issuing price was only possible because the brokerages which underwrite shares throughout China are themselves state-run or quasi-state enterprises, subject to state directives through their parent agency and the People's Bank of China, and isolated from the pressures of competition on the market place. Every brokerage in Shanghai had institutional links either with one of China's specialized banks or with a large investment and trust company, all of which are government or quasi-government agencies. Thus, to name only the largest in Shanghai, Haitong Securities Company operated under the Bank of Communications, Shenyin Securities Company under the Industrial and Commercial Bank, and Caizheng Securities Company under the national Ministry of Finance. Even International (Wanguo) Securities Company, which was itself a joint-stock company, had as its principal share-holder the quasi-government Shanghai Investment and Trust Company. This is not to say that brokerages did not compete, sometimes even fiercely, with one another. However, following the logic of the tributary mode, they competed for reputation and influence, that is, for advancement in the state-based system of rewards (which could frequently be converted to personal profit) and not for a healthy bottom line. Brokerages could point out the problems of primary share pricing to their parent agencies (my interview material suggests that all were aware of these problems), but

---

[19] This argument is appealing but misleading. In theory, a small investor can just as well buy one share costing 200 *yuan* as four shares costing 50 *yuan*. In fact, however, she may be reluctant to do so. This psychological tendency to avoid shares with too high a unit price irrespective of their worth gives rise to the practice of share-splitting in stock markets internationally.

[20] The "face value" of state shares is simply an accounting baseline. By contrast, the "premium value" of shares issued to the public is a real price: it represents the amount of money which new investors must pay to buy a share of the enterprise. This difference was not generally understood by Shanghai investors.

their freedom to negotiate on their own behalf with the issuing company was highly circumscribed, and the system of rewards for good performance lay elsewhere.

In addition to "legal person" and "individual" shares, a third form of share was offered to foreign purchasers by officially designated enterprises. Beginning in late 1991, a certain number of Shanghai enterprises were granted permission to issue "special *renminbi* stock" (*renminbi tezhong gupiao,* or "B shares"), that is, shares valued in Chinese *yuan* but denominated in US dollars and sold internationally to foreign individuals and institutions. All efforts were made to keep the market in B shares separate from the market in domestically traded "A shares" ("individual shares"), although some cross-over did occur.[21] The legal framework regulating the B share market was developed earlier and applied with more consistency than that governing the domestic market. Government "interference" in price movements, if it existed, was performed with great discretion; and issuing companies were held to international standards of accounting and disclosure.[22] Prices on the B share market varied independently from movements on the domestic market, and B shares competed with other Chinese enterprise issues in Hong Kong ("H shares") and New York rather than with domestic shares. Thus, while these shares were exceedingly important for Shanghai's image as an international financial center, they were not in 1992 and are still not today important to the market's functioning and they are generally exempt from its "special" logic. Throughout this book, I will refer only incidentally to this distinct market.

Table 1 summarizes the date of issuance, industry sector and ownership structure of the fifty companies on or about to come onto the Shanghai market as of December 31, 1992. It should be apparent from the table that "stockification," or transformation to the share-holding system, is in no sense equivalent to "privatization." As can be seen, genuinely private ownership occupies a minor, sometimes minuscule, place in the share structure of previously state-owned enterprises. Nonetheless, the term is frequently

[21] Some well-connected Chinese purchased shares designated for foreigners; however, because the B share market was sluggish in comparison with the domestic market, the temptation to circumvent government regulations in this regard was minor. I also knew of some Taiwanese investors (technically required to purchase B shares) who came to Shanghai to trade on the domestic market. This was potentially a far more lucrative affair, but it was an opportunity open only to overseas Chinese investors who were willing to install themselves in Shanghai and work the market in person, or who had Shanghainese relatives whom they trusted and who were willing to work the market on their behalf.

[22] For an English translation of regulations concerning B shares applicable at the time of this study, see the appendices in Y. Hu (1993).

found in the Western mass media, and beyond: for example, the word "privatization" was amply employed in the promotional literature of a large Swiss bank involved in underwriting China's international offerings.[23] This bank was one of the best informed foreign presences participating in share-holding experiments in Shanghai. Their use of this term thus reflects ideology or marketing strategy, not ignorance. Hu's *China's Capital Market* (1993) is also vague on the structure of ownership on China's stock markets. Of course, both Chinese and foreign brokers banking on the China market (one of whom employed Hu at the time he wrote his book) have an interest in maintaining this confusion, for an introduction to ownership structure in Shanghai such as the one I present here would likely as not scare away a significant number of potential foreign investors.

Turning from ownership formally defined to control, it becomes even clearer that these new joint-stock companies were still, for the most part, state run. The previous manager (*changzhang*) and Party secretary (*dang zhibu shuji*) were most commonly reappointed as the company's new chief executive officer (*zong jingli*) and chairman of the board (*dongshizhang*), respectively. Untrained in management techniques and unfamiliar with the enterprise, the National State Assets Administration Bureau did not attempt to exercise its rights as majority share-holder, except to supervise the initial transformation of the enterprise into the share-holding form. The real functions of the board of directors were delegated to share-holders (or "honorary" members of the board) more familiar with the enterprise in question, that is, to the same ministries and parent companies that administered the enterprise prior to transformation to share-holding. As mentioned in chapter 1, individual investors participated in management to an even lesser degree than the percentages listed in table 1 would indicate. Most company charters included provisions that individual share-holders must possess a minimum (usually rather high) number of shares before they could participate in shareholders' meetings. Groups of individual investors who combined their shares to meet this minimum could delegate a representative, but these representatives, unfamiliar with the procedures for shareholder democracy and cynical about the real possibilities for exercising their vote, did not usually participate actively. As of December 1992, no companies provided for share-holder vote by written proxy.

---

[23] In February of 1993, I attended a seminar in Geneva on the Shanghai stock market, organized by this bank and one of Shanghai's principal brokerages.

Table 1. *Ownership structure of Shanghai joint-stock companies, 1992*

Name of company	Year approved	Product or service	Percentage of shares owned by			
			State	"Legal persons"	Chinese individuals	Foreigners
Feile Yinxiang (Xiao)	1984	stereo equipment manufacturing	–	14	86	–
Yanzhong	1985	office equipment manufacturing	–	9	91	–
Aishi	1985	electronics manufacturing	–	30	70	–
Shenhua	1987	transport, investment	–	32	68	–
Feile Gufen (Da)	1987	stereo equipment manufacturing	65	27	8	–
Dianzhenkong (Vacuum)	1987	vacuum tube manufacturing	50	16	1	33
Fenghuang (Zhejiang)	1989	chemical products manufacturing	79	3	18	–
Xingye	1991	real estate investment	–	75	25	–
Erfangji (ETM)	1991	textile industry manufacturing	46	3	10	41
Lianhe Fangzhi (UT)	1991	textile machinery promotion	–	82	18	–
Qinggong Jixie	1991	light industrial machinery	94	–	6	–
Yixing Gangguan	1991	pipe manufacturing	65	13	22	–
Jiafeng	1992	textile manufacturing	84	2	14	–
Yuyuan (Shangcheng)	1992	tourist industry	14	72	14	–
Jiaodai (Rubber Belt)	1992	industrial belt manufacturing	50	7	7	36
Fenghua	1992	pen manufacturing	68	21	11	–
Yongsheng (Wingsun)	1992	pen manufacturing	54	9	6	31
Zhongfangji (China)	1992	textile machinery manufacturing	53	6	7	34
Diyi Qianbi (CFP)	1992	pencil manufacturing	45	8	8	39
Dazhong (DZ Taxi)	1992	taxi service	59	6	6	29
Jiabao	1992	lighting products manufacturing	–	91	9	–
Shuixian	1992	electronics manufacturing	71	20	9	–

Longtou	1992	textile manufacturing	74	17	9	—
Shibai Yidian	1992	retail sales	56	25	19	—
Dongfang Mingzhu	1992	broadcasting investment	—	95	5	—
Luntai (T & R)	1992	tire and rubber manufacturing	69	1	3	27
Xin Shijie	1992	retail sales	55	19	26	—
Lujiazui Kaifa	1992	Pudong promotion	94	4	2	—
Hualian Shangxia	1992	retail sales	45	34	21	—
Lianghua	1992	wholesaling staples	—	88	12	—
Jinling	1992	electronics manufacturing	—	88	12	—
Shanghai Dianqi	1992	electronics manufacturing	89	5	6	—
Waigaoqiao (WDC)	1992	Pudong promotion	75	9	3	13
Diyi Shipin	1992	retail sales	34	40	26	—
Shangye Wangdian	1992	real estate investment	—	85	15	—
Liannong	1992	wholesaling, agricultural products	32	44	24	—
Bingxiang (Compressor)	1992	compressor manufacturing	47	18	6	29
Lujian (Chloro-Alkali)	1992	chemical processing	61	8	2	29
Hainiao	1992	electronics manufacturing	—	—	100	—
Lingqiao	1992	drinking water supply	66	21	13	—
Jinqiao (JDC)	1992	Pudong promotion	59	7	7	27
Lianhua Heqian	1992	textile manufacturing	73	21	6	—
Fuhua	1992	high-tech research and development	10	55	35	—
Shenda	1992	textile manufacturing	74	17	9	—
Lengguang	1992	optical equipment manufacturing	56	12	32	—
Xinya	1992	fast food manufacturing/sales	59	18	23	—
Pudong Qiangsheng	1992	taxi service	57	—	43	—
Zhongcheng	1992	real estate investment	84	—	16	—
Xin Jinjiang (XJJ)	1992	hotel services	32	29	6	—
Shuanglü	1992	refrigerator manufacturing	—	95	5	33

Source: This table was compiled on the basis of figures in Guan and Wu (1992), Jin, Xiao and Xu (1991), and *Zhengquan Shichang* (*Securities Market Weekly*), a magazine published by the Stock Exchange Executive Council in Beijing.

Because the three, sometimes four, types of shares making up the owner-ship structure of Shanghai's joint-stock companies could circulate only among themselves and not across categories, the percentages of ownership set forth in table 1 were fixed. However, reformers were well aware that this separation of shares into distinct markets limited the market's potential and ran counter to many of the goals which transformation to the share-holding system was thought to promote. It was precisely this problem which so preoccupied the Shanghai economists in their meeting with the Taiwanese delegation. One issue, always underlying discussion of the state's role in the market, was whether the state had the right to reap the windfall profits created by "stock fever." A second, more political, was the question of state control over industry. Over the course of 1992, the atti-tudes of central and local authorities on this second question underwent a certain evolution: a number of well-positioned informants told me that even Party conservatives had come to recognize that a controlling minority of state shares would be sufficient to guarantee state control over the board of directors. A third question was then posed: how to implement the decision to decrease the state's ownership share. Changing the proportion of state to legal person/individual shares for enterprises not yet "stock-ified" was relatively simple: the People's Bank had only to authorize the issuing of a higher percentage of shares to the public. Selling off state shares in enterprises which already had their shares listed on the Exchange was more delicate. In April 1992, rumor had it that the state planned to sell a certain number of state shares on the Shanghai Exchange. However, this plan, if it ever existed, was postponed when these rumors caused a sharp drop in the market. It was decided that until the Exchange had enough volume to absorb large quantities of new shares without serious effects on price, no state-owned shares should be approved for trading.

This detour through share-holding reforms on the primary market is crucial to our understanding of the role of the state in regulating the sec-ondary market. However, whereas the issues discussed for the primary market centered around the question of state action, the secondary market posed the problem of popular reaction. We turn now to a description of the government agencies responsible for the Shanghai Securities Exchange, and to an interpretation of the logic underlying their activities.

Regulating the secondary market
Like all provinces and provincial-level municipalities in China, the Shanghai government is formally under the direct control of central authorities. Each arm of the municipal government has its equivalent arm

in Beijing (as with the local and central arms of the State Assets Administration Bureau, examined above), and receives directives from its parent administration. In practice, however, the relations between central and local authorities are far more complex than this simple centralized picture indicates; indeed, central–local relations are one of the most delicate and dynamic areas of change in China, both under the reforms and preceding them.

Shanghai has earned a reputation as a relatively well-behaved locality, in contrast to Guangzhou and Shenzhen, but also to other important cities such as Wuhan, Shenyang and Tianjin. Pye (1981) suggests that this docility is based on a particularly Shanghainese way of relating to Beijing. More probably, it seems to me, Shanghai's reputation for obedience to central authorities reflects a particularly Pekinese method of relating to Shanghai, through tight controls over the local administration, and through the practice of promoting prominent Shanghai leaders to key positions in the central government,[24] thus coopting key players capable of resisting Beijing at the local level. This is not the place to enter into a theoretical discussion of this complex problem.[25] Rather, I will illustrate this dynamic as it works itself out in the area of the stock market.

At the inception of share-holding reforms and throughout the period of my fieldwork, the principal agency responsible for regulating the Shanghai stock market was the Shanghai Branch of the People's Bank of China, more specifically, its Finance Administration and Regulation Office (Jinrong Xingzheng Guanli Chu, or Jinguanchu).[26] It was this office which

[24] President Jiang Zemin and Vice-Premier Zhu Rongji are the most high-profile results of this strategy today.

[25] Lieberthal's much read analysis focuses on the notion of "fragmented authoritarianism" (1995). Gates provides a compelling bottom-up model for regional variation, arguing that where the state tributary system is weakly installed, one will find a strong petty capitalist mode of production. Her chapter on "Cities and Space" is a breath-taking, air-clearing re-examination of Skinner's influential "market town/central-place" model of Chinese regional variability (1996:62–83).

[26] Just after I left the field, the State Council created its Securities Policy Committee (Guowuyuan Zhengquan Weiyuanhui, or Guozhengwei), charged with overseeing the overall development of the securities market nationally by drafting laws and setting the pace of securities reforms. Under this Commission is a specialized agency, the China Securities Regulatory Commission (Zhongguo Zhengquan Jiandu Guanli Weiyuanhui, or Zhengjianwei) which is meant to act as a watchdog agency, much like the US Securities and Exchange Commission. The Zhengjianwei was to have authority over local regulatory bodies – in the case of Shanghai, the Shanghai Securities Regulatory Commission (Shanghai Zhengquan Guanli Weiyuanhui, or Zhengguanwei), to be discussed below. From media reports, it appears that a fierce but hidden struggle on the part of this agency to exercise its authority over competing national and local-level agencies is still under way. (Contrast *Far Eastern Economic Review* article of March 10, 1994, claiming that central control is merely nominal [*FEER* 1994b], with an article of the same month from the same source suggesting that the battle is far from over [*FEER* 1994c].) Meanwhile, the central

authorized initial experiments with transformation to the share-holding system in mid-1986, which approved the "stockification" and listing of all companies on the market, and which issued initial and subsequent written regulations governing the primary and secondary markets in Shanghai.[27] The People's Bank's formal mandate was to set down the basic goals (*jiben yitu*) for stock market regulation. Mere administrative and technical problems, such as the ins-and-outs of the computerized trading system or the practicalities of establishing customer accounts and services, were to be handled by the Shanghai Securities Exchange and the securities brokerages.

From interviews with members of this office, it was clear that they were fierce defenders of their independence from both central and other municipal government agencies. When asked whether central authorities helped to formulate the conceptual framework for the market, one interviewee said flatly, "No. If the locality thinks it can handle it, then it goes ahead" (*Difang renwei keyi gao, jiu gaoqilai*). When asked whether the laws being drafted would require central approval, his response was that "the center" (*zhongyang*) would have a look at them but would not make any public statement (*buchumian*). However, when asked whether his office identified itself as a central or local agency – after an initial and important difficulty translating the notion "identify as" – his response was: "We must remain consistent with the Central Bank" (*gen zhonghang baochi yizhi*). As for competing local agencies, this interviewee bluntly claimed that: "All concrete decisions are made by this office, even if they are publicized in the newspaper as if they were taken by the Exchange." Even in this brief exchange, it was evident that competition for authority, power and prestige between these different agencies was a very real but strictly tacit part of regulatory practice. There is also every reason to doubt the accuracy of this interviewee's claims to power. Other well-placed acquaintances told me that all major decisions were regularly discussed and negotiated with both city government and central authorities.

The administrators in charge of the stock market at the Shanghai Branch of the People's Bank struck me as highly competent and responsi-

---

People's Bank has been formally excluded from the stock market regulatory business, but still maintains a certain influence (pers. comm.). In Shanghai, the heads of the Finance Administration and Regulation Office of the People's Bank have been transferred to the new Shanghai Regulatory Commission (pers. comm.).

27 See regulations collected in *Shanghai Zhengquan Nianjian 1992* (*Shanghai Securities Year Book 1992*). For a careful commentary on these regulations, see P. Potter (1992). In addition, this office was helping to prepare basic laws on joint-stock companies, financial accounting standards, and internal shares at the time of my fieldwork.

ble officials. (They were also obviously aware that my study could have an impact on the international image of their market, and kept themselves at a healthy distance from me outside of official settings.) Most top officials had received graduate training in economics, law or finance, mainly in Chinese universities, and many had been abroad for long enough periods to understand how stock markets work in the West and Japan, and to measure the kinds and dimensions of the "problems" in the Shanghai market. Indeed, the rhetoric of these officials was – during my interviews with them – entirely adapted to Western ears. Not even *pro forma* references to socialism or "Chinese characteristics" were to be heard. Rather, the problems they mentioned were precisely those problems which Western observers tended to point to: an inadequate legal framework governing such issues as disclosure and insider-trading, "abnormal" (*bu guifan*) accounting standards detracting from the reliability and comparability of company financial statements, and a tendency towards speculation rather than rational investment on the part of the investing public. When pressed, these officials also talked in very Western ways about the necessity of getting the government out of the business of day-to-day regulation. These tendencies to "intervene" (*canyu*) in the normal functioning of the market were always laid at the door of another agency, either the Shanghai Securities Exchange itself or the Shanghai Securities Regulatory Commission.[28]

However, interviews with other agencies and with employees lower down on the bureaucratic ladder suggest that the People's Bank conducted its fair share of "intervening" in the market, following a logic which I have identified as part and parcel of the tributary mode of government action.[29] This intervention could take many forms, all of which will be discussed shortly. What is important here are the justifications offered for intervention. In the words of one lower echelon employee at the Bank, the stock market was now in a "period of adjustment" (*tiaozheng jieduan*). "Investors' psychological ability to stand losses was very poor" (*gumin de xinli chengshou nengli tai cha*). It was their office's job to "diminish as much as possible the shock to society" (*jinliang jianshao dui shehui de zhengdang*) and "avoid social unrest" (*bimian shehui gaoluan*) by exercising control over the market.

---

[28] One of my interviewees was openly contemptuous of these other agencies, stating frankly that the people in charge "don't understand the market" (*bu dong shichang*).

[29] I conducted interviews with employees lower on the echelon in March and April 1992, and put off interviewing the heads of this office until November and December. The difference in rhetoric which I noticed between these two sets of interviews may also reflect the fact that a Western line on how to regulate stock markets was learned over the course of the year.

I retranscribe the details of this interview because I was never again to hear these justifications offered openly by any agency involved in regulating the stock market. Perhaps, this line was increasingly perceived as "abnormal" (*bu guifan*), that is, unsuited to international discourse on financial regulations. Perhaps, this silence simply reflected the standard government prohibition surrounding discussions of its motives. However, the unanimous consensus among interviewees outside the government was that concerns over the social effects of the stock market were extremely important to all regulators, and often determined the direction of specific policy decisions. One of the most striking examples of this reasoning was the worry, frequently expressed in non-governmental circles, that someone would commit suicide after losing money on the market.[30] During the early part of my fieldwork, I was assured that if anyone were to commit suicide, it would put the whole stock market project in jeopardy, for suicide was supposed to be a possibility only in the context of an exploitative capitalist stock market. However, over the course of 1992, an indeterminate number of people did commit stock-related suicide (seven cases were publicized, but rumor had it that more than twenty people had died), without a subsequent halt in the reforms. This suggests that unlike the issues of state control which form the basis for the tributary logic under examination, questions of popular reaction operate principally at the level of fantasy. This question will be taken up in detail in the following chapter.

The primary place where these concerns over social order were acted on was the Shanghai Securities Regulatory Commission (Shanghai Zhengguanwei). I repeatedly asked for and was never given interviews with members of this Commission, which leads me to think that it was the most powerful agency operating in Shanghai. It was made up of the Vice-Mayor of Shanghai in charge of the stock market, and top officials from all related municipal bureaux and agencies. These ranged from the Bureaux of Finance and Taxation to the Commissions for Economic Reforms and Commerce, to, more surprisingly, the Bureau of Public Security. It also included representatives from the major brokerages in Shanghai and, of course, from the Exchange itself.

The Commission met regularly a minimum of once a week. Its primary

---

[30] Virtually everyone who mentioned this risk used the phrase "to jump from a tall building" (*tiaolou*), and not the Chinese term for suicide (*zisha*). The same imagery appears in popular mythology about the 1929 stock market crash in New York. Notice the mimetic quality of this metaphor in both English and Chinese; the man drops as the stocks dropped.

concern was with the secondary market, that is, it was concerned with those aspects of the stock market which touched directly on "the masses." As contrasted with officials at the People's Bank, members from city government were not necessarily trained in law, economics or finance. They were reform-minded Chinese bureaucrats, concerned with the governance of their city, not the law of supply and demand. The Commission rarely issued directives or regulations in its own name. Rather, it worked through the Shanghai Securities Exchange, over which it had direct influence though no formal authority.

The Shanghai Securities Exchange was the third-most important institution in the municipal regulatory framework. The official structure of the Exchange was that of a fully independent, "not-for-profit membership organization" (*feiyingli huiyuanzhi*). Members rented chairs on the Exchange, for which they paid a yearly fee pegged to their assets. The Exchange was governed by a board of directors which met annually, and which was comprised of officers at many of the principal banks, broker-ages, and investment and trust companies in Shanghai. This board of directors was important for the connections they brought to the Exchange but appeared to exercise little authority. Within the organization itself, all important decisions taken by the Exchange were approved by the Shanghai Branch of the People's Bank of China, its "head" (*tou*), and the municipal government through the Shanghai Securities Regulatory Commission.

The fourth set of institutions with the capacity to "intervene" in the market were the brokerage houses, called collectively securities organiza-tions (*zhengquan jigou*). As already mentioned, these companies were linked to major government agencies via their parent companies (banks, ministries, and investment and trust companies) and through their repre-sentatives on the Shanghai Securities Regulatory Commission. Authorized to buy and sell shares on their own accounts, these companies were fre-quently called upon to execute decisions about market "intervention" taken by various government agencies, central and local. As we shall see, an important part of government "regulation" consisted in ordering these brokerages to buy up or sell out large quantities of a given stock or stocks in order to influence market price and direction.

Finally, it appears that Shanghai was frequently subject to suggestions or pressure from central authorities who wished to see the market acting in one way or another. These pressures were never made public, although the visits of all central leaders to the Exchange made front page news in the *Shanghai Securities Weekly* (*Shanghai Zhengquan Bao*), the official organ of the Shanghai Securities Exchange.[31] One of the most frequent topics of discussion in the rumors which circulated among investors throughout the city were the allegedly weekly trips which then-Chairman of the Exchange Wei Wenyuan took to Beijing. Generally, on the Monday after such a trip, a version of what the center (*zhongyang*) wanted the stock market to look like circulated around the city, causing a certain number of price flurries. When the market entered its period of prolonged decline in the fall of 1992, it was even said that Vice-Premier Zhu Rongji had personally come to Shanghai to tell securities organizations how to behave. "And, do they respect him?," I asked. "They don't respect him," was the immediate reply. "They're afraid of him."

An ethnography of administrative function
I have outlined the principal agencies with authority over and responsibility for the primary and secondary markets in shares. However, it should already be apparent that the task of determining how the market was regulated involves far more than a routine account of institutional design. Ascertaining which of the various agencies with regulatory authority over the stock market was behind which policy decision turned out to be one of the more difficult tasks I set myself during my fieldwork.

In the operations of Chinese government, decisions are regularly made by an agency other than the one issuing the public announcement of the decision. This secrecy is a crucial element of administrative functioning, and is a source of enormous difficulty in the study of the Chinese state in action. My attempts to discover exactly who was behind a given policy position were met with suspicion and trepidation, suspicion on the part of those whom I was asking, trepidation on the part of my assistant or advisor, roped into helping me with my inquiry. Revelations, when they came, were made in a tone of hushed intimacy which was both thrilling and disconcerting. It seems to matter little that the content of the decision had already been made fully public, or that it was innocuous in its design and its effects. Throughout my fieldwork and even as I write, I found this working principle of Chinese government difficult to contemplate with that matter-of-factness which should characterize the anthropological perspective. I became particularly infuriated when I heard Chinese officials complain about the "immaturity" (*bu chengshu*) of Shanghainese investors, and the difficulties this created for constructing a truly "normalized"

---

[31] Photos of all important visitors to the Exchange appeared in the *Shanghai Securities Weekly* (*Shanghai Zhengquan Bao*), and constituted valuable political capital for officials supporting securities experiments.

(*guifanhua*) international stock market. Trembling with conviction, I would suggest that lack of transparency in government was a far greater problem in foreign eyes than investor psychology. These outbursts met with varying responses. From those who felt safely out of the line of fire, there was hearty agreement. From those who felt implicated, I received bland statements about how everything is published but perhaps, as a foreigner, I simply did not know how to find the sources. The Chinese government apparently reserves the right to operate incognito.

For the most part, Chinese investors did not even attempt to follow through on the institutional origin of government decisions. The degree of sophistication which went into interpreting the actions and motives of "the State" was not matched by a sophistication about which institution was acting for "the State." Gossip centered on individual leaders, and the relations between individuals and cliques, not on institutional function or "culture." I frequently asked investors which arm of the state they thought was the author of a given policy change or declaration. Rarely did even well-informed investors know the answer, nor did they seem to care.

The foregoing is all by way of a large caveat. While I tried repeatedly to figure out the source of each administrative decision affecting the stock market so as to chart differing institutional functions, I can say that I only succeeded in a very few cases in coming up with what I take to be reliable information. This is because I did not want to over-tax the patience of those people in a position to help me, for every such demand was a demand of some importance. Furthermore, officials themselves were in no small degree of confusion about who should be doing what – confusion which was frequently attributed to the "youth" of the stock market regulatory apparatus.[32] To give credit where credit is due, many of the administrative structures put in place to regulate the stock market were indeed new, and undergoing rapid evolution.

The most basic type of regulation – what a Western reader might be tempted to call "real" regulation – took the form of directives issued by the Shanghai Securities Exchange to govern the technical aspects of the Exchange. These included decisions to fix the minimum price difference which counts as a "bid" at 5 *fen* or 5/100 of a *yuan*, or decisions about how the opening price for the day will be fixed. These directives, called "administrative regulations" (*xingzheng guanli*), were published regularly in the

---

[32] Of course, confusion has its strategic advantages. It promotes greater caution and greater secrecy, goals generally approved by all concerned. It also provides a way for central authorities to reprimand subordinate agencies for making mistakes, while taking credit for all positive achievements. Confusion is and has always been a principal element in Chinese military strategy and statecraft (von Senger 1991).

Shanghai Securities Weekly, and occasioned little interest from investors.

The next important set of regulations, also published regularly in the *Shanghai Securities Weekly*, were all those measures taken during the first half of 1992 to fix ceilings and floors for maximum price movements. During the second half of the year, these measures also included decisions about when to release onto the secondary market the twenty-nine newly approved joint-stock companies for 1992. These decisions were routinely issued in the name of the Exchange. However, it is unlikely that they were taken without prior consultation with the Shanghai People's Bank and city officials on the Shanghai Securities Regulatory Commission.

Needless to say, these regulations occasioned far more popular interest as they generally had immediate effect on price. Indeed, some people speculated that officials had an incentive to issue as many of this type of regulation as possible, as they could then profit from their insider knowledge by buying and selling on their own account. Of course, officials with any connection with the stock market were strictly forbidden from buying or selling stocks. However, it was the opinion of everyone I talked with, including rather high-placed officials and academics, that the vast majority of city officials were nevertheless engaging in various forms of insider trading through friends and relatives. It is impossible to prove that this is the case, nor did I choose to put my research or the lives of my acquaintances in jeopardy by trying to verify specific allegations. However, public government declarations about the dimensions of corruption in China give us every reason to believe that insider-trading on the Shanghai market is a very real problem (see Rocca 1992). What I could observe, however, was that as with all news of any importance on the stock market, all well-informed investors knew of these decisions hours if not days before they were made public.

A third form of "regulation," which investors qualified as "interference," were those public pronouncements by city officials connected with the stock market which commented on the propriety of various prices, or the problems of the market as they perceived them. These pronouncements were not decisions as such, but they were taken to mean – and most people would say intended to be taken to mean – that some unspecified government action was imminent. Because the consequences of such action were left intentionally vague, these declarations generally had an even stronger effect on market prices than the official regulations mentioned above.

A fourth form of "regulation," often called "adjustment" (*tiaokong*) by the government and "manipulation" (*caozong*) by the investing public, were orders given to stock-broking companies to intervene in the market in one way or another. In the fall of 1992, when this action was most visible, this involved ordering securities organizations to "prop up the market" (*tuoshi*) by buying in large quantities of shares on their own account. These measures, while issued secretly, were visible to all through the computer terminals at brokerages which reported each trade with the number of the purchasing agent.

I managed to trace one such "regulation" – designed to slow the selling spree which was infesting the autumn market – to its real source, the Shanghai Securities Regulatory Commission. This act of regulation, which was not publicized, took the form of a temporary order given to all brokerages forbidding them to sell shares prior to seven days after they had bought them. It was this measure which had caused one official of the Shanghai People's Bank to declare that city officials "don't understand the market," for predictably it had precisely the opposite effect from that desired as brokerage houses rushed to rid themselves of unwanted shares at any price as soon as the seven days had passed. Soon after its implementation, this measure was revoked with the same secrecy that it had been promulgated in.

Finally, city officials and perhaps even the Shanghai People's Bank sometimes chose to "regulate" the market through the judicious spreading of rumors. I was told, but cannot verify, that city officials ordered the Exchange to send out plants among the crowds of stock investors who discussed policy on the curbside, with the hopes that these rumors would set off a buying or selling spree. In another case, one that I followed, a securities company leaked advance policy information to its large investors in order to encourage them to buy into the sinking market. It was up to these investors to decide how to interpret this kind of information: at times, advance policy leaks circulated in response to administrative pressures on the brokerages to get the market moving in the desired direction; at other times, news was leaked to large investors in that spirit of cautious collegiality which reigned between brokerages and their important clients.

State ownership and state control

In the context of the primary market in shares, I have demonstrated the high degree of state presence in the ownership structure of Shanghai companies. However, it remains to demonstrate the particularly "tributary" logic of this ownership. After all, many European states own large portions or absolute majorities of national companies, but this ownership, in and of itself, is consistent with the capitalist economic environment in which these companies operate.[33] The "special characteristic" of the Chinese state as owner is that it does not act as an owner should act according to neo-classical theories of the corporation. In less reified terms, this means that the administrative system responsible for safeguarding the state's ownership position does not single-mindedly pursue the goal of maximizing returns on its "investments." Rather, it acts as part of a complex hierarchy of administrative organs whose job it is to promote the overall political, ideological and extractive interests of the state.

A hint at the way the state perceived these interests in 1992 comes with a closer examination of the State Assets Administration Bureau. As described above, the entire process of assets assessment which this Bureau oversees leaves the state considerable leeway in valuing its own past investment and in claiming shares in new joint-stock companies. However, despite the consequent possibilities for the over-valuing of state holdings, the incentive structure in this administrative system tended, to the contrary, to result in the under-valuing and under-utilization of state shares. The most flagrant example of this was the Bureau's reluctance, despite published regulations, to assess land-use rights and intangible property in its determination of state holdings.

In 1992, the Bureau was directed to attend to the principal worry of central and local reformers – getting the market off the ground. This meant that state assets were assessed "flexibly" and tax and dividend policies applied "appropriately" to encourage the new joint-stock companies. In Shanghai, the local State Assets Administration Bureau was housed in the offices of the Bureau of Taxation, and took many of its officials from this Bureau or from the Bureau of Finance. Of course, this situation contained the risk that appropriations, taxation and assets management policies would be treated as a bundle of possible rewards and deterrents, with the appropriate distribution of each negotiated on a case-by-case basis in consultation with the ex-administrative superiors (*zhuguan bumen*) of the new joint-stock company.[34] My interview material suggests that this risk certainly materialized in 1992.

Further indications of the state's perception of its role in the new

---

[33] More or less. The collapse of France's flagship public corporation, the Crédit Lyonnais, in 1995, and the scandals that have emerged around it suggest that the French government and Crédit Lyonnais were linked through tributary bonds of loyalty and mutual promotion which violated the spirit and the letter of public ownership in capitalist economies.

[34] Note that there is no capital-gains tax on dividends and interest for individuals or for corporations in Shanghai. The taxes which state administrators had at their disposal were income-based.

market for shares come from the Bureau's attitude towards corporate governance. As administrative "trustee" for the principal share-holder in virtually all of the companies on the market, the Bureau had the right to sit in on board meetings and elect management. Typically, however, the Bureau, unacquainted with the companies it now "owned," delegated this right to other arms of the state supervisory structure. Most commonly, these other arms were again the new joint-stock companies' old administrative superiors. Furthermore, at the time of my study and as late as 1994, the Bureau frequently voluntarily surrendered its rights to receive dividends and interest on state shares, reasoning that the health of the company and of shareholding reforms generally would be better served if this capital were plowed back into the enterprise.

We may attribute the particular form which state control of the stock market took in 1992 Shanghai to the newness of the market, the inexperience of government regulators, and the "conservative" habits of mind still common among state officials. Certainly, there is some degree of truth to this view. However, the overall justification for the high degree of state ownership in Shanghai companies is consistent with what Gates has identified as a

tributary mode managed by state officials who put their own requirements for reliable revenues, stable class relations, and continued hegemony above any perceived need for economic expansion (1996:8).

"Regulatory" activity on the secondary market is perhaps an even clearer indicator that something more complex than mere inexperience guided the hand of municipal and central authorities. The many forms of "regulation" found on the Shanghai market were responses to a single, pressing objective: controlling prices on the Exchange. Prices were to be high enough to attract investors, or else the entire experiment would be put in jeopardy. But prices should not rise too high or too rapidly, for such movements created the risk that too many investors would be too badly hurt when prices fell again. Furthermore, shares should be available to all who wanted them, for a shortage of shares pushed prices higher and increased the ungainly speculative character of an already highly speculative market.

In the context of regulating the secondary market, then, state power was conceived of as the power to intervene directly and immediately in the affairs of "the People" to establish order, and in this case, order centered around the notion of appropriate price. In the eyes of government officials, the opposite of state power was not power in the hands of someone or something else: it was chaos. That this conception of the role of the state caused problems – "contradictions" in the mainland vocabulary – for the formation and regulation of the stock market was clear to all mainland observers. The question was, in the words of the mainland economists of chapter 1, how much should the government "interfere" and what could possibly take the place of government "interference"?

These questions were not answered during the time of my fieldwork, and may not be answered for years to come, if at all. However, over the course of the year, an evolution in the area of stock market "regulation" could be observed, an evolution which was not so much voluntarily put in place as forced on state officials by the very nature of the market they were trying to regulate. It was not, as the guide at the Shanghai Securities Exchange implied, that market pressures led to market results. Rather, market pressures made it clear to all those observing the stock market that in the great dialectical struggle between "the State" and "the People," sometimes "the People" got the upper hand.

Let me avert a misunderstanding at the outset. The "triumph" of "the People" through the market is not democracy, nor is there reason to be optimistic that it will lead to more democratic political–economic practices in any near future. Rather, it is a form of counter-hegemony. It is in the context of state hegemony and popular counter-hegemony that our discussion of the stock market in China today must be placed. And, it is to that context that I now turn.

3

Stock fever (*gupiao re*)

I arrived in Shanghai in February 1992 to begin my fieldwork and got into the car sent by my host institution to meet me at the airport. Two minutes into our ride into the city, the official who had met me turned to me and said: "It's a good thing you came now. If you had come last year, your topic wouldn't have been interesting. Next year, we don't know what will happen. But this year, the stock market is *re*."

The social fact
And so I encountered what was to become one of the guiding concepts for this study minutes into my stay in the field. *Re* means "hot" or "in," and in this context is often translated as "fever." "Stock fever" (*gupiao re*) was manifested by the fact that "everyone" was talking about the stock market; stocks were in, and not to invest in – or at least to have an opinion about – the market was to be out of it. Long lines of people waiting to buy and sell stocks spilled into the streets outside the many stockbroking offices scattered throughout the city. Next to these lines were other crowds: large crowds straining to catch a glimpse of computer screens in the brokerage lobbies, smaller crowds gathered in circles discussing the market's activities, and other even smaller groupings engaging in various forms of deal-making. At night, the city was dotted with groups of (mostly) men standing on the streets in circles of five to fifty, sharing information and predictions. I could eavesdrop on conversations about particular stocks, recent trends, and government policy shifts in virtually every restaurant I ate in, on every bus I took. Perhaps most importantly, while literally "everyone" was not, of course, talking about stocks all of the time, literally everyone agreed that the stock market was *re*. Stock fever is a social fact.

In this chapter, I analyze the form and function of stock fever in the light of other "fevers" which spread through urban Shanghai, for it is through the notion of *re* that one can see with particular clarity the symbolic relation between "the State" and "the People" in contemporary urban society. However, a note of caution is necessary at the outset of this enterprise. The notion of Chinese "stock fever" conjures up powerful images in the Western imagination, images which should be handled with great care. On the one hand, it is deceptive in its familiarity. We in the West have also been prone, for centuries now, to epidemics of speculative "mania" (Mackay 1980 [1841], Kindleberger 1989 [1978]). With the spread of financial markets to Asia, bourses in Bombay, Taibei and Tokyo have experienced similar booms and crashes. As capitalist evolutionism gains ground in its claim of universal historical inevitability, it seems merely a matter of course that the Chinese would participate in these moments of speculative fever along with the rest of us.

On the other hand, though it may be a matter of course, Chinese stock fever is also the object of particular curiosity. As already argued, the Chinese stock market is the *pièce de résistance* in the West's ideological triumph over Communism. This structure is only reinforced by recent Western presumptions about a particularly capitalist "gene" shared by the Chinese nation.[1] In 1959, Freedman identified overseas Chinese "sophistication in the handling of money" (1979 [1959]) as a factor in their remarkable economic success once arrived in their new homelands. What Freedman describes is an extremely elaborate use of credit and debt among social networks in the mainland, an outgrowth of the petty-capitalist mode of production. Among overseas Chinese, freed from the tributary state, this economic sophistication became a "capitalist gene." With the challenge to Euro-American dominance posed by east Asian economic development in general, and Chinese economies in particular, we see a growing tendency to view this sophistication as an immutable "Chinese characteristic," an instinct for petty commerce, thrift and industry (see Gates 1996:13–14). Redding's (1990) widely read study of managerial attitudes among overseas Chinese exemplifies this tendency to essentialize Chinese culture's relation to capitalism. Though Redding does not resort to genetic metaphors, the "heritage" which overseas Chinese carry about in his account appears positively hardwired into them. After describing for us a "typical Overseas Chinese", Mr. Lim – a composite created from in-depth interviews with seventy-two successful businessmen – Redding assures us that "Mr. Lim has over 40 million compatriots, people with a

---

[1] I heard the term "gene" used by a French sinologist in a television interview about China's economic reforms.

common heritage, many common ideals, shared norms of social behavior, similar strengths and similar weaknesses; in sum, a distinct cultural type, and one moreover which has remained consistent and true to itself for centuries" (18).[2] What is lost in this culturalist account, as Dirlik (1996) demonstrates, is any consideration of the particular place which Chinese capital occupies under current conditions of advanced capitalism, and the ways in which this new economic role reinforces old cultural stereotypes.

Finally, "stock fever" conjures up other images particular to China. Crowds of black-haired, brown-eyed Chinese squeezed together on the streets remind us of other crowds, revolutionary crowds, and the fanaticism associated with them. The image of crowds has a particular potency in what the West has called "Asia." The loss of individuality associated with crowds (Canetti 1984 [1960]) is accentuated by our deep-seated conviction that Asians all look alike.[3] In the Western collective unconscious, Asians are natural crowds.

Thus, the Western fascination with Chinese stock fever draws simultaneously on stereotypes of Chinese as instinctive capitalists and brain-washed hordes. It is worth noting at the outset that these two images are in some degree of tension. If all that the Chinese want to do is get down to the business of making a buck, how are we to account for the revolutionary and millenarian movements which, while they reached a historical highwater mark under Mao, have been an important part of Chinese history throughout the imperial and Republican periods? Or vice versa? In sum, how are we to reconcile these qualities of fanaticism and rationality (or, "capitalism," a word which has become its synonym)?

The very contradictory nature of these images is a hint as to the sociocentrism in their formulation.[4] Anthropology as a discipline is not immune to these forms of sociocentrism. In this regard, it is instructive to make a brief detour by way of a famous anthropological site, a theoretical place

[2] What Mr. Lim really has is a list of traits, comparable to the list of "Chinese characteristics" drawn up one hundred years ago by Arthur Smith (1894) in his monument of sociocentric missionary writing.

[3] It would be interesting to date this popular conviction. Was it part of Western perceptions of "Asians" from our first contacts, or has it developed more recently, and if so why? Note by way of contrast that "Africans" do not fit this perceptual scheme. In the American cultural context, we do not believe that "Africans" all look alike, nor do we think of "Africans" as crowds in the sense described by Canetti.

[4] Note also that the element of comparison with Western speculative manias has disappeared. This tacking between universal and particularist logics is the result of what Louis Dumont has identified as the implicit hierarchy within Western universalist individualism [Dumont 1986 (1983)]: in practice, Western universalism frequently boils down to the belief that all peoples are alike except when they're different from us, in which case they're irrational.

where money-making and frenzy appear to go hand in hand, the famous "cargo cults" of Melanesia.[5]

Anthropology and the myth of the cargo cult

The traditional anthropological treatment of cargo cults serves as a guide to some of the underlying assumptions about wealth, production, exchange and rationality which have structured the discipline's apprehension of non-Western socio-economic forms. The "cargo cults" which animated various tribes inhabiting the islands of Melanesia have been an object of fascination in anthropological theory since their "discovery" in 1948 (Kilani 1983:24).[6] These cults were seen as an expression of the Melanesians' "hopeless envy" of the material wealth of their Western colonizers (Mair 1948:67). Through various fanatical activities – invocation of the ancestors, worship of certain Western consumer items, and sometimes the large-scale destruction of indigenous goods – the Melanesians, it was said, were trying to bring about the arrival of "cargo," Western wealth and commodities. That their system of belief had not yet evolved to a state which could be considered rational was evident in their failure to fit the means employed to the ends desired. With time, these anthropologists predicted, this irrational relation to wealth and production would evolve along Western lines, and the Melanesians would come to see that hard work, investment and technological progress are the only routes to genuine prosperity.

A careful rereading of the ethnographic record demonstrates that the cargo cult is an invention not of the envious Melanesians but of their Western observers. Numerous cult and millenarian movements did exist in Melanesia – both before the arrival of the colonial powers and well after the period when these movements were to have evolved away under the influence of Western rationality. However, none of them appears to have been motivated by "envy" for Western prosperity. Rather, in the manner of comparable revitalization movements among native Americans, or traditionalist movements in Africa (Wallace 1956), Melanesian cult movements were motivated by a desire to assert a revived tribal solidarity, thereby bringing about more balanced relations with white and other neighboring

---

[5] Appadurai (1986:51–53) too compares Western stock and futures markets to cargo cults, but at a different level of analysis and for different reasons.

[6] Lucy Mair coined the term "cargo cult" in *Australia in New Guinea* (1948) and applied it retrospectively to the numerous millenarian movements which had been observed by missionaries and colonial administrators since the mid-nineteenth century. For this critique of the anthropological treatment of cargo cults, I draw on the excellent study by Mondher Kilani (1983).

ethnic groups. Wealth and commodities were one medium among others by which Melanesians acted out and worked through issues of intra- and inter-ethnic identity in a rapidly changing environment.

I mention this example not because I wish to apply it directly to the Shanghainese context. Shanghainese are not Melanesians (indeed, they would most likely be offended by the comparison). "Cargo cults" are instructive indirectly, both for what they can tell us about the discipline's preconceptions, and for what they suggest by way of alternative inter-pretations. Despite the teachings of Mauss and Malinowski, the prevailing disciplinary ideology interpreted this complex social phenomenon as a simple economic one; means–end rationality was then used as a criterion for evaluating the effectiveness of this imaginary economic institution; and it was concluded that the Melanesians did not measure up.[7] Interestingly, however, the term "cargo-cult mentality" *has* been used to describe the Chinese relation to their new stock markets.[8] Here we find the boomerang effect (or as Bourdieu [1980] calls it, the "Montesquieu Effect") that typ-ifies the relation between popular and scientific sociocentrisms: fed by economistic proto-conceptions, anthropologists read a loosely related series of social movements in Melanesia as cults to Western goods or cargo; these cults then take on a life of their own, and in this reified form re-enter popular discourse in entirely different social and historical con-texts as a "mentality."

Any description of a "feverish" Shanghainese interest in their stock market – how the "fever" arises and is maintained, what forms it takes, how it is interpreted by the Shanghainese themselves – cannot overlook this history of Western investments, both economic and symbolic, in what it takes to be other peoples' irrational relation to the production of wealth. Furthermore, it must look to the ethnographic record for hints as to alter-native approaches. If the cargo-cult analogy teaches us anything, it is that the Shanghai stock market is not merely a mechanism, more or less ratio-nal, for the production of wealth; the phenomenon of stock fever is richer than a feverish interest in getting rich. Rather it is an avenue through which issues of urban identity and intra-societal dynamics are elaborated,

---

[7] Perhaps it is not too far-fetched to remind ourselves of the context in which Mair coined this concept in late 1940s England: the Western world had just emerged from a paroxysm of violence and fanaticism, set off, at least in part, by one nation's fantasies about another ethnic group's relation to wealth and power.

[8] See Lincoln Kaye of the *Far Eastern Economic Review*, quoted in *The Nation* (1992:740). In an even more far-fetched analogy, the building of the Goddess of Democracy during the 1989 student protests in Tiananmen has been characterized as "a kind of cargo-cult to the coming of democracy in the absence of a coherent political strategy" (Godement 1993:293, my translation).

and Shanghai's relation to what it takes to be modernity worked out. Properly read, the native concept of "fever" leads us to this social-cultural context.

Forms of *re*

The Chinese notion of fever (*re*) is a constant and important element of contemporary urban culture, and applies to many phenomena beyond the stock market. The year I was in Shanghai, a number of things were in (*re*): wearing black, hanging a picture of Mao on the rear view mirror of one's taxi, hula-hoops, even emigration were described to me with the suffix "*re.*" Frequently, these descriptions were accompanied by a particular kind of commentary. "Chinese have no individual personality" (*gexing*), I was told by Shanghainese friends and acquaintances. "They always follow fashion (*gan shimao*), they have the psychology of a beehive (*yiwofeng*), they 'rush headlong into mass action' (*yi hong er shang* [a proverb])." Putting stock fever in the context of other fevers demonstrates that beyond purely economic motivations, a "feverish" interest in the stock market follows a pattern which we should analyze as deep-structural.

The fundamental notion underlying a *re* is that everyone is doing the same thing at the same time. The Chinese commentary on *re* frames this notion as a problem of relationship between the individual and the group. Furthermore, this commentary was generally delivered with an air of contempt, as if it went without saying that I, as a Westerner, would find this "psychology" (*xinli*) absurd. At first, I assumed that my Chinese interlocutors were simply parroting for me what they took to be a Western stance on "fevers," for they appeared to participate actively in these moments despite their criticism. However, I came to believe that their ambivalence toward *re* was part and parcel of the way in which *re* functions in the modern world, a world in which "Western" individualist ideology is always present but never fully realized (Latour 1991).

If fevers "worked" to such a spectacular degree in urban China, it is because they provided an idiom for the expression of group and individual identity simultaneously: the person who wore black with the most style, who managed to go abroad under the best conditions, or who made the most on the stock market distinguished herself from the group but on the group's terms. While some of the urbanites I met stubbornly refused any association with "fevers," and others threw themselves foolishly into the most ephemeral of passing fads, most Shanghainese played the fever game with discretion, choosing when they participated, how they participated and with what attitude.[9]

Clearly, different forces propel different types of fever. Some are principally commercial, as with the sudden arrival in the spring of 1992 of millions of hula-hoops for sale by thousands of small distributors in Shanghai. From one day to the next, it seemed, hula-hoops were everywhere: young and old, women and men were to be found hula-hooping throughout the city and state-run television programs vaunted the merits of hula-hooping as entertaining, low-impact exercise, while all remained apparently oblivious, as Americans did in the prudish 1950s, to the grinding hip motion which must have been part of the sport's appeal. And then, just as suddenly as they had appeared, the hula-hoops disappeared, replaced by portable computer games such as Tetris. Likewise for the color black, which disappeared during the summer in favor of lime green, bright orange and fluorescent yellow.

Fads form part of commercial culture throughout the industrialized world, and work in much the same sudden and evanescent way in the West. Indeed, we have come to celebrate fads as a crucial force in keeping consumer economies in motion. However, commercial fads in Chinese urban centers are followed by a wider spectrum of consumers than we are used to. This may be because "market engineers" in China have not yet similarly segregated the market to parallel and demarcate the class/status system. This in turn may be a reflection of the fact that the urban class/status system in contemporary China is not as rigorously determined.[10] Commercial fads in urban China are also more noticeable than their Western (especially bourgeois) equivalents, as lack of space forces city-dwellers to spend large amounts of time on the streets, and much of that time is spent doing what we might think of as private activities.

However, commercial *re* are but one form of fever in urban China. Proverbs and "in" phrases (*shunkouliu*) circulate throughout the city for a moment, and then pass out of fashion. Popular puns, frequently political in nature, are another form of *re*. For example, during the Anti-Spiritual Pollution Campaign (1983–1984) to combat Western influence and alienation (*yihua*), popular discourse labeled alienation "the fifth modernization" in a play on Deng's famous "Four Modernizations" campaign. Punning and *double-entendres* form part of a long tradition of what we could call dissident uses of language in Chinese culture. Similar

---

[9] For an insightful analysis of precisely this multiplex relation to "modernity" in the context of Nepalese healing practices, see Pigg (1996).

[10] The question of the urban class/status system will be picked up again in chapter 4.

phenomena are common in the United States among minority groups, particularly among African-American and Hispanic youth. These practices are generally thought to be linked to processes of identity formation and group membership in a context in which the dominant culture is hostile to or ignorant of the culture of the minority group; they form a minority "counter-culture." The parallel is instructive as it alerts us to the ways in which all of popular culture in urban China has the structural potential to work counter-culturally.

The potential for popular reworking of state ideology through *re* is best exemplified by another and far more widespread "fever," the sudden appearance of millions of small laminated pictures of Chairman Mao in the shops and stalls of private entrepreneurs and on the rear view mirrors of taxi cabs some time in the early 1990s.[11] The outbreak of "Mao fever," as it was labeled, merits detailed examination, for it takes us beyond the consumer culture of contemporary urban China and back to traditional popular religious/mythical practices.

The first appearance of Mao fever can be dated to 1990 when small-scale producers in Canton began distributing inexpensive laminated images of Chairman Mao through private entrepreneurs and hawkers.[12] One standard double-sided image prevailed, in which the Chairman was pictured before and after the Chinese Revolution – on one side, Mao the young revolutionary, on the other, Mao the seasoned leader[13] – but numerous versions were put into circulation, occasionally including pictures of Zhou Enlai or other members of the Long March pantheon. Drivers of state- and privately owned cars hung these picture on their rear view mirrors to ward off accidents. Private entrepreneurs hung them in their shops alongside or in place of the Fortune God (Cai Shen), the popular deity whose help in bringing prosperity and warding off evil is frequently invoked.

---

[11] The English-language mass media cannot get enough of this "absurd" phenomenon. See *FEER* 1991c, 1993a, 1993b, 1993c, 1993–1994, *IHT* 1992a.

[12] I put these events in the past tense as they came into and went out of style during the year I was in Shanghai. However, more recent newspaper reports suggest that these practices have been revived or that in certain parts of the country they never died out (*FEER* 1993b).

[13] Mao as a young revolutionary has a distinctly feminine look about him for reasons that merit further analysis. My suggestion would be that this double-sided image works to highlight the enormous transformation (*hua*) which the Chinese Revolution wrought on Mao as a person, but also on the entire nation, as Mao is seen "as having become synonymous with the Chinese nation" (*Beijing Zhoubao* [*Peking Review*], cited in *FEER* 1993–1994). The femininity of the young Mao serves to highlight the mature masculinity of the post-revolutionary Mao. Chinese deities are frequently ambiguously sexed (see e.g. Hodous 1929:104, cited in J. Watson 1985:298, n.18), perhaps because transformation is a central element of their supernatural power.

When asked why Mao was in (*re*), most people I talked with answered that "people" thought he was a god. When asked whether they themselves held this belief, they generally expressed skepticism; they hung his picture in their store or taxi because it was "fashionable" or, at the most, "to bring good luck," they told me. Again, we may explain this hedging by the fact that no reasonably worldly Chinese would admit to engaging in such "feudal thinking" (*fengjian sixiang*) in front of a foreigner. However, as with the discourse on *re* in general, the discourse on *Mao re* did not seem addressed at me; rather, the "voice" – in Bakhtin's sense (Amorim 1996) – of the modern West was present as an imaginary Other in all discourse in modern China in which objects of tradition and belief were at issue. Slavoj Zizek (1989) and Bruno Latour (1991) have suggested that belief in the modern world often takes the form of the mere belief that others believe, and that this indirect structure of belief is sufficient to produce all the effects of direct belief. Of course, the quintessential example of this structure of indirection is the stock market itself, but as Pigg (1996) has demonstrated, in a world in which the ideology of modernity is everywhere immanent, an ambivalent, context-driven relation to belief defines practice in even the most "traditional" of settings.

Differences in "political culture" as between north and south China also affected the terms in which "Mao fever" was understood. Over dinner one night, I asked four acquaintances for their interpretation of the central government's attitude towards Mao fever. One diner, from Hangzhou – a historically important, sophisticated coastal city – found the whole subject "backward" (*luohou*) and declined to give an interpretation. Two others, both from inland Hubei Province, offered directly contradictory interpretations: one suggested that central leaders supported Mao fever as a way of giving ordinary people a sense of security, an object to believe in; the other suggested that they opposed it because it exalted Mao over Deng. Finally, the diner from Beijing proposed a factional interpretation: the entire fever was being tacitly supported by the "conservative clique" (*baoshou pai*) against Deng and the "reformist clique" (*gaige pai*), and depending on the results of power shifts after the Fourteenth Party Congress in October, we would see the Mao images either suppressed or openly promoted.[14]

That Mao the man should become Mao the god is not unusual as the line between the human and supernatural worlds in Chinese tradition is

---

[14] As it turned out, though the Dengist clique "won" in the Fourteenth Party Congress, the images did not disappear, suggesting that this Beijingese suffered from an exaggerated conception of central leaders' power to dictate popular culture.

notoriously porous. Indeed, it is probably incorrect to speak of a line at all, for as Potter (1970) and Wolf (1978) have pointed out, all humans take on some form of supernatural power when they die, either benevolent (ancestors), malevolent (ghosts), or quixotic (gods). Historian Barend ter Haar (1993) argues that supernatural power in the Chinese tradition is essentially linked to the god/hero's capacity for violence: the more violent the human being, the more powerful the god. Ter Haar's interpretation resolves a "contradiction" frequently noted in mass media reports of Mao fever.

That millions died as a result of disastrous Mao initiatives such as the Great Leap Forward and the Cultural Revolution seems to matter little to the more than four million people [who have come to visit Mao's place of birth],

complains the *Far Eastern Economic Review*, attributing this apparent paradox to forgetfulness and youth (*FEER* 1993b). But, perhaps Mao's power to cause harm in his lifetime is directly proportional to his powers as a god after his death. This would also explain why many Chinese believe that Zhou Enlai, while a more respectable human being than Chairman Mao, is not a god. In the words of one acquaintance: "People who have met Mao say that when they saw him they became so frightened they couldn't speak. Zhou Enlai did not frighten people, he was just like us."

If Mao fever engages popular conceptions of supernatural power, it also has a familiar mytho-religious structure. It began after Mao gave a certain number of signs of his powers to harm disrespectful citizens and/or to protect those who paid him homage. The first of these occurred during the student demonstrations in Tiananmen, when three protesters threw paint at his portrait overlooking the square. Hours later, Beijing was drenched by a torrential rain storm (*IHT* 1992a). Since then, the Chairman has been implicated in the miraculous survival of numerous car accident victims. While the place of these miracles varies with the teller, they are always located in a city of symbolic importance. In many versions, the miracle took place in or near Canton, that is, the center of the most radical economic reforms under Deng, creator of its own economic "miracle." In others, it occurs near Mao's birthplace in Hunan Province. Finally, in others it occurs in or near Beijing, the national capital and symbolic site *par excellence.*

The circulation of these anecdotes follows the form in which myths of local deities or miraculous events have circulated in China since at least the twelfth century. Anecdotes of a heroic exploit performed by a local hero lead to the creation of local cults. These cults bring pilgrims seeking to tap the god's powers, who in turn spread the cult over large areas of the country, as with the Song dynasty cult of Guan Yu explored by ter Haar (1993). Frequently too, deity cults spread by means of official promotion and promulgation.[15] Beyond cults, the circulation of rumors, panics, and of course, rebellious thought on a large scale seems to have been a constant feature of popular culture throughout the imperial period, a feature which attests to the high degree of complexity of urban–rural networks (Kuhn 1990, Wakeman 1977).

Through the indigenous concept of *re* we may thus place stock fever alongside a long list of other activities which have little or no immediate pecuniary benefit. With *re*, we avoid the pitfalls of a crude reading of Shanghainese interest in the stock market, a reading, I should add, which is found in both Chinese and Western accounts of stock fever: structurally speaking, it is not the simple desire to make money which feeds stock fever, but stock fever which creates this apparently simple desire to make money. Fevers are moments when a particular conception of the relation between the individual and the group in urban Chinese society is given expression. They provide a means for distinguishing oneself from real and imaginary others in society, while simultaneously articulating the changing framework within which society evaluates the individual. They spread by means of the extraordinarily complex and far-reaching networks linking different sectors of urban and rural China. In their strongest form, they make reference to mythical conceptions of power, both the power to do good, as in the cult of Mao or Guan Yu, and the power to harm, as in the Qing dynasty sorcery scare discussed by Kuhn (1990). Finally, with fevers, differences between "commoners" are temporarily muted while the commonalities linking "the People" are ritually enacted. *Re* act out the binary class division between "the People" and "the State" which characterizes the tributary mode of production.

Official *re*: the *yundong*

Re have close cousins in the political campaigns (*yundong*) that have shaped Chinese history throughout the Communist period, and which, in diluted intensity though similar form, have played an important part in imperial history as well.[16] Indeed, we could say that *re* are simply popular *yundong*, or that *yundong* are official *re*. Both create moments when an

---

[15] See J. Watson (1985) for a rich discussion of official–popular relations in this context.
[16] This observation graduated from the state of a vague intuition to that of a fully-fledged thought with the help of Christopher Reed, historian and brilliant anthropologist *manqué*.

entire cultural area (often all of urban China, sometimes the nation as a whole) is unified by a common activity. Whyte and Parish's *Urban Life in Contemporary China* confirms this characterization:

In Canton [during the 1970s], the mania for hobbies and card games became known among some as the "mass movement," welling up from below, as opposed to the numerous "political movements" which descended from above. Among others, it became known as the "army, air force, navy movement," with crickets being the army, birds the air force, and goldfish the navy (1984:321).

Interestingly from our point of view, the Chinese term *yundong* is translated variously as "campaign" or "movement," that is, it specifically does not distinguish between conscious and directed mobilization from the top down (as implied by the English word "campaign") and spontaneous or popular mobilization from the bottom up (as implied by the English word "movement"). However, the differences between bureaucratically led "campaigns" and grass-roots "movements" did not go unnoticed; their relative merits were an important point of discord between Mao and other leading Party members (Meisner 1977:288–293), and led to more or less effective incursions into the lives of Chinese citizens. *Yundong* – either in the form of campaigns or of mass movements – were a central element of Mao's successful revolutionary military strategy (Kim 1969), and were extended to the political arena even before the Communist reunification of the country in 1949 (Bennett 1976). With the success of the Revolution, the Chinese Communist Party's principal goal became assuring the triumph of the "revolutionary classes" over the "bourgeoisie"; to this end, political campaigns became the Party's primary means of mobilizing "the People" to wage class struggle against its "enemies."

Campaigns varied enormously in character and importance, from two-day campaigns to kill sparrows, pick up litter or plant trees, to the enormously influential Great Proletarian Cultural Revolution. At times, they accompanied and enacted aspects of other policy decisions, as with the Three-Antis and Five-Antis campaigns against corruption, waste and bureaucratism, and tax evasion, bribery, fraud, theft of government property and theft of state economic secrets, respectively (1951–1952); at other times, they were the implementation of far-reaching policy decisions which profoundly changed the structure of rural and urban life in China, as with the land reform campaigns which began in the occupied territories as early as 1946 and spread to the entire country in 1949, or the *xia fang* movement to send cadres and intellectuals to factories and villages in 1957 and 1958 which, along with the communization drive, radically if temporarily altered the relations between city and countryside, intellectuals and manual workers, women and men, home and work life, and center and periphery throughout the country.

An (ideological) emphasis on ideology has prevented us from analyzing with care the particular representation of politics which lies behind the *yundong*. There are many ways to view this political technology: from a Western liberal point of view, mass mobilization connotes peer pressure and lack of liberty; others point to the positive effects of a high degree of participation in the doing of politics (Cell 1977). I would like to focus on a third element, the representational logic of mass mobilization. In social terms, *yundong* are characterized by what I will call, for lack of a better term, a dramatization of politics: the Party or the state mobilizes a target population (cadres, intellectuals, peasants, "the People") to enact the application of a new policy. In *yundong*, one can hear, see and read the application of policy in the words and deeds of all citizens concerned. This point is best illustrated by contrasting the *yundong* with Western bureau-cratic techniques of policy implementation. Euro-American policy design tends to adhere to a logic of systems: the "incentive environment" of the target population, be it institutions or individuals, is modified so that the desired behavior is produced, as it were, naturally. Taxation is thus the quintessential model for the application of positive state power in Western societies (Nader 1978). By contrast, *yundong* follow the principle of ritual: policies "work" when they are visibly enacted by the populace.[17] With *yundong*, society is transformed not gradually, through the workings of structures and incentives on individuals, but immediately, through the mobilization of a monolithically conceived society for immediate action. The consequences of this ontology of state power for the short-term economic well-being of the nation have been undeniably negative. Its conse-quences for the social, political and cultural coherence of New China are far more complex.

Reform through "revolution"

With the death of Mao and the ascent to power of Deng Xiaoping, the focus of Communist Party policy shifted from class struggle to economic

---

[17] This contrast is overdrawn, but a theoretical discussion of Western conceptions of state power would take us too far afield. However, even from this brief discussion, it should be clear that I have hesitations about the by now common use of Foucauldian theory in China studies (see e.g. Dutton 1992, Yang 1989). Foucault traces a very particular "arche-ology" of power over five centuries of Western European (read French) history. By the force of his own arguments, there is no reason to believe that China would have experi-enced a similar trajectory, and every reason to resist correlating China's particular archeol-ogy of power to the formal political turning points of modern Chinese history, as Dutton seems to do.

development in the form of the Four Modernizations. Popular perception dates the end of the *yundong* and the beginning of a recognizable program of capitalist development – or, to return to the imagery we began with, the substitution of the brain-washed hordes by the innate capitalists – to this moment in recent Chinese history. But here again, the form as much as the content of these reforms merits attention. For while the word "campaign" is rarely used today, the form in which policy shifts are announced and applied in Deng's China bears important resemblances to the practices of mobilization detailed above.[18]

The image of China's reform program which dominates the Western press – in particular that of the US – is one of a complete rupture with past practices. "Once regarded as the epitome of radical communitarianism, China [is] suddenly pictured by many outside observers as a budding capitalist society alive with the spirit of entrepreneurial individualism" (Perry and Wong 1985a:1). This impression is reinforced by a parallel effort in the Chinese press to emphasize what Deng has called "a revolution in urban and rural economic policies" (Riskin 1987:342). Clearly, recent reforms have brought about very important changes in China's economic, political and social structures; indeed, this study is born of those changes. However, the ideological dimension of claims for change on both sides must not be overlooked.

The most fundamental sense in which the ideology of rupture serves the interests of both China and the United States is as a justification for the normalization of relations, even friendship and economic cooperation, between two countries that had, only a matter of years ago, been formal enemies.[19] Beyond this coincidence of motives, however, the notions of

---

[18] Many Chinese today speak of *yundong* with the same note of irony and derision used to discuss *re*, as evidenced by a popular pun: *yundong* means "movement" in the physical sense as well as the political sense, and a *yundongyuan* is an athlete; however, *yundongyuan* is also used ironically to refer to someone who participates frequently, actively and opportunistically in political campaigns.

[19] For a good discussion of normalization, first undertaken, we should remember, by Zhou and Mao, not Deng, see Hsu (1982:56–90). It is not too outrageous, I think, to compare this event with the sudden shifts in allegiance parodied in Orwell's *1984* (1949); indeed, the very word "normalization" has a slight odor of Newspeak about it. What Orwell captures is the contrast between the eternal nature of the principles evoked to justify enmity or friendship between nations, and the ephemerality of their effects. We might think that diplomatic relations could be conducted in the language of *Realpolitik*, as they are analyzed in the press or the academy. But, it seems that states cannot speak the language of the *Real*; allegiance or enmity between "Peoples" invokes Principles.

The jarring nature of these sudden realignments is all the more remarkable when viewed cross-culturally. Compare the distinct rhetorics of friendship (i.e. trade) versus war employed by modern nation-states with the apparently more dialectical ideologies of tribal societies, where trade and war are quite consciously seen as two sides of the same coin. The potlatch, practiced by Northwest Native Americans (Codere 1950), is the classic ethnographic example of this dialectical logic.

rupture propounded by US and Chinese commentators part ways. US portrayal of China's abandonment of Maoist practices follows the American Manichaean tendency to view political economics in terms of a binary opposition between free markets and democracies on the one hand, command economies and totalitarianism on the other. The Chinese Communist Party has a more complex set of reasons for propounding the notion of a Dengist "revolution."

Undeniably, a major factor prompting Deng to undertake reform was widespread and mounting popular discontent with economic performance during the ten years of the Cultural Revolution (Perry and Wong 1985a:2). Added to this was cynicism and fatigue after countless campaigns for political mobilization (Whyte and Parish 1984:319–325). In proclaiming a "revolution," Deng aimed to garner popular support with promises of immediate and tangible improvements in the general standard of living. However, dissatisfaction with economic performance followed by changes in policy and promises of increased yields were a mainstay of pre-reform politics. As Perry and Wong point out, the fact of "abrupt swings in policy which occur when the locus of decision-making authority shifts from one set of leaders to another" is a "commonplace in the study of contemporary China" (Perry and Wong 1985a:5). It is, in other words, rather a point of continuity with the past than a rupture. At one point in the early 1960s, then-Premier Liu Shaoqi had even suggested restoring the stock market (Dittmer 1989:49). What makes Deng's reform policies more "revolutionary" than this?

Blinded by the content of the reforms, we have overlooked the form in which they were announced; the call for "a profound and extensive revolution" to carry out socialist modernization (Chinese Communist Party Central Committee Documentary Research Office 1979:168) is an example of the precise rhetoric with which mobilization campaigns had been announced throughout the Maoist period. The claim of revolution must be understood not so much as a statement of fact but as a political linguistic act, an act by which Deng simultaneously reappropriated the Maoist past and marked his distance from it. Mao, it should be remembered, was the only Communist leader in world history ever to put the Trotskyite theory of "permanent revolution" to the test, most spectacularly during the Great Proletarian Cultural Revolution of 1966–1969.[20] True, these experiments have not been held up as successes; they may even account for most of the 30 percent of error which the Party's re-evaluation of Mao's

---

[20] On the Chinese interpretation of "permanent revolution," see Meisner (1977:204–216) and Wakeman (1973:320–327).

contributions to socialism was to assign him (Hsu 1982:44–52, 142–167). However, this has in no way tarnished the glow of the term "revolution" in the Party lexicon. After all, China's own national revolution was just thirty years old. "Revolution" within the context of continued Communist Party rule involves elements of continuity and change; it is the Party bowing to its own capacities for continual self-renewal (see Spence 1990:653–692).

And beyond this rhetorical structure, there is more fundamental continuity in the manner in which politics is conducted in Dengist and Maoist times. That continuity is most apparent in the delicate and charged area of law reform. With the Four Modernizations and policy of "reform and opening," one important area of reform has been the law (Baum 1986, Dicks 1989, Keith 1991, Leng 1989, Lubman 1996). However, while enormous efforts have been made to develop a comprehensive statutory code and judiciary system, particularly in areas touching on foreign trade and investment with China, not law but "policy" (*zhengce*) remains, as in the Maoist era, the primary locus for the articulation of norms and their application (Potter and Potter 1990:245).[21] As Article 1 of the new Constitution of 1982 makes clear, the legal system is subordinate to the "people's democratic dictatorship," which is guided by Marxist–Leninist–Mao-Zedong Thought, and articulated through the Party. Political direction comes from the "spirit" of the Party leadership, and this spirit guides the application of law to facts through "policy."

The subordination of law to policy is apparent in numerous domains. In the prosecution and sentencing of criminals, both the way in which crimes are defined and the seriousness with which they are handled vary with the political climate (see Clarke and Feinerman 1996). In 1983, shortly after the enactment of the new codes of criminal law and criminal procedure, a "Decision of the Standing Committee of the National People's Congress Regarding the Severe Punishment of Criminals Who Seriously Endanger Public Security" was adopted, followed (and preceded) by massive arrests and public executions. Likewise, the near yearly "cleaning-up" campaigns launched against corruption and economic crime routinely net twice as many criminals as during non-campaign times (Rocca 1992:407). During

---

[21] The position of law in Chinese society today is a point of contention (see Keith [1991] for a review of the Chinese debate on the "rule of law"). No unified attitude, even among top leadership, can be distilled: some believe that economic development depends on a fully independent legal system on the model of Western democracies; others believe that "socialist legality with Chinese characteristics" requires that law maintain its position as a tool of Party policy (Dicks 1989:542; see generally von Senger 1985). Whatever the disagreements at the highest level and the intentions behind the reforms, in practice today law remains in a secondary and instrumental position in relation to policy.

such drives, defendants who would in laxer moments be sentenced to long prison terms may find themselves sentenced to death.[22] Policy and not law governs the application of state power in other domains as well. In the controversial area of birth control, law, formulated at a very general level, has consistently been supplemented by policy which is refined as it descends down the bureaucratic ladder to take into account "local circumstances" (S. H. Potter 1987, Palmer 1996). In the cultural area, campaigns against "Spiritual Pollution" (Larson 1989) and "Bourgeois Liberalization" can lead to the arrest of artists and writers through the application of policy, broadly supported by laws against "counter-revolutionary activities," and activities that "disrupt the socialist system" (Dicks 1989:548).

In none of these areas do campaigns have the dimensions of Cultural Revolution mass movements, and it is clear that real changes in the conception of appropriate forms of popular mobilization have occurred. What has not changed, however, is the belief that sporadic mobilization itself is an appropriate technique for the application of policy. The Western press tends to treat these "campaigns" as residual, hangovers from Maoist practices, or political posturing by "Leftist" leaders. Clearly, this is an area in which changes are occurring. However, I would argue that the dramatized conception of policy application which lies at the base of *yundong* has not been fundamentally altered. Furthermore, following the cultural logic of the tributary mode, to this conception of state power corresponds an equally dramatized vision of the practice of popular resistance (see Nathan 1985, Esherick and Wasserstrom 1990). Despite their varying goals and vastly different consequences, grassroots movements, mass campaigns, fads, fevers and popular demonstrations of discontent all share a totalistic vision of society in which the individual and the group melt together to form "the People," as contrasted with, and sometimes as opposed to, "the State." What appear to disappear during these (necessarily) momentary scenarios are all of those localized entities (institutions, lineages, associations, networks) and time-consuming practices (negotiation, rule-making, status differentiation) which govern relations among "the People" and within "the State" when they are not engaged in this primordial opposition.

---

[22] Crime, particularly economic crimes and "corruption" as the Chinese state defines it, is increasingly an enormous problem. For a general survey of the statistics, see Rocca 1992. According to an official pronouncement by Deputy Procurator General Liang Guoqing in September 1993, "corruption is now worse than in any other period since New China was founded in 1949" (*FEER* 1993c:16).

Time and politics: the importance of opportunity
The most important area in which the processes of mobilization are visible today is in the economic arena. Since the launching of economic reforms in 1980, and their extension to the areas of urban and industrial policy in 1984, China has experienced waves of change that touch on virtually every area of economic life. With more than ten years of urban reforms accomplished, a pattern or cycle of economic action and reaction can now be clearly delineated: when central authorities loosen control over credit and decentralize authority, localities react with a flurry of investment projects, as often as not over-ambitious and wasteful from the perspective of China's overall development needs. This boom in investment causes inflation, which in turn leads to price and wage hikes (Bowles 1990, Naughton 1991). The center then tightens the reins again, slowing the tendency to over-investment while simultaneously restraining the general economic climate through wage and price freezes. It is this cycle that reached acute levels in 1988 and helped fuel the fires of student protests, with the ensuing crackdown in Beijing in the spring of 1989. The following two years, 1990–1991, have generally been described as "conservative"; that is, new experiments in economic reform were kept to a minimum as central authorities exercised tighter controls over the investment activities of local governments. However, a new "liberal wind" was inaugurated at exactly the moment I arrived in Shanghai, in February 1992.

The ebb and flow in the application of reform policies is generally attributed to struggles within the Party leadership between "conservative" and "liberal" factions. An exclusive focus on inner-Party power struggles, however, may blind us to the broader formal continuity between waves of economic reform and *yundong*. Whether this wave-like pattern of policy application represents a cultural pattern, a series of last-minute decisions caused by power struggles within the Central Committee, or conscious choice on the part of central authorities, as some of my Shanghainese acquaintances implied, remains unclear. The result, however, is a particular cultural conception of "opportunity" (*jihui*) that is central to all "fevers" in urban China and indispensable for an understanding of the "stock fever" set off by Deng's trip to Shenzhen in the spring of 1992.

The events at the origin of this change in political climate are deceptively simple. From January 18 to February 21, 1992, retired government official Deng Xiaoping visited Wuchang, Shenzhen, Zhuhai and Shanghai to examine the effects of economic reforms on these four localities. There he announced his general satisfaction, and urged that Party authorities "quicken the pace of reforming and opening" (*gaige kaifang yao maikai buzi*).[23] There followed a spate of editorials throughout China's important state-run newspapers affirming the principles laid forth in Deng's "talks" (*jianghua*), and then an extraordinary meeting of the Politburo of the Party Central Committee, during which the official call to increase the pace of economic reform was issued.[24] Deng's visit to the south – which was soon labeled the "Southern Tour" (*Deng Xiaoping Nanxun*) after the numerous voyages to the south taken by the Kangxi Emperor between 1684 and 1707 (Spence 1966:124–165) – set the program for economic policy developments throughout 1992 and beyond. That an entire country can be thrown into motion by the pronouncements of a retired official taking a trip is perhaps the quintessential illustration of the subordinate role of law in contemporary Chinese politics.[25]

Behind this event lay a complex series of maneuvers in which Deng successfully rallied key Party players to his side in a bid for power against more conservative factions, power which he was then to use to place loyal reformists in key positions in the coming Fourteenth Congress of the Chinese Communist Party in October 1992 (*FEER* 1992). In the version of this behind-the-scenes tale I heard, Deng's visit to Wuchang had garnered him little support. Rather than return to Beijing weakened, Deng decided to continue his trip to Shenzhen. In Shenzhen, Deng met by chance with top military authorities Yang Shangkun and Yang Baibing, who manifested their loyalty through public pronouncements in favor of reforms. Bolstered, Deng then proceeded to Shanghai, where he convinced ex-Mayor Wang Daohan to urge Party Secretary Jiang Zemin, Wang's "student," to fall into line. The final piece in this edifice consisted in convincing Chen Yun, a powerful conservative economist (also from

---

[23] Deng's "talks" during this trip were widely publicized in different forms in March and April 1992. I make reference to a version published by the Chinese Communist Party Shenzhen Municipal Committee Propaganda Bureau, *Deng Xiaoping yu Shenzhen. Yijiujiuer chun* (*Deng Xiaoping and Shenzhen. Spring, 1992*) (Zhonggong Shenzhen Shiwei Xuanchuanbu 1992).

[24] "Zhonggong Zhongyang Zhengzhiju zai Beijing Zhaokai Quanti Huiyi Taolun Woguo Gaige he Fazhan de Ruogan Zhongda Wenti" ("The Chinese Communist Party Central Committee's Political Bureau Calls a Full Meeting in Beijing in order to Discuss Certain Important Questions concerning Reform and Development in Our Country"), March 11, 1992, reprinted in Zhonggong Shenzhen Shiwei Xuanchuanbu (1992:37–39).

[25] From 1988, until his death, Deng held no official position of leadership in the Chinese government or the Chinese Communist Party. This monumental fact is rarely pointed to by Western scholars of Chinese law and politics. True, Western journalists frequently made snide references to Deng as "the strong man of China," but this only confused matters by characterizing Deng's authority as a kind of brute force. If Deng indeed maintained his central position in Party politics with the backing of large portions of the Chinese military, this simply meant that for these military officers, Deng represented an authority, not a "strong man."

Shanghai) who had consistently weighed in in support of greater reliance on planning mechanisms, that Shanghai's Pudong New Development Zone should become the new center for reform experiments. This Deng did with the help of China's most renowned anthropologist, Fei Xiaotong, who has vaunted the merits of Shanghai as the "dragon's head," and Pudong as the "dragon's eye," of the Yangzi River Delta since the 1930s.[26]

In his "talks," Deng repeatedly urged Party cadres to be bolder in promoting the reforms. Deng stressed the tremendous opportunity (*jihui*) which lay before them, and the need not to be afraid of making political errors.[27] His tone was dramatic, perhaps reflecting his awareness that he was nearing the end of his life:

Surrounding countries and regions are experiencing more rapid economic development than we are. If we do not develop, or we develop too slowly, ordinary people will compare and have questions [or, there will be problems]. . . .[28] Developing at a slow pace is equivalent to standing still, even to regressing. We must seize this opportunity; now is a good opportunity. My only worry is that we miss this opportunity, that we fail to seize it. If we don't seize it, we lose the opportunity before our own eyes, and in a flash time will have gone by.[29]

[26] I received this scoop from a Shanghai intellectual with friends in high places in Shanghai and Beijing. However, there is no reason to think that my friend's version is "correct," and this for reasons that have everything to do with the way power works in China. No one, not even Deng himself, can know "what really happened" because what really happened is a political stake that can be and is manipulated by all manner of participants and bystanders. Clarity is to no one's advantage, for it rigidifies an otherwise dynamic system. It is interesting that in the version told to me (an anthropologist in Shanghai), Shanghai and an anthropologist emerge as the cornerstone of the entire Deng edifice.

[27] The notion of "opportunity" is linked with widely shared Chinese beliefs in personal fate or destiny (*mingyun*). One's personal fate (legible in one's hands, one's physiognomy, one's *Yijing* (*I-Ching*) readings, and in one's life history generally) is a natural tendency or pattern in which one can and should actively intervene. The belief in fate is thus in no sense fatalistic; quite the contrary, fate presents itself in the form of opportunities which are to be seized upon and worked with. To remain blind to signs of one's personal fate is as foolish and counterproductive in the Chinese moral universe as to disregard one's personal psychological history in contemporary US culture. For careful treatment of this complex topic, see Basu 1991, Harrell 1987.

[28] Note again the power which the fantasy of popular dissatisfaction exercises over Chinese leaders. Here we see the "questions" of "ordinary people" (*laobaixing*) being used by Deng as a scarecrow to ward off conservative trespassers in the field of economic reform, much as our guide at the Shanghai Securities Exchange used the market, and behind it "the masses," as an argument for continued stock market experiments. In chapter 2, we saw fears of suicide or "an event happening" (*chu shiqing*) exercising a similar fascination over Shanghai municipal leaders responsible for the stock market. In the spring of 1989, the world saw this phantasmagoric relation to "the People" in its most tragic light.

[29] "Zhoubian yixie guojia he diqu jingji fazhan bi women kuai, ruguo women bu fazhan huo fazhan de tai man, laobaixing yi bi jiu you wenti le . . . Yao zhuazhu jihui, xianzai jiu shi hao jihui. Wo jiu danxin sangshi jihui. Bu zhua ya, kandao de jihui jiu diudiao le, shijian yihuang jiu guoqu le" (Zhonggong Shenzhen Shiwei Xuanchuanbu 1992:6, my translation).

It is most important to note the self-confirming nature of this discussion. As Deng must have known, for the Chinese nation reading these speeches it was he who had the power to create the opportunity which he was urging them to seize. The fear of political error – in Deng's words, the worry over whether economic reforms belonged to the socialist or capitalist "lineage" (*xing she xing zi*) – was not a vague or theoretical concern about China's future, but a concrete fear held by all those in positions of responsibility that if they were seen supporting the reforms too openly, a change in political winds could bring about personal and professional reprisals. Deng's highly publicized appearances were a signal that this change of political wind was not imminent. His ability to bring the major instruments of state propaganda in line with his rhetoric was the surest sign that existed in Chinese society of the direction of current policy. This self-confirming structure was apparent in the notion of "opportunity" itself. The content of Deng's speech suggested that the opportunity currently presenting itself to China was an event with natural causes: it was a series of circumstances lying beyond China's control which boded well for her economic development. However, for Chinese cadres, investors in the stock market, and just "ordinary people," the opportunity opening up before them had entirely political roots. Indeed, it was the pure product of Deng's pronouncements on the opportunity of opportunity at the time.

The political nature of opportunity in China brings with it certain consequences. For one, it is the result of an act of communication: through his Southern Tours, Deng successfully sent a message to the entire population. There is thus little place for differing interpretations. This becomes clearer if we contrast this notion of opportunity with the kind of market analysis which employs millions of functionaries in the West: analyzing the opportuneness of investing in real estate in Thailand, for example, is an endlessly complex process, in which differences of opinion are more than commonplace. Analyzing the opportunity opened up by Deng's pronouncement is not. The inevitable result is that a far larger proportion of the population will immediately throw itself into the breach opened up by such a political moment. Secondly, being eminently political, and hence shrouded in the mystery that surrounds China's centers of power and decision-making, it is virtually impossible to predict how long this opportunity will last. All the more reason, therefore, that it be seized immediately, in the perspective of profiting as fully as possible in the shortest time possible. In early 1992, the stock market presented itself as the biggest, most open, most interesting, and potentially most short-term opportunity around.

The stock market: between *re* and *yundong*

Deng Xiaoping's Southern Tours set off the biggest wave of interest, both official and popular, in the Shanghai stock market in Shanghai history. However, when they are read attentively Deng's comments about stocks and stock markets are not as unambiguously positive as one might think:

> As for securities and the stock market, are they finally good or bad, are they dangerous, are they things which only capitalism has, or can socialism also make use of them? We are allowed to try and see, but on a resolutely experimental basis. If we think they work, if after a year or two we think this is right, then we expand; if they are wrong, we correct, we close them down. Even if we close them down, we can do so quickly or slowly, and we can even leave a little tail (Zhonggong Shenzhen Shiwei Xuanchuanbu 1992:4).

The operative element in this discussion is clearly not the assertion that stock markets are correct policy, but the implication that those responsible for experimenting with stock markets will not be punished if there is a change of policy. Thus, the conditions for speculation in the Shanghai market were laid down by the fact that the very existence of the market was itself a matter of speculation.

Put together with Deng's positive comments about "capitalist mechanisms" in general and, particularly, with his manifest support for the Pudong project – Shanghai's New Development Zone – energy for the stock market arrived from all corners. The Mayor of Shanghai announced that central authorities had given Shanghai special privileges and conditions for developing Pudong, including the right to more independent control over the issuing of stocks and bonds. For 1992, this meant that the Shanghai Branch of the People's Bank had the right to approve a total of 200,000,000 new shares over and above the quota of 400,000,000 already set for it by central authorities (*SHZQ* 1992a). The Shanghai Composite Share Index, which had been hovering at around 300 since the end of 1991, began a spectacular rise which peaked at 1,953 on June 1, more than six times its January value (*SHZQ* 1992b).

We are now in the position to place "stock fever" in its full context. Unlike other urban *re*, "stock fever" was kicked off by government policy changes. Indeed, "stock fever" was kicked off by what comes awfully close to a "movement" (*yundong*) as Deng's new "spirit" of bold experiments with "capitalist mechanisms" filtered down from central authorities, through Shanghai municipal authorities, through the directors of Shanghai's state-run Exchange and brokerage houses, to individual investors. Stock fever represents a complex intersection of bottom-up and top-down action, of official and unofficial discourse.

Like other *re*, stock fever is the forum for a dramatization and reworking of the relation between the individual and the group in urban Chinese society. Those who participate are "in," in sync with the times; those who refuse cannot keep pace with change. Among those who participate, there are those who succeed, those who fail, and those who succeed beyond everyone's wildest dreams. The stock market thus provided a mechanism for status differentiation in a society where few of the familiar trappings of status (education, profession, place of residence) can be relied on.

But, does stock fever manifest the third characteristic which we identified for *re*: does it make reference to mytho-religious conceptions of power? The answer to this question must be both yes and no. The discourse of stock fever, both official and unofficial, speaks of three suprahuman actors behind the movements of the stock market: "big players," "dispersed players," and "the State." These actors are mythical to the extent that they are built on a very particular abstraction of a set of characteristics attributed to society under Chinese socialism. They are real to the extent that the sum total of the actions taken by individuals grouped into these three categories makes up the stock market, with its very real movements, entailing very real gains and losses. To elucidate the relation between these mythic social actors and the individuals who make them up, the following chapter outlines the dynamics of social change in Maoist and post-Maoist Shanghai.

4

City people, stock people

When I arrived in Shanghai in February 1992, there were a reported 300,000 stock accounts at brokerages throughout the city; when I left in December, that number had jumped to 1,300,000 (Wei 1993:7). Approximately 50 percent of these accounts were held by investors outside Shanghai who purchased shares through regional brokerages with seats on the Shanghai Exchange (*ibid.*). Granting that Shanghai investors would frequently band together to play the market through a single account, we may presume that at least 700,000, very likely a million Shanghainese, were actively investing in stocks at the height of the fever – that is to say, 8 percent of Shanghai's 13 million inhabitants. We are thus faced with a puzzle: why do the activities of 8 percent of the population constitute a "fever"? Why was I consistently told that "everyone" was playing the stock market?

Clearly, the rhythm of entry into the market had something feverish about it. In the course of twelve months, participation in the market more than quadrupled. But, the social fact of stock fever is constructed culturally, not mathematically. What struck the Shanghainese was that, unlike many of the new opportunities created by the policy of "reform and opening," participation in the stock market cut across all social classes and categories. Only the very well connected could send their children to study abroad, and only "ex-prisoners and the unemployed" would stoop to opening an individual business. But "everybody" – that is, in Chinese terms, peasants, workers, hooligans, intellectuals and government officials, to name just a few of the most general categories – was getting on the stock market bandwagon.[1] In the special room for wealthy investors which

---

[1] In my observations of stock market-related gatherings, I regularly controlled for participation based on sex. In public places connected with the stock market (brokerage houses, informal courses, and discussion groups), 10% of the participating public were women.

I visited regularly, one of the more respected "big players" was a woman of peasant background, in her sixties, who had started investing with the money her son had sent her from his temporary work in Australia. My research assistant, a graduate student in finance, had borrowed a significant sum from his family and teachers to play the market. I was introduced to the editor of a literary magazine who had made a neat fortune investing on a whim in share-purchase lottery tickets. I was also befriended by a worker from a Shanghai factory who had been hired by a group of co-workers to buy and sell for them. For each of these people, the social implications of investing in the stock market were quite different, both in terms of the image they had of themselves, and in terms of the skills and social resources they called upon to invest.

The "everybody" with stock fever extended well beyond the boundaries of Shanghai Municipality. While Shanghai and Shenzhen were the only official exchanges, various forms of stock had been issued in virtually all of China's provinces (Jin, Xiao and Xu 1991:64–65), unofficial or black market exchanges had been documented in Chengdu, Chongqing, Guangzhou, Nanning, Tianjin, Shenyang, Wuhan, Xiamen (*FEER* 1991a:29), and most Chinese observers told me that stock trading had spread throughout the country to cities and townships of even relatively minor size. It was in part this sense of a nationwide, all-status "everybody," in which the Shanghainese saw themselves as particularly implicated, which lent the stock market much of its power of fascination.

In Shanghai, the choice to invest in the stock market was of much greater consequence than a similar decision in the West. It was also – potentially – far more lucrative. The stock market was a new, politically sensitive, intimidating institution. The decision to invest fell in the category of those activities colloquially labeled "setting out to sea" (*xia hai*). The term *xia hai* can apply to any attempt to make a living outside state bureaucratic channels; it is the decision to explore uncharted waters. Because personal financial decisions frequently became public knowledge in Shanghai's close-knit neighborhoods and work units, entering the stock market generally put not only one's finances but also one's "face" on the line. It was this quasi-heroic endeavor which attracted or repelled potential investors, for it meant drawing upon all of the resources offered by the complex and shifting logics of urban life in Shanghai.

Investors had to inform themselves about the virtues of listed stocks with very little reliable published material to go by. They had to wait long hours, sometimes even days, in lines outside the brokerage offices to place their orders. Depending on the market's "temperature" at the moment, they sometimes had to meet minimum deposit requirements to open a stock account, or work through a lottery system even to have the right to purchase shares. Furthermore, in all of this, they could not rely on Shanghai brokers for anything but paperwork, for at the time of my field-work an unpublished directive forbad brokers from advising their customers on purchase and sales decisions for fear that they would engage in rampant insider-trading. And, even had these brokers not been forbidden to counsel their clients, they would not have had the time, nor would investors have trusted them to do a good job.

Thus, becoming an investor in Shanghai meant having at one's disposal, or at that of a friend, co-worker or relative, enough time, energy, sources of information, confidence, and, of course, money to tackle a new and complex institution. Understanding where these financial and informational resources, expertise and confidence came from – who had them and how they deployed them – requires understanding the varied strategies of urban living which Shanghainese have developed and perfected over the course of the dramatic events of their recent history. The personal and family situations of the vast majority of Shanghai's citizens have altered significantly, often more than once, over their lifetimes and those of their parents and grandparents. These changes are unlike the patterned shifts in prestige and wealth which standard sociological categories – income, education, age – capture with a certain grace for more stable political regimes. Neither are they tied in any direct way to those sociological categories which have been essentialized as the conceptual building blocks of many contemporary societies – race, ethnicity, religion and language.[2] Indeed, the notion of social structure is perhaps inappropriate to describe institutions which have been abolished, reconstituted, abolished again and reconstructed once more over the course of China's forty-plus years of Communist Party rule. Status differentiation in urban Chinese society is as much a product of the shifting logics of Chinese politics as it is a result of the functional divisions of labor which have enabled the creation of the imperturbable class-status systems of Western capitalism.

By transcending divisions between social statuses in urban society, the stock market highlights the assumptions and practices grounding these divisions in the first place. It provides an ideal context in which to discover how status markers and social logics operate in urban Chinese society. In

---

[2] However, a good case can and has been made that classifications based on perceptions of something like ethnic difference have been more important in the building of contemporary Chinese social structure than official discourse would allow (see Honig 1992, Schein 1993).

this chapter, I address this question by sketching out a generalized description of Shanghai social dynamics since the Chinese Revolution. Stock fever is a social fact, even a "total social fact," to borrow Mauss' famous phrase, because the stock market in one way or another draws upon all of the institutions, systems and practices – bureaucratic, revolutionary, connections-based, and market-oriented – which have formed and reformed urban Chinese society since the Communist Revolution.

Shanghai's pre-Revolutionary stock market

Before launching ourselves into a discussion of urban Chinese social dynamics, brief mention of Shanghai's pre-Revolutionary experience with the stock market is called for. As China rehabilitates its financial past, a recounting of Shanghai's role as financial capital of Asia during the Republican era has become standard fare in Chinese and foreign textbooks on the new securities industry. Chinese and foreigners alike are attracted by the romantic image of this modern (for the former), exotic (for the latter), "adventurer's paradise" (*maoxianjia de leyuan*), and it is probably fair to say that much of the investment interest thus far manifested in the city is based on the belief that the expertise, enthusiasm and, most importantly, wealth associated with Republican-era Shanghai will magically reappear under the correct political–economic conditions.

Nothing is more misleading than this re-incarnation theory of the Shanghai stock market. As I will demonstrate, the socio-cultural contours of the contemporary market were formed most immediately by more than forty-five years of Communist Party rule. Underlying the varied events and changing policies of these years is the powerful dynamic of the combined tributary and petty-capitalist modes of production. It is with this background in mind that we must examine the exceptional, though not anomalous, years of experience with high finance in Shanghai.

The sources are unanimous that China's most intimate experience with capitalism was in Republican-era Shanghai (1911–1949).[3] As in all of China's treaty ports,[4] this experience began with the compradors, Chinese

---

[3] The fascination which Republican-era Shanghai exercises on the Western scholarly imagination parallels popular interest, both Chinese and Western. See the recent outpouring of literature devoted to studying this already well studied period: Bergère 1964, 1981, 1986, Coble 1980, Cochran 1980, Elvin 1969, 1974, 1977, Fewsmith 1985, Henriot 1991, Heppner 1993, Jones 1974, Journal of Asian Studies 1995, Mac Elderry 1976, Murphey 1953, 1970, 1977, Perry 1993, Rankin 1971, Sanford 1976, Wakeman 1988, Wakeman and Yeh 1992, Wei 1987, Zhang 1956, 1990.

[4] The Treaty of Nanjing (1842), signed after China's defeat by Britain in the First Opium War, stipulated that five Chinese cities (Canton, Fuzhou, Xiamen, Ningbo and Shanghai) were to be opened to British citizens for residence and trade.

entrepreneurs who served as middlemen between Chinese and foreign merchants. Though the Qing (Ch'ing, 1644–1912) made every effort to contain these economic exchanges within government controlled channels, the cultural impact of Western and Japanese capitalism flowed far beyond the boundaries officials had originally set for it. In 1882, Chinese merchants opened, with government approval, the Shanghai Standard Stock Company (Shanghai Pingzhun Gupiao Gongsi) which posted share prices for jointly run government–merchant enterprises (*guan shang he ban*), bought and sold on its own account, and granted loans with shares as collateral. Investor enthusiasm was instantaneous. The *Shenbao*, Shanghai's most important newspaper at the time, reported that "with each new company, thousands of people compete to buy in and equate obtaining shares with good fortune" (cited in Gu 1994:16, my translation).

By the turn of the century, a small number of Chinese-owned and operated industries had sprung up in the lower Yangzi region. Over the next few decades, these industrial "petty capitalists," as Gates would call them, blossomed into a full-blown capitalist bourgeoisie through a combination of circumstances: the weakness of the dying Qing and new-born Republican governments; links with foreign capitalists; and the opportunities provided by the paralysis of foreign trade during World War I (Bergère 1986). Paralleling these developments in industry and commerce, China's first recorded securities exchange was established in 1914 by the Stockbrokers' Trade Association (Gupiao Shangye Gonghui) (Gu 1994:15–20). However, the Exchange's economic impact was minimal, for by far the greatest part of this new activity was purely speculative in nature as illustrated by the infamous "tempest of the bourses" (*xin jiao fengchao*) of 1921–1922, during which 140 new "stock exchanges" – generally companies whose only business was trading in their own shares – were established within the space of six months, all but seven of which collapsed during the year that followed (Bergère 1986:86).[5]

When the Guomindang (Nationalist or KMT) Party solidified its control over Shanghai in 1927, the city's capitalists became the principal source of financial support for war efforts against the Japanese and the Communists (Coble 1980). Much of this support took the form of government and military bonds foisted upon the banking community by the Guomindang government. The Shanghai Chinese Merchants' Securities Exchange (Shanghai Huashang Zhengquan Jiaoyisuo), officially established in 1920, became a forum for rampant speculation, prices fluctuating

---

[5] I am currently carrying out historical research into the socio-cultural structure of this "tempest" as compared with the 1992 "fever" I witnessed.

wildly with each new rumor of military success or failure. Closed during the Japanese occupation of Shanghai, the Exchange re-opened again (as the Shanghai Securities Exchange [Shanghai Zhengquan Jiaoyisuo]) in September 1946, but only a handful of company shares were traded. In June 1951, two years after the Communist entry into Shanghai, the Shanghai Stock Exchange was discreetly closed down (Howe 1981a:419).

Most of Shanghai's indigenous capital and "talented managers" fled to Hong Kong and Taiwan with the Communist takeover (Pye 1981:xii). Clearly, the kinship links with overseas Chinese in Taiwan, Hong Kong and the West created at that moment have become an important asset in Shanghai's recent economic development. However, this asset accrued precisely because these "Shanghai capitalists" were operating elsewhere than in Shanghai during the subsequent forty years. Thus, Shanghai leaders, eager to establish a fictive continuity between the city's pre-Revolutionary financial glory and her reform-era prospects, have sought out and cultivated relations with the by now rather elderly men who worked as brokers in Shanghai's pre-Revolutionary securities industry. These men receive "honorary membership" in securities agencies and investment houses, and act as titulary "advisors" to government think-tanks and consultancies, but exercise no actual power whatsoever when it comes to decisions about how to regulate the contemporary market. And, why should they? These were young men, often of low rank, at the time they worked for firms such as Big Elephant Trust and Investment Company, and they are now in their seventies and eighties and out of touch with all aspects of financial regulation in contemporary China.

One such group of elderly ex-brokers met weekly for tea in a neighborhood teahouse, and I had the pleasure of sitting in on one of their morning chats. The conversation, when it concerned the stock market at all, generally turned on the incompetence of today's government regulators, and the bizarre structure of the entire experiment as compared with the pre-Revolutionary market. Indeed, these men expressed much the same sort of bafflement over the presence of state shares or the form of government "regulation" that I had heard from the Taiwanese delegation discussed in chapter 1. To their minds, the principal point of comparison between Republican-era markets and today's was the stock fever surrounding them.

Shanghai social dynamics since 1949

When the Communists entered Shanghai, they came with contradictory images of this international metropolis. As a capitalist, corrupt, foreign-dominated, sophisticated coastal city, Shanghai represented all that the CCP's nationalist leadership, generally of inland peasant background, felt most uncomfortable with (Gaulton 1981:40). However, as one of China's most industrialized cities, Shanghai was of central importance to the Party's economic policy. And, as the birthplace of the Chinese Communist Party, Shanghai's revolutionary heritage could not be ignored (*ibid.*:39). The ambivalence of central authorities was to be felt throughout the thirty years which preceded Deng's rise to power and beyond; indeed, Shanghai was only officially targeted for the beneficial treatment many of its citizens felt it deserved in 1992, with Deng's decision to develop Pudong (discussed in chapter 3, pp. 89–90 above).

Beijing's economic dependence on Shanghai was patent. One year after the establishment of the People's Republic of China, Shanghai was responsible for producing one-fifth of China's industrial output (Pye 1981:xii). During the First Five-Year Plan, Shanghai contributed more than 14 percent to the total increase in gross value of industrial output, while receiving only 1–2 percent of national investment (Howe 1981b). In addition, Shanghai sent between one and two million educated workers to help with economic development in other parts of the country (Pye 1981:xiii). Shanghai can legitimately claim to have given far more to the national economy than she received in return (Pye 1981), a fact of popular knowledge among Shanghai citizens and a source of both resentment and pride.[6]

Getting a grasp on the complex and entrenched structures of urban life in Shanghai involved an effort at deep penetration into society by the Party/state bureaucracy, a process which was paralleled throughout urban China. Once in place, however, this bureaucracy began to take on a life of its own. It was the rise of this independent bureaucratic class which, for reasons of power and ideology, frightened Mao into launching the Great Proletarian Cultural Revolution, radically altering for a second time the structure of Shanghai society. Then, it was disillusionment with this radical vision and its unintended consequences which led to the reappearance of a third social system, the system of *guanxi*, or connections. Finally, with the reforms, these three social systems – the bureaucratic, the radical egalitarian, and the *guanxi*-based – were countered and complemented by a fourth, the market.

In this section, I discuss the historical and social organizational logics

---

[6] For a careful calculation of changing standards of living in Shanghai after the Revolution, see Reynolds (1981).

underlying each of these systems. However, we would be wrong to think of them as independent entities. Rather, these different logics intertwine, creating the conditions for the varied strategies of urban living in contemporary urban China. Furthermore, each is related in a particular way to the more general historical dynamic which I have traced using Gates' notion of the "tributary" and "petty capitalist" modes of production (TMP and PCMP). Clearly, the "bureaucratic system" is the quintessential site for the operation of Gates' TMP, while the "market sphere" is largely, though not exclusively, made up of petty capitalists operating under the PCMP. What I am calling the "continual revolutionary dynamic" and "the *guanxi* system" are permutations: the first, as argued in chapter 3, is essentially a mass egalitarian inversion of the primary class division established under the TMP; the second, as we shall see, represents the infiltration of PCMP logic into the TMP. In contemporary Shanghai, all four systems must be taken together as a dynamic yet frequently conservative complex. Only then can we fully appreciate who was in the position to undertake the complicated and risky business of playing the stock market.

The bureaucratic system

With the Communist victory in 1949, the Party set out to reorganize the nation into an all-encompassing social, political, economic and cultural "New China." In urban China, three systems of control form the keystones for this ambitious project of bureaucratization, all of which still function, in muted form, today. Though modeled on a Leninist bureaucratic blueprint, these systems perpetuated many of the qualities we have identified as adhering to the tributary mode of state production, distribution and hegemony. The state embraces "the People" in interlocking networks of obligation and loyalty, setting ideological conformity over productive efficiency.

The first of these systems is the household registration system. All families are issued a household registration booklet (*hukoubu*) in which the names of each individual in the household are recorded. A strict division between rural and urban residents – Sulamith Potter calls it a "caste-like system of social stratification" (S.H. Potter 1983) – was thereby institutionalized as a means of controlling rural migration.[7] Parallel records are

---

[7] The consequences of this division for China's peasants have been harsh indeed: while urbanites are, or at least were until very recently, part of an all-encompassing system of social welfare, peasants have no such guarantees from the state in matters of employment, health care, social welfare and retirement benefits. Contrary to official ideology, urbanites are citizens in a way that peasants are not.

kept at the local police station. Virtually all of the activities which made up urban life before the reforms involved showing one's household registration booklet: gaining access to rationed goods, schools and officially assigned jobs, receiving permission to marry and divorce, and, more recently, having one's child. One's household registration can be transferred to another location only with the permission of public security, residential committee and work place authorities.

If the household registration system guaranteed control over who lived in China's cities, it did not solve the problem of how these city residents were to become participants in New China. Two parallel systems made up the core of this ambitious project: the "work unit" (*danwei*), or simply "unit" in a direct translation from the Chinese;[8] and the residential system. The features of the Chinese work unit have been described in detail by others, and I will only sketch their general outline here.[9] The unit was first and foremost the place of employment for urban residents. With this job came the privileges of membership in the state system: heavily subsidized housing, a retirement pension, health and child care benefits, and access to rationed goods.[10] It is important to note, however, that contrary to the logic of system equality at the heart of bureaucratic ideology, all work units did not receive equal treatment, and hence not all units provide the full panoply of rights and privileges (Pieke 1996:61–66, Whyte and Parish 1984:25–26). Most disadvantaged in this hierarchy were the "collective" units, enterprises created by low levels of government such as a neighborhood committee, or by another enterprise (Whyte and Parish 1984:28–33).

---

[8] The phenomenological force of China's bureaucratic ideology translates poorly into the language of Western rationalist individualism. Perhaps the importance of bureaucracy is best illustrated by the word "unit" itself. It implies that these complex organisms, in which sometimes thousands of people work, eat and live, are the primary cell of social reality, the building blocks out of which society will be constructed. It is not that the Chinese ideology of governance does not recognize the existence of the individual people within a "unit." It simply grants them no ontological priority.

[9] Henderson 1982, Henderson and Cohen 1984, Lewis 1971, Li 1993, Lu 1989, Pieke 1996:59–91, 101–109, Southall 1993c, Walder 1986, Whyte and Parish 1984:25–26. Whyte and Parish make the interesting point that the unit occasionally figured in Republican-era work place organization (1984:359).

[10] Whyte and Parish provide a good overview of the rationing system as it functioned in urban China up until the reforms (1984:86–93). The concept of "rationed goods" is a difficult one in China today. While rationing for staple foods and articles (rice, oil, eggs, meat, soap, etc.) has been progressively phased out over a period of eight years from 1984 to 1992, more complex goods, services and, most importantly, permissions are still rationed, in fact if not in theory. For example, permission to go abroad is still controlled primarily by one's work unit, which must comply with quota systems established by superior organs. More importantly, subsidized housing is rationed out by one's unit. As we shall see, access to share-offerings on the primary market is also occasionally rationed through the work unit.

The second system, put in place as early as 1950 in Shanghai, was the residential or neighborhood system (see generally Whyte and Parish 1984:22–25). Shanghai's urban center was divided into districts, subdivided into wards, and these wards were in turn subdivided into units of about 100–800 families called residence committees (Whyte and Parish 1984:22). While the entire structure makes up the state system of residential control, not all of the officers on the ladder receive a state stipend. Generally, retired people or housewives are called in at the level of the residence committee and below. These citizens carry out directives from superior levels, report back to these offices on unusual activities or problems in their jurisdiction, and generally act as go-betweens between the state bureaucracy and city residents (Whyte and Parish 1984:22–25). The residential control system is closely tied in with the police and public security system, particularly through control of the household registration books, allowing the state easy access to information on such things as residence permits, marriage, divorce and child-births, place of employment, class background, etc.

Paralleling these organizational systems was the cultural/ideological system of class labels (G. White 1976, Kraus 1982, Billeter 1985). These class labels seem at first glance to correspond to a Marxist vision of productive relations. However, further examination reveals that the "class status" system was rather a *sui generis* creation, reflecting traditional hierarchical values, Marxist analysis, and the political needs of the Communist Party at any given time (Billeter 1985, Kuhn 1984, Watson 1984a). The system of class labeling changed nature over the thirty years of its application as Mao alternated between the view that class consciousness was based uniquely on social origins and the view that class consciousness could be demonstrated through revolutionary virtue (Schram 1984, Shirk 1984, Watson 1984b).

In Shanghai, the class status system had to be adapted to the very particular circumstances of that city. It was necessary to find a means for distinguishing between those "bourgeois elements" who could be useful in the reconstruction of New China, and those who threatened it. The urban household registers thus contained two entries – "family social origin" (*jiating chushen*) and "individual class status" (*geren chengfen*). In this way, sufficient flexibility was built into the system to accommodate a wide variety of people within a wide variety of categories.

The "new class" of managers in Shanghai was made up of two elements: managers from the bourgeois management class of the Republican era who were necessary to maintaining industrial production (and who usually qualified for their positions through their "individual class status" as "revolutionary worker"), and proletarian or peasant recruits into Party schools whose "family social origins" were "correct" (L. White 1984). According to White, the tensions between these two factions of the new elite were dissipated over the ten years between the Communist victory and the Great Leap Forward.[11] By 1963, the new management class was to divide on the question whether economic or political factors were more important to China's socialist reconstruction, but this division was not based along old class lines. In other words, a short fifteen years after the Revolution, "family social origins" ceased to be a useful category for understanding the political, social and economic worldviews of Shanghai's new elite.

These bureaucratic systems sought to give a socialist shape to China's new cities. And, clearly, many aspects of urban life did change. However, the bureaucratic incursions into Shanghai society did not alter certain of its fundamental features, or altered them only partially. Part of the reason for this can be found in the history of Shanghai's urban planning and housing policy (see Howe 1968). Chinese city planners faced with the complex problems of urban management following the Revolution turned initially to Soviet models (Fung 1981). Very quickly, however, these models were abandoned for a vision of Communist urbanization which kept urban growth to a minimum, moved factories out of the city center to sub-urban neighborhoods where worker residences could be built close to their place of work, and tried to maintain a balance between urban and sub-urban conglomerates (*ibid.*). This pattern, followed in Shanghai, left pre-existing urban neighborhoods largely intact.[12]

In 1949, a significant number of Shanghainese were living in relatively well-built and modern apartments or row-houses (*shikumen*) in neighbor-hoods separated by a network of small alleys (*longtang*) built specially by Chinese or foreign employers for their employees.[13] Little of this housing was destroyed with the arrival of the Communists. Rather, through shuffling and partitioning, much of the population remained in the areas developed before 1949. New-style buildings were located in the expanding outskirts of the city (Pellow 1993). Despite bureaucratic ambitions, then, many Shanghai work units were not able to provide housing for their

[11] In a fascinating article, L. White (1984) reconstructs the chronology of this melding.

[12] Whyte and Parish found that the average length of residence in the same home in urban China was eighteen years (1984:21).

[13] A significant proportion, but by no means the majority. Sprawling slums existed in Shanghai prior to the Revolution and in modified form still exist today, particularly in the working-class district of Nanshi.

employees in the same physical complex as their job. Rather, employees frequently lived scattered throughout the city. While relations among co-workers did become increasingly important with the work unit system, neighborly relations continued to represent an independent source of acquaintances, friendships and mutual aid, and kept Shanghai citizens in touch with a wide variety of their co-citizens.

Similarly, the implementation of class/status ideology did not entirely transform pre-existing Shanghainese notions of social status. An indication of class ideology and social stratification as they affected popular values and behavior can be gained through an examination of marriage choice. Croll (1984) traces these developments by examining expressed choices in marriage partners between 1949 and 1979. She found that despite the radical free-choice ambitions of the 1950 Marriage Law, Chinese continued to prefer status homogamy; what changed were the factors influencing popular perceptions of status. While the political class/status system outlined above played an important role, social factors such as level of education or training, wealth, looks and family influence were equally important.[14]

Thus the bureaucratic system's main impact was to further compartmentalize the already tight-knit though highly labile social groups making up Shanghai society. No doubt its most important contribution was to bureaucratize the distribution of goods and services through these new cellular structures (Solinger 1984a). This not only represented a significant change from the market economy which had flourished in pre-1949 Shanghai, it placed a new class of bureaucrats in positions of control over life essentials. We shall see that the power thus distributed and the opportunities for its abuse played an important role in future developments. However, this bureaucratic system was itself essentially static. To understand the energy behind the dramatic reversals of fortune which characterize Shanghai history, we must turn to the revolutionary dynamic.

The continual revolutionary dynamic
I label the continual revolutionary dynamic that series of policies and practices designed to intensify egalitarianism and counter the creation of a new class of bureaucratic elites. These radical policies are generally associated with Mao Zedong, but as the Shanghai example illustrates extended far beyond his personal influence. The revolutionary dynamic ebbed and flowed, following changes in political wind determined both in Beijing and

---

[14] For a careful discussion of post-reform urban status hierarchies in a northern Chinese city, see Jankowiak 1993:60–96.

at the local level. In general, radical discourse stressed the need to dismantle China's "semi-colonial, semi-feudal" class structure and build a new social structure on the foundations of the revolutionary alliance between workers and peasants. This general goal translated into numerous specific policy moves. At times it meant that citizens with "good" class-status labels ("worker," "staff," "poor peasant") were given priority in access to education and jobs. It led to periodic criticism of what were identified as bourgeois ideological criteria for governing promotions and production, such as "slavish reliance" on expertise and individually based incentive structures. At moments when radical discourse was in the ascendant, factory and office managers, teachers and administrators were encouraged to place full faith in the People's revolutionary fervor.

This discourse is frequently identified as "ideological" or "utopian" by both Chinese and foreign commentators. However, radical egalitarian discourse generally corresponded with very tangible changes in policy, changes which addressed what were perceived as pressing social problems. In the process, these policies tended significantly to increase the Communist Party's hold over Chinese society. The 1951 Five-Antis campaign examined by Gardner (1969), or the urban commune experiments discussed by Schurmann (1968:380–399), are cases in point. So is the egalitarian discourse which brought women into the work force in massive proportions, calculated to earn the CCP "the women's vote" by strengthening women's position in Chinese society, but perhaps as importantly, strengthening the Party's hold over the education of children.[15]

Perhaps the clearest example of the pragmatic aims behind radical egalitarian policies can be found in the rustification campaigns that relocated no less than 10 percent of China's urban population to the countryside (T. Bernstein 1977, Ivory and Lavely 1977, Whyte and Parish 1984:39). As Whyte and Parish point out, the "up to the mountains and down to the villages" campaign was promoted "as a measure to foster revolutionary fervor and class solidarity with peasants"; however, the program served perhaps a more pressing purpose as well, that of alleviating "the crisis situation of educated unemployed" (*ibid.*). Like many developing and developed countries, Chinese cities of the 1960s were unable to absorb the enormous number of educated young people which increased political stability and standards of living had produced. In the Party's view, rustification provided an ideologically forward-looking means for solving this practical problem.

---

[15] Nader (1990) has pointed out that state-sponsored rhetoric promoting the position of women often masks state moves for control over the education of children.

The cry for continual revolution reached its heights with the Great Proletarian Cultural Revolution (1966–1969). With the contemporary focus on Shanghai as a commercial megalopolis, it is easy to forget that Shanghai was also the site where the Cultural Revolution attained its "greatest" (Goodman 1981), its most "proletarian" (Wylie 1981), its most "cultural" (Gardner 1981, Ragvald 1981) and its most "revolutionary" (Chang 1981) expression. Launched from Shanghai, the Cultural Revolution took a radical turn with the creation of the Shanghai Commune in January 1967, but this moment was to be very short-lived indeed.[16] The assertion of "actual proletariat" (Meisner 1977:319)[17] interests along genuinely egalitarian lines frightened Party leaders, Mao among them. In mid-February 1967, Mao declared the situation one of "extreme anarchism, it is most reactionary ... [i]n reality there will still always be leaders," thereby quietly but effectively putting an end to the Commune experiment (Meisner 1977:323).

The various waves of radical egalitarian policy which swept Shanghai, beginning with the Five-Antis campaign in 1951 and culminating in the Shanghai Commune of 1967, worked significant changes on the composition and rhythms of Shanghai society. The effort to promote people of "good" class background gave power and privileges to categories of society which would not otherwise have entered the ruling elite. Conversely, members of the pre-Revolutionary elite frequently suffered personal and familial downfalls which left them utterly destitute until Deng set about "correcting leftist errors" in the early 1980s. These changes took place in the context of the tight work place and neighborhood communities described above, the fate of all being known to most. Furthermore, the element of a-morality – the detachment of private assessments of virtue and vice from public structures of reward and punishment – led to a general disillusionment with the Communist Party leadership which was to have profound effects on future developments.

Many observers of China have concluded, along with Whyte and Parish, that "the new socialist values and rituals failed to provide meaning and structure to urban life in the 1970s [and beyond]" (1984:324).[18] It is undeniable that most Chinese, assessing the senseless suffering and chaos

---

[16] This account is based on Meisner (1977:309–324).

[17] Meisner's use of the term "actual proletariat," like White's attempt to distinguish a "real" bourgeoisie from the Chinese-labeled "bourgeoisie," suggests the degree to which virtually all Western intellectuals are more Marxist than virtually all Chinese. By this I mean that the Western intellectual tradition grants an ontological reality to the Marxist notion of class, correctly analyzed, which we find incompatible with the Chinese politicized use of this term.   [18] A more subtle analysis is provided by Jankowiak (1993:60–164).

of the Cultural Revolutionary years, turned against the "strident dogmatism" (*ibid.*) of radical egalitarianism when promoted from above. It was clearly perceived that the rhetoric of mass mobilization could be and had been used to reinforce the power of (portions of) "the State" over "the People," in direct contradiction to its manifest content. However, as discussed in chapter 3, radical egalitarianism is not simply a "socialist value." Rather, it echoes and amplifies on the counter-hegemonic dialectic within the tributary mode of production. It is this counter-hegemonic appeal which makes radical egalitarianism a permanent fixture, not a passing phase, on the Chinese ideological scene.

For that generation of people, now in their forties, who served as Red Guards or who were "sent down" to the countryside, Cultural Revolutionary rhetoric is still, at times, a powerful source of inspiration. At the very least, the Cultural Revolution impressed on China's youth the tremendous fragility of the status quo. At its most powerful, Cultural Revolutionary rhetoric reinforced a strong aversion to elite power and privilege that is reflected in popular discourse at all levels. This bottom-up egalitarianism is a key element in the construction of stock fever in Shanghai.

The origins of guanxi

The sources are unanimous that it was with the end of the Cultural Revolution, and the chaotic years that followed (1970–1976), that a new "feudal" phenomenon re-entered the Chinese social scene: connections or *guanxi* (Cheng 1986:497, Gold 1985, King 1991, Pieke 1996:92–93, Yang 1989:35).[19] *Guanxi* means "relation," "connection" or "importance," as in the common phrase "it is not important," literally "there is no connection" (*meiyou guanxi*). The "social art" of *guanxi*, or *guanxixue*, as defined by Yang, "lies in the skillful mobilization of moral and cultural imperatives such as obligation and reciprocity in pursuit of both diffuse social ends and calculated instrumental goals" (1989:35).

Guanxi were an important part of imperial and Republican-era Chinese social dynamics (Fried 1953:102–123, M. Yang 1945). With the rise of the bureaucratic system during the 1950s, the *guanxi* system was suppressed in favor of the universalist logic of Communist bureaucratization. By the

---

[19] Equally important evidence of the recent reappearance of *guanxi* on the Chinese scene is the fact that *guanxi* are barely mentioned in Whyte and Parish's otherwise thorough study of urban life (1984). Given that most of their interviews were conducted with refugees from the 1960s and early 1970s it is reasonable to conclude that these refugees, whose political memories were based on China of the 1950s and 1960s, were simply not acquainted with the practice of *guanxi* on the mainland.

early 1970s, however, the use of *guanxi* was back, and permeated all levels of the Chinese social system. Acquaintances in Shanghai told me that the use and abuse of *guanxi* began in that city with parents attempting to have their "sent-down" children transferred back to Shanghai and granted a Shanghai residence permit. If, as we have seen, the rustification policy touched at least 10 percent of Shanghai's urban youth (not to mention the 1 to 2 million skilled workers sent to other parts of the countryside), the mobilization of *guanxi* to obtain their return must have been a massive phenomenon.

The subject of *guanxi* is a book in itself (see Yang 1994, Yan 1996), but a brief review of its basic features is indispensable for any coherent description of contemporary China. In this discussion, I prefer the more commonly used term *guanxi* to *guanxixue*. *Guanxixue* is a term which has emerged as self-consciousness about *guanxi* grew among the Chinese populace. It promotes the *guanxi* phenomenon to an "art" or set of skills to be developed by the upwardly mobile. In translation, the word is not only cynical, it mischaracterizes the sociological nature of *guanxi*, portraying the use of *guanxi* as an individual strategy, not a social system. *Guanxi* as individual strategy exists in US society as well, but *guanxi* as a pervasive distributional logic does not.

Guanxi, or what Pieke calls "personalized transactions" (1996:128–138), take many forms and have many contents: from the mutual small favors which two factory workers might render each other, to long-term relations of reciprocity developed between a petroleum processing and a synthetic fibers plant; from the purely instrumental doing of favors to the deep loyalties of friendship and mutual aid common among Chinese friends and colleagues. (Interestingly, one cannot speak of developing *guanxi* with one's relatives, the presumption being that long-term loyalty and mutual aid are built into the relationship. When this presumption proves false, however, one can say that one "does not have any connection" with one's relatives.) Whatever their form, however, *guanxi* relations share certain qualities which merit their being considered as a category. These qualities are the creation of a long-term relationship in which reciprocity and continued obligation are presumed, and the invocation of "feelings" (*ganqing*) or "human feelings" (*renqing*) as the basis for the relationship.

In most cases of *guanxi* mobilization, official channels of distribution are circumvented as the partners to the exchange assure themselves access to scarce commodities. The use of connections is undoubtedly intensified by what Kornai has called "the economics of shortage" (Kornai 1980).[20]

---

[20] See Whyte and Parish on shortages in urban China before the reforms (1984:93–100).

The converse is true as well: the use of *guanxi* exacerbates shortages in a command economy by distorting the planned flow of goods and services (Clarke 1991). On the industrial level, an increase in the use of *guanxi* between work units reflects the need to procure primary materials and distributors in an allocative system which crumbled into a state of anarchy and paralysis with the chaos of the Cultural Revolution (Donnithorne 1972, Perry and Wong 1985b). However, there are two important reasons to find the scarcity-based theory of the development of *guanxi* inadequate. First, *guanxi* are an important part of the Taiwanese and Hong Kong economies, economies which are hardly troubled by shortages (de Glopper 1972, Jacobs 1979, King 1991, Moore 1988, Silin 1972, Smart 1993). Second, the shortage-based perspective fails to account for that particular form of surplus value produced by *guanxi*, the supplement of "face" which *guanxi* transactions provide.

As commentators on traditional and Republican-era China have noted (Fried 1953:102–123, Hu 1944, Yang 1945), face (*mianzi* or *lian*) was a central element in the conception of the person in Chinese culture. Contemporary anthropologists have demonstrated that it is no less so for urban Chinese today (Jankowiak 1993:60–96, King 1991, Pieke 1996:130–131, Yang 1989:42–43, Yan 1996:136–138). *Mianzi* is a quality which adheres to a person not as a lone individual, but in her relations to those around her; it is by definition interpersonal. The accumulation of *mianzi* comes with the maintenance and development of wide-spread harmonious relations in society. As the size of one's personal network depends on one's power to provide desirables, face inevitably correlates with social status. However, *mianzi* has a universalist, subjective component in the form of *lian* (which also means "face," Hu 1944). Thus, the large amounts of face (*mianzi*) which generally accompany power and status can be diminished by personally reprehensible behavior, which causes loss of face (*lian*).

One of the clearest roles of the *guanxi* system is to serve as a forum for the expression and negotiation of face. One of my Shanghai acquaintances was what might be labeled a "connections junkie" (*guanxigui*), a person for whom cultivating connections was more than a necessity, as with most urban Chinese, but rather an obsession. This man staked his honor on his ability never to pay full price for anything, never to obtain anything as an anonymous consumer on the market, and never to adhere to bureaucratic channels meant to govern access to desirables. He was also an astute observer of his own behavior. He had calculated, he told me, the amount of money he spent – in "gifts, favors and banquets" to borrow

Yang's (1994) elegant phrase – in order to maintain his *guanxi* network and concluded that it exactly equaled the amount of money he saved by mobilizing this network. "But," he explained with didactic self-satisfaction, "no matter what, people always needs face" (*danshi, buguan zemma yang, ren zongshi yao mianzi*). The ability to obtain or grant desirables through one's social network is a measure of one's social status, and hence one's face. Conversely, the fact of waiting one's turn, like everybody else, for the distribution of a desired good or service is more than an inconvenience: it is a loss of face, or a patent demonstration of the narrowness of one's social relationships. This has remained true even as market reforms have made consumer goods and special privileges more freely available.

Clearly, the particularistic ties of *guanxi* relationships help to maintain the Chinese sense of self and social order in a way that universalistic "free" markets cannot. This is true from the lowest level of society to the highest, although the Chinese moral evaluation of the use of *guanxi* by a taxi-driver and by a high-level official tend to differ greatly. In political terms, *guanxi* work to reinforce the power and prestige of those in the position to distribute goods and services. The widespread (most Shanghainese say universal) abuse of *guanxi* by officials at all levels cuts against the egalitarian distributional logic of the state bureaucratic system, while simultaneously reinforcing the personal power of its officers. Indeed, the rampant use of *guanxi* by state officials – which the Chinese state labels corruption – causes a problem for the use of the term "state" in descriptions of Chinese politics. Is the "state" that collection of officers and institutions which are currently fighting against internal corruption, or is it the system of corruption which keeps these officers in power? This tension cannot be resolved, and both notions are reflected in the Chinese use of the term *guojia* (nation/state) in popular – though not official – discourse.[21]

The widespread use of *guanxi* is generally decried in official and popular discourse, although popular discourse also reflects a grudging admiration for those who have managed to ascend the social hierarchy through the skillful mobilization of *guanxi* (Yang 1989:36). These discussions, however, fail to recognize one of the paradoxically "socialist" side-effects

---

[21] For this reason, I cannot agree with Yang's use of the term "state" in "The Gift Economy and State Power in China" (1989). She argues that "the State" attempts the normative exercise of bio-power (Foucault 1979) through its distributive bureaucracy, and that something like "the People" resist and circumvent this power through the "gift economy." This is a teleological interpretation of power and intransigence which builds on de Certeau's (1984) work on strategies of resistance in everyday life. Such a morality tale is only possible if we can maintain a reasonable distinction between those exercising power and those resisting it. In China, such a distinction is simply not tenable.

of the *guanxi* system. Because all acquisitions bring face when obtained through *guanxi*, all people in the position to control a desirable commodity or service are to be cultivated for eventual mobilization. The result is criss-crossing networks of people of widely different social statuses. Whyte and Parish report a bit of popular wisdom which circulated in Canton during the 1970s:

one should maintain relations with "three valuables" (*sanbao*) – a doctor, a truck driver, and a sales clerk. The doctor would help one beat the lines and medical shortages at hospitals. The truck driver could get one cheap goods from markets outside the city. The sales clerk could notify one when scarce goods like electric fans, televisions, and better clothing were about to appear on the market and might "forget" to check purchases off on one's ration book (1984:98).

What is interesting here is that the "three valuables" in this scenario may well have a lower status background than those seeking to maintain relations with them. (Doctors do not enjoy particularly high status in socialist China.) This cross-cutting of relations does not equalize social statuses, for it has no effect on the general cultural perception that a driver is lower on the status hierarchy than his boss. However, the boss must engage in the cultivation of his driver, and must be prepared to render him services in return. This structure of reciprocity works to soften the impact of the Chinese status hierarchy in practice.

The widespread use of *guanxi* which began in the 1970s has introduced a new element of dynamism to urban life in China. While it has strengthened the power of state officials, it has done so in ways which cut against both the distributional logic of the bureaucratic system, and the egalitarian logic of revolutionary discourse. Furthermore, despite economists' predictions, the *guanxi* system has not disappeared under the pressure of market reforms, to which we now turn.

The market sphere

Under Deng, a number of important urban reforms were designed to increase the role of market forces in the urban economy: the gradual phasing out of rationing for foodstuff and basic consumer items in favor of a system of "guidance pricing," the legalization of free markets, the encouragement of small-scale entrepreneurial activities,[22] the increased possibilities for job mobility (Davis 1992a) and the creation of something

---

[22] "Encouragement" is perhaps too strong a word. While individual entrepreneurs (*getihu*) have served as a partial solution to the urban unemployment problem, the government has remained on guard against excessive accumulations of private wealth, and has tended to burden individual and private entrepreneurs with far heavier taxes and administrative hurdles than it has the collective sector (see Gold 1991, Bruun 1993, Rocca 1996).

resembling a market in real estate (Vucinic 1993). The literature on market reforms in China is vast.[23] Again, I limit myself in this section to emphasizing those aspects of market-oriented reforms which have created the possibility for new configurations of social status and power in urban China.

The clearest change wrought by market reforms is to decrease the power of state officials to control the distribution of goods and services in the bureaucratic system. Indeed, in some sense this is the express aim of market reforms. With food, clothing and consumer commodities available to all without ration coupons, the state has lost an important hold over the behavior of state workers. With the opening of a limited labor market, state and collective units have lost another source of control over their employees. Most people who wish to can now elect to exit the work unit system altogether and find work in the joint-venture or private sectors, provided, of course, that they can arrange housing for themselves. Furthermore, while the household registration system is still in operation today, markets in foodstuffs, jobs and housing have made it possible to live in urban areas without official permission.[24]

Davis' (1992a) study of job mobility under reforms demonstrates, however, that job mobility has not increased in the way that reformers would have predicted. Rather, a number of forms of "muddling through" (*hun*) seem to occupy a large percentage of the population. In some cases – as with journalists, researchers and other professionals – one's job officially takes up only about 20 percent of one's time. The rest can be devoted to one's chosen path for social and economic advancement, entirely outside the confines of one's job. Those who work in supervised situations frequently ask for one of a number of forms of unpaid leave from their state or collective unit (see Davis 1992a), and then use their free time to earn money through other channels. Researchers at the Shanghai Academy of Social Sciences, with which I was associated, were a case in point. Officially, they were required to come into the Academy only twice a week. A small percentage spent the rest of their time doing research related to their job. Most were engaged in different – and more lucrative – lines of business: running trading companies, writing for television and radio, consulting for Shanghai companies seeking foreign investors, etc.

Leaving the work unit system does not end one's relationships with

---

[23] See Chossudovsky 1986, Lampton 1987, Meaney 1989, *Modern China* 1992, Perry and Wong 1985b, Pieke 1996:109–128, Riskin 1987, Solinger 1993, World Bank 1990, 1992.

[24] As feared, this has created problems of massive rural migration, with consequent poverty, vagrancy and crime (*FEER* 1994a, Zhou 1993).

urban bureaucracy. Personal records once kept by work unit leaders will be transferred to one's street committee, and each new job or change of civil status will require permission from these officials. Those who launch themselves into business must satisfy numerous registration and tax requirements set by the local Ministry of Industry and Commerce. Tales of encounters with these officials tend to be tales of how and how much one must bribe them to receive the required stamps and letters in a reasonable length of time. Likewise, while the real estate market is being opened up, especially to foreign purchasers, the allotment of state-subsidized housing remains highly bureaucratized and riven with corrupt practices.

The second important change brought about by market reforms is the birth of an urban group of *nouveaux riches*. Many of the people who have launched themselves outside state channels – either in black market activities or as individual entrepreneurs (although the two are frequently equated in popular ideology) – have become remarkably rich. The story of the social trajectory of these *nouveaux riches* is far from written, but even over the ten years since their appearance on the urban scene a certain evolution is apparent. During the mid 1980s, as opportunities for doing business, legal or illegal, were just opening up, these new black marketeers and individual entrepreneurs were so looked down upon that only those individuals with few other options entered these lines of business: a common urban stereotype had it that most individual entrepreneurs were people who had been released from prison. However, as the reforms have continued and as money has become a more explicit object for many urban Chinese, all manner of professions and social strata have been "taking the plunge" (*xia hai*), leaving the state sector for business. Of course these "businesses" are stratified – high-level cadres and their children frequently capitalize on their connections to act as deal-makers;[25] intellectuals and lower-level cadres tend towards professional activities such as computer sales and programming, cultural promotional activities or night-school teaching; and workers lucky enough to have an apartment which can serve as a storefront often open small clothing or food stands.

Thus, market reforms have indeed created opportunities for more individual risk-taking and entrepreneurship; they have also, of course, reintroduced the tensions and rhythms of petty capitalism into urban life. While the tempo of work in the state and collective sectors is languid at best, individual businessmen and -women work long and tiring hours, knowing that while they are taking a break their competitor might not be.

---

[25] Chinese newspapers report that 70% of top officials' children have opened "trading companies" in Shanghai (Rocca 1992:415).

Those who have launched themselves into the joint-venture sector get a first taste of capitalist discipline international style.

Urban living: *qian, quan* and *mianzi*

Whyte and Parish conclude their sociological portrait of urban China with the observation that "there is but a single status hierarchy" (1984:363), the hierarchy of government officials. This observation marks the limits of a study based on interviews from the 1960s and 1970s. It may or may not be correct to say that up until the Cultural Revolution, the only edifice of social status was the Party/state hierarchy; Croll's study (1984) of status homogamy in marriage choice indicates that the situation was more complicated even in the years of alternating bureaucratic and radical egalitarian policies. It is certainly not an accurate description of contemporary reality, when a variety of strategies for attaining social prestige are open to urban residents simultaneously.

Two principal changes in urban Chinese social dynamics have opened the way for a more complex system of status classification. First, the Dengist era has put an end to the officially sponsored egalitarian rhetoric which I have called continual revolutionary discourse, and reversed many of the dramatic changes of fortune which struck China's ruling elite during the Cultural Revolution. With the rehabilitation of Deng, numerous other victims of these "Ultra-leftist deviations" were also rehabilitated. This, of course, left those cadres who had risen to power during the Cultural Revolution badly situated, and many were demoted or "retired" (Manion 1992). A moratorium was called on "class struggle," and policies designed to equalize class disparities fell thoroughly out of favor.

The Cultural Revolution also deprived an entire generation of young Chinese of an education. Urban youth averaged about seven years of schooling during "the ten lost years," and became proficient in none of the skills demanded by an increasingly technological urban economy (see Davis 1992b). With the reforms, these young people often found themselves in jobs for which they were not trained. The overall result is that a wide range of positions are occupied by people who have developed the fine art of improvising. As we shall see, this anti-professional spirit was to come in handy in the creation of a stock market.

The second great change was the re-emergence of the *guanxi* system, followed by the advent of market reforms. In what follows, I center on the new domains for deploying the strategies of urban living opened up by these two developments. These strategies can best be labeled techniques of conversion, centering on the ability to convert the "goods" of one system into the "goods" of another.

The first of these convertible social "goods" is *quan*, associated with the bureaucratic system. The Chinese term *quan* is translated in dictionaries as "power" or "authority." In the context we are discussing, the choice of one or the other of these translations is a very close call. "Authority" implies legitimacy. This legitimacy comes, in theory, from the position within the state bureaucracy held by the person with *quan*. However, many uses of *quan* are considered abuses in contemporary urban ideology, hence mere exercises of power. The choice of the term "authority" emphasizes the fact that the bureaucratic (tributary) social logic still rests on a legitimating "behavioral/ideational system" (Gates 1996:7): the difference between extortion by a government official and extortion by a local thug is still recognized, even if the former is often compared to the latter in popular discourse. The choice of the term "power" emphasizes the fact that the legitimacy of the bureaucratic system rests on weak ground indeed (Whyte and Parish 1984:362–363, Jankowiak 1993:60–96). Popular disgust over official morals and the state's virulent efforts to control what it defines as corruption are constant features of contemporary Chinese culture, though it should be remembered that this has been true of one thousand years of tributary state culture as well.

Perhaps the best translation – at least, the one I will adopt here – is one not included in any dictionary definition of *quan*, that of "position." If we grant the term "position" all of the cultural force which this concept implies in Chinese bureaucratic ideology, we can understand how *quan* works as a feature of criss-crossing modes of production without resolving the constitutive ambivalence of moral standing. The *quan* susceptible to conversion from one system to another is based on an external criterion, the ability, because of one's position in the bureaucratic hierarchy, to make decisions and/or obtain privileges. With the growth of market reforms, however, much of what was once available only through position is now available with mere money. Indeed, expensive consumer goods may be beyond the reach of officials on state salaries, who watch with consternation as newly wealthy entrepreneurs and black marketeers parade about in expensive suits or ride expensive motorcycles. It has thus become necessary to find ways to convert position into wealth (*qian*). This is accomplished through *guanxi* (Pieke 1996:142, Yang 1989:44–49).

Under the *guanxi* system, the privileges of position can be transformed into the privileges of wealth, and, to a certain extent, vice versa. High-, mid- and even certain low-level officials, by carefully capitalizing on the particular privileges associated with their position, may cultivate networks of connections (*guanxiwang*) with those able to procure them the signs of wealth and status. As noted above, a surprising number of jobs within the vast state tributary system lend themselves to conversions of this sort: journalists are in the "position" (*you quan*) to publish flattering stories about officials; drivers, to travel relatively freely around the city and beyond; clerks in personnel departments, to weight the file of one up-and-comer over another; hotel managers, to reserve rooms for special guests; and teachers in a good middle school, to let one child enter their class over another. When properly deployed, position thus translates into material goods or services otherwise out of reach.

The conversion of money into position is somewhat more tricky, suggesting that the interlocking system of conversions remains weighted in favor of the bureaucratic hierarchy. As contrasted with the heyday of Republican government in Shanghai, those who make their wealth at low-status illegal activities – such as black-marketeering, prostitution, illegal speculation – are not coopted by the power structure for its own ends.[26] These "bad elements" may become rich, may become very rich, but without the trappings of respectability they will not develop real *guanxi* relations with those in "position." There were isolated examples of individual entrepreneurs or rich stock investors who were brought into a low-level function by the municipal government in order to serve as a kind of mascot of the government's support for the reform policies, but these coopted individuals generally lost the respect of their old friends without really gaining the respect of their new official relations.

A far more complicated and interesting set of possibilities exists, however, for those on the edge of the state economy as, for example, in that vaguely legal area of economic reforms touching on the renting and contracting out of state and collective enterprises. As Pieke points out, the continued bureaucratic monopolies over certain goods and services have been put to the service of private interests largely through the system of "contracting out" (*chengbao*) (Pieke 1996:101–106). As part of industrial and managerial reforms, state-run enterprises were encouraged in the mid 1980s to contract out portions of their operations to individuals. These individuals generally promised to pay a fixed portion of their profits to the parent enterprise; the rest of their after-tax income they were free to

---

[26] The most notorious case is, of course, Du Yuesheng and the Green Gang's long-term *guanxi* relationship with Chiang Kai-shek. In my view, this particular pattern of social symbiosis is not about to repeat itself in Shanghai. Southern China and Hong Kong may be another story (see Hertz 1996a).

dispose of as they liked. While these reforms were designed to put the state sector to more efficient use by creating incentive structures for private undertakings, they were quickly coopted by the very officials they were meant to circumvent. Unwilling to see profits being made in which they did not participate, these officials quickly established *guanxi* relationships with their contractual partner, in which the official in charge of the parent enterprise facilitated business for the contracting party in return for an additional cut of the profits. The easiest way to do this was through the practice of *guandao*. *Guandao*, literally "official speculation,"[27] is the practice whereby officials use their position to buy products at state-subsidized prices which they then sell at market prices. As these price differences have remained significant in many sectors, this is one of the greatest sources of wealth for officials and for the entrepreneurs whom they hire to work for them.[28] More importantly, for those outside the bureaucratic system, this is a way of converting wealth into the privileges of position.

The mobilization of *guanxi* relationships to procure wealth or position brings into play the third "good" of urban social life, face. Face is a most delicate commodity, which demands of its seekers strict adherence to certain formalities. That one has become wealthy through the strategic use of one's position does not in and of itself give face; indeed if one allows one's behavior to have the look of crude corruption, one loses rather than gains face. By contrast, to gain access to the privileges of position through strategic deployment of one's wealth gives face in virtually all circumstances – except, interestingly, in a certain version of stock market discourse. Face is guaranteed by the breadth and depth of one's social network, not by the profitability of any particular *guanxi* relation. Face demands adherence to the rhetoric of personal loyalty and commitment, to displays of generosity and largesse, and to the ability to make oneself useful as well as to use others.

Gaining and maintaining position, money and face in urban China is a tightrope walk which few can perform well, if at all. A state-sector factory worker on a production line with no education or family ties and no particular talent to trade on is excluded from much of this activity. The kind of face which he or she may accumulate is principally the internalized moral face or *lian* which comes with upright behavior and cooperative, harmonious relations with one's friends and relations. However, I did have

---

[27] See Pieke 1996:150, n.36 for a thorough discussion of the etymology of this word.
[28] *Guandao* takes many forms, as indeed it must in order to escape constant bureaucratic efforts to suppress it. The practice of contracting out is merely one of its most easily described manifestations. For further discussion, see Rocca (1992).

the mixed privilege of knowing one expert tightrope-walker during my fieldwork.[29] A description of his activities in Shanghai during my fieldwork may help to illustrate the polyvalent possibilities of urban living in China.

The social origins of my acquaintance are mysterious. It seems that his family suffered during the Cultural Revolution and that he was raised by an aunt. When I met him, he was working as a journalist with a large state-run newspaper. Through the careful use of flattering articles, he had befriended a number of high-level municipal officials and industry managers. On the side, my friend dealt in the black market in postage stamps.[30] By cultivating connections in the postal administration, he had been able to make a small bundle from this speculative market. He had also made money on the stock market through active use of his journalistic connections. Putting these resources together, my friend had rented a facility and opened a club for a select group of officials and managers.[31] There he organized cultural activities such as lecture series and, more importantly, provided an "exclusive" setting in which he and club members could make still further connections.

All of these activities were couched in a rhetoric of mutual assistance and friendship. "I've just invited a few friends to dinner to thank them for supporting me," he would say, encouraging me to come along. On the numerous occasions when I did so, these "few friends" turned out to be Shanghai's top industry managers and municipal officials. I should add that I myself never succeeded in establishing the slightest "connection" with any of these officials, who well knew that they had everything to lose and nothing to gain from a US graduate student in anthropology. My friend, on the other hand, would dash about madly making sure that each of these big-wigs felt sufficiently important and flattered, and that each was seated next to someone who could be of service to him. The payoff for all this effort tended to be enormous: tens of thousands of *yuan* to support a new and improved project to launch my friend in business; a letter from the Vice-minister of Shanghai requesting that such-and-such a consulate grant him a visa to go abroad, and so on. My friend had success-

---

[29] My acquaintance was something of a pathological liar who had befriended me with specific ends in mind. His wife was studying abroad and he had learned that she was having an affair there. I deduced from the fact that he kept parading me about at the high-level banquets he was incessantly organizing that he aimed to avenge himself on his wife and gain back a little face by pretending I was his girlfriend.

[30] The speculative market in stamps, which provided many investors for the new stock market, will be discussed in chapter 5.

[31] The notion of "selective" clubs, restaurants and vacation sites, a tacit fact of political life under Mao, has been rehabilitated with "market" reforms.

fully deployed all three of the assets of urban life: authority, money and face.[32]

For all Shanghai residents, not only advancement within the urban status hierarchy but even the simple pursuit of one's livelihood with no further ambitions was based on the ability to navigate smoothly between the four social logics – bureaucratic, revolutionary, *guanxi*-based and market-based – which I have described here. For those with little to trade on, these back-and-forths were circumscribed; for those with many resources and talents, they were endless. Many Shanghainese I interviewed talked explicitly in terms of the notion of "conversion" (*ba quan huancheng qian*) and the need for social lability (*linghuoxing*). However, they viewed the notions of conversion and lability as an accurate description of an aberrant social structure. The general sense that order and virtue had become confused in contemporary urban society was summarized in a popular jingle: "One must walk the black road and the white road simultaneously" (*heidao, baidao, tongshi zou*). Whether this generalized moral condemnation of contemporary urban social dynamics represents a threat to China's future stability, or whether it is merely a cynical adaptation to a stable reality, is a question I do not attempt to answer here.[33]

In the market (*gushi shang*)

The stock market is one avenue for advancement among many now available to urban residents. What were its particularities? Who were the people likely to venture down this path? And, how did it fit within the quadruple logic of urban social dynamics described above?

The first people to consider are all those who had not invested, for despite the fever infecting the city, they represented the vast majority. Clearly, some of these were people who lacked the money, connections or confidence necessary to "take the plunge." However, many people with at

---

[32] An interesting incident occurred just as I was leaving the field, indeed at the airport where my friend insisted on accompanying me as is the polite Chinese custom. He confessed that he had gotten as high as he could get in Shanghai, and that he had relations with just about everybody he needed to make a brilliant career in the municipality. However, he said, he had decided to go back to school and earn a graduate degree, as if he wished to make the next step to Beijing, he would have to have educational credentials. Whether this is a story about the new professionalism in reform China or about the unbridled ambitions of my acquaintance, I am not sure.

[33] China specialists are often lured into predictions of the kind I try to resist, and this for two reasons. First, the frequently dramatic tones in which urban Chinese talk about the fate of their country lends itself to imitation. Second, in the Manichaean struggle between Free Market Democracy and Communism, clear storylines are desired. In the process, both foreign and Chinese observers forget that the relation between "the will of the People" and the stability or longevity of a social system is a vastly complicated affair.

least some of these resources at their disposal chose nonetheless not to invest, and for reasons which were telling. Some Shanghainese, both investors and mere observers, were highly skeptical of what they considered to be a new government gadget: in their view the stock market was the latest trick the Communist Party had thought up to make money out of ordinary people (*laobaixing*). Others insisted that its main function was that of showpiece for Western investors. Furthermore, some "intellectuals"[34] found playing the stock market a frivolous and/or immoral way of using one's money. Finally, many simply did not have the time or energy necessary to stand in line and fight the crowds.

For those who did choose to buy shares, the most obvious prerequisite was money. Surprisingly, perhaps, this was also the most easily satisfied. China has one of the world's highest individual savings rates (World Bank 1988:12–33), and it was estimated in the spring of 1992 that Shanghai citizens possessed thirty-seven billion *yuan* in untapped savings (*SHZQ* 1992a). One source of money available for investment was savings from state salaries. Here, Chinese displayed their incredible talent for economizing, for while state salaries are not high, many families still managed to put away some portion of this salary every month for future use.

A second important source of money came from overseas. A significant proportion of the Shanghai population had relatives living in Taiwan, Hong Kong, or North America, and many of these people sent regular sums to their relatives in Shanghai. Investment capital also came from relatives, mainly children, who had recently gone abroad to work. From Shanghai, most of these people went to Japan, but I knew people with sons or daughters in Australia, Singapore, Africa, Vietnam, and the United States. These children were expected either to send regular remittances to their parents in Shanghai, or to bring back a considerable sum upon their return. Thus, kinship obligations played the same role in the stock market that they have been found to play in all aspects of petty capitalist activity in reform China (see e.g. Bruun 1993, Whyte 1993). However, the money earned by children was not always pooled for family use. Children, particularly sons, frequently considered the money they made abroad their own, and used it for investments as they saw fit. This was the case with a number of my stock investor acquaintances.

Money sent or earned by relatives abroad was money earned outside the complicated urban social dynamics described above (although the connections necessary to arrange for one's child to go abroad were not). By far

---

[34] An "intellectual" is formally defined in Chinese discourse as anyone with any tertiary education.

the greater proportion of investment capital, however, came from some combination of individual enterprise, "business" conducted through connections, part-time work on the side, black marketeering, and previous investments. This was the area where actual wealth was most difficult to track, for it quickly lost any direct connection both with official salary and with class/status. It is also what allowed for the remarkable diversity in status background among the investors I met during my fieldwork.

Armed with capital and the decision to "take the plunge," the question remained how best to negotiate one's entry into the market. The simplest formula involved investing through the work unit. As outlined in chapter 2, some state workers had been urged or forced to buy "irregular" "enterprise internal shares" during the early stages of share-holding reforms. These shares were not listed on the official exchange, and hence could not be sold, but they did entitle their owners to regular dividends, and to the right to call themselves "stock people" (*gumin*). However, the number of "irregular" shares was by all accounts small in Shanghai.

A second form of share-ownership also directed by the work unit was far more common. This involved what were called "collective legal person shares" (*jiti farengu*). Work units collected funds from their employees which they used to purchase "legal person shares" on the primary market in the work unit's name; these shares were then held in trust for employees. Because legal person shares could not be sold by individuals on the Exchange (and could only be sold with difficulty and in blocks by institutions with access to specialized over-the-counter trading networks) these shares, like employee internal shares, allowed investors merely to participate passively in dividends which the work unit collected and distributed in proportion to their initial investment. (Investors could also entertain the hope that as stock market policy "loosened" [*fang song*], they might be able one day to sell their shares individually on the Exchange.) The extent of this practice was difficult to measure, as it resided in that gray zone of institutional activities in China which are neither clearly legal nor clearly illegal, but in my own contacts with a variety of work units in Shanghai, I encountered a number of "stock people" of this sort.

These collective legal person shares represent a pure example of the state tributary logic at work: work units used their position in the state bureaucracy to purchase shares at what amounted to subsidized prices[35] as a way of giving their employees access to a market from which they were

---

[35] See discussion of share-price determination on the primary market, chapter 2, pp. 50–53 above.

otherwise excluded. The work unit itself did not generally benefit financially from these transactions. Rather, the assumption guiding its decision to invest in legal person shares was classically tributary: helping scarce goods flow down to its employees helped loyalty flow up to their superiors.

The vast majority of Shanghai "stock people," however, entered the market under a different distributional logic, that governing the state-run lottery system which allocated "individual shares" on the primary market. The social logic behind the state-run lottery for shares in Shanghai might be labeled "random egalitarianism." In organizing the share-purchase application lotteries, Shanghai officials were responding to what they perceived as the single most important criterion for the orderly implementation of share-holding experiments: the necessity to prevent access to shares from being entirely governed by the system of *guanxi*. Should "the People" perceive that the stock market was a game in which they were being left out, "disorder" (*luan*) would surely ensue.[36] Compared with this threat of social unrest, the fact that the share-purchase lottery system failed to produce the benefits of a veritable "market mechanism" – that is, failed to provide the avenues for consumer choice which are the minimal prerequisite for allocative efficiency – was for municipal authorities a fact of little importance.

Thus, *guanxi* logic indirectly determined possibilities for access to shares in Shanghai. It also structured it directly. As everybody knew, work unit officials used their position within the state bureaucracy for personal gain; this was "official speculation" (*guandao*) in a form adapted to the stock market. Shares purchased in the name of an enterprise but actually owned by individual leaders were referred to by a special term: "social legal person shares" (*shehui farengu*), colloquially called "leader" or "head" shares (*lingdaogu* or *toutougu*). These shares were purchased on the primary market by high cadres, frequently with enterprise money, and then, through the proper connections, leaked onto the secondary market as "individual shares," allowing these officials to reimburse the work unit and pocket the difference. This practice was strictly illegal but generally thought to be quite common, as the confusion surrounding the nature of "legal person shares" made it difficult to prosecute offending cadres. Moreover, sources were unanimous that those in positions of sufficient power were able to guarantee that some portion of shares in newly issued companies be set aside for them personally without maneuvering through their enterprises.

---

[36] This official fear was well founded, as the share-purchase application riots in Shenzhen in August 1992 attest (see p. 180 below).

The logic of *guanxi* was also crucially important in the secondary market. Many of my investor friends, particularly the wealthier ones, told me that it would be sheer folly to buy stock without adequate connections. These connections were mainly necessary for gathering adequate and accurate information about internal government regulations and policy shifts. They were also helpful for speeding the processing of trade orders, for gaining access to particular stocks in times of high demand, and, if one had kept one's job in the state sector, for facilitating one's long and repeated absences from one's post. All of these forms of *guanxi* as they operated in the stock market will be discussed in more detail in chapters 5 and 6 below.

It remains the case, however, that the overwhelming majority of investors in 1992 entered the market by winning the right to buy shares on the primary market through the lottery, and this in response to an egalitarian imperative which picked up the threads of the radical egalitarian policies already described above. Egalitarianism was mandated from above, but in response to pressures, imagined and real, from below. At the popular level, egalitarian discourse was directed against the perception of power discrepancies structuring the relations between "the State" and its officials on the one hand, and "the People" on the other. Only secondarily did differences in wealth and power among "the People" come under attack. It should come as no surprise by now that this egalitarian logic mirrored the class structure of urban China under the tributary state/petty capitalist dialectic. The multiple and shifting hierarchies of status and wealth amongst "the People" paled in comparison with the great binary divide separating "the People" from "the State."

The egalitarian interpretation of the stock market was central to the events which moved the market during the year of my fieldwork. The stock market, it was argued by both "large" and "small" investors, was one of the few, perhaps the only, truly egalitarian forums for making money in Shanghai society. Buying primary issues was open to all and buying on the secondary market as well, even if big investors received slightly better treatment. Equally important was the fact that skillful predicting and "manipulating" (*caozuo*) of one's investments did not depend merely on connections but also on knowledge of how the market worked, and this knowledge was available to anyone willing to make the effort to gain it. Not surprisingly, perhaps, this line was generally expounded by that generation of investors, now in their forties, who had grown up in the bubbling, sometimes boiling, egalitarian atmosphere of the Cultural

Revolution. My most interesting friends and acquaintances were all from this generation. For them, more than for those in their twenties who had lived most of their adult life under the reforms, the stock market was something which needed explaining, both in ideological and in historical terms. Its implications for Party power, national development and socialism were frequent topics of discussion. The stock market was much more than a way to make a fast buck. Playing the stock market meant participating in a historical moment, a moment which one friend called a "second Cultural Revolution."

Why was the stock market revolutionary in the eyes of these investors? What were the forces at work behind this "social movement"? To answer these questions we must dive headlong into the dramatic and dramatized world of Shanghai "stock people" (*gumin*).

PART II

"Out of a population of a billion,
Nine hundred million are business people.
Together they will counter
The Party Central Committee."
(aphorism in circulation in urban China, c. 1988)

共同对付党中央
十亿人民九亿商

5

The big players (*dahu*)

In 1992, when Shanghainese investors, regulators and the press discussed the market, when they attempted to figure out the reasons for its ups and downs, when they tried to make sense of the kinds of people playing it, they did so in terms of three large categories of actor: "big players," "scattered players" and "the State." In this and the following chapters, we analyze these imagined collective actors, asking what is particular about each in relation to the market. We begin where the Shanghainese begin, with the most novel of the three.

The *dahu*: larger than life
Over the past few years, Shanghai society has been disrupted and enlivened by the advent of a new phenomenon: the *dahu*. A *dahu* – translated in the Western press as "big player" – is a category of person, a social stereotype, an ideal type. Much like the US "Yuppie" of the 1980s, the *dahu* has come into being to give expression to the discomfort surrounding the dramatic new possibilities for making money in contemporary Shanghai.

Like the Yuppie, the *dahu* is an ambivalent character, both despised and admired. However, while few young urban professionals in America today voluntarily describe themselves as Yuppies, many Shanghainese strive to accede to the status of a *dahu*. But, what is the status of a *dahu*? At its origins, this term designates a "rich or influential family."[1] Today, *dahu* is,

---

[1] The word "*dahu*" poses problems of translation. The literal meaning of "*hu*" is door, more precisely, the tall wooden doors which marked the entrance to houses (of the not-too-poor) in traditional China. By extension, *hu* came to mean the family behind the door, a *dahu* being a large (*da*), rich or influential family, and a *xiaohu* being a small (*xiao*) or poor family or one lacking in social connections. In contemporary imagery, however, *hu* has lost its relation with the family. English-language Chinese and foreign newspapers are thus not wrong in translating *hu* as "player." However, "player" – which conjures up images of the

first and foremost, a person (ideally a man; I return to this in a moment) with a lot of money. However, as we have seen, the relation between wealth and influence or "position" is complex and occasionally contradictory. *Dahu* today are clearly rich, but it is unclear what kind of influence they wield. Furthermore, given the history of Communist economic policy, *dahu* money has almost certainly been earned in the last few years. Much of the ambivalence surrounding the figure of the *dahu* stems from the fact that the cultural schemes for categorizing these people are in rapid flux, if not total disarray, in contemporary urban China. The over-nightness of *dahu* wealth is clearly one of its most disturbing and intriguing aspects; this phenomenon is best explored through the related term, "*baofahu*."

A *baofahu* is explicitly a person who has suddenly become very rich or important, an "upstart," in the words of the Commercial Press' *Chinese–English Dictionary*. Morphologically, it is made up of the verb "break out" or "burst forth" and the same suffix "*hu*" found in *dahu*, meaning "a person who..."; it could thus be translated as a "burster." Semantically, however, the term is ambiguous, for it is unclear who is doing the bursting forth – the *hu* himself or something around him (his business, the stock market, etc.). Furthermore, *baofa* has a homophone in *baofa*, "to explode," adding to the violence of its imagery. Unlike *dahu*, *baofahu* is a term with no positive connotations. It is loaded with moral opprobrium (few people would describe themselves as *baofahu*) and connotes violence. The sudden "bursting" of the *baofahu* suggests an ugly lack of control (over oneself, one's surroundings). The connotations of *dahu* are more ambivalent and complex.

To qualify as a *dahu*, one must be wealthy – with one telling exception: people who became rich playing the stock market and then lost all of their money in the great slump of the second half of 1992 (and this was no small number) did not lose their status as *dahu*. This is our first indication that the notion of the *dahu*, while emerging in the context of an broadened range of opportunities and choices under economic reforms, is not reducible to an economic category; qualification as a *dahu* is based not on wealth *per se* but rather on a complex of socio-cultural traits associated with certain kinds of wealth. Furthermore, not everyone who is wealthy is a *dahu*. As noted in chapter 4, wealth has many origins in contemporary

lone black-jacker tempting his luck – gives us only half the picture, for the connotations of *hu* still hint at a group of backers behind the individual operating as their "front." *Dahu* and *xiaohu* are entwined within webs of connections, large and powerful for the former, small and weak for the latter. For this reason, I would be tempted to translate "*dahu*" and "*xiaohu*" as "big front" and "little front" were it not so awkward.

Shanghai. Some families are currently wealthy because property which they owned before the Cultural Revolution has been returned to them; others are wealthy because they have even wealthier relatives overseas who have sent them regular remittances. None of these wealthy families properly qualify as *dahu*, although they may produce *dahu*. Still other families may have become rich by profiting from their position in the Party/state bureaucracy. These families are not only not *dahu*, they cannot even produce them, for the sons and daughters of Party/state officials are reserved a special term, *gaoganzidi* (literally, "the sons of high cadres"), with its own set of ambivalent connotations linked to the system of *guanxi* economics discussed in chapter 4.

As opposed to these families, a *dahu* in contemporary urban imagery is a single individual. Indeed, in his manifestation as an ideal type, the *dahu*, like the cowboy, has no family. The *dahu* gains prestige by earning his money without support from the two basic institutions of Chinese society: the state and the family. Thus, quite apart from the practical difficulty of becoming rich working at a job in the state sector, one cannot become a *dahu* at such a job because one would lack the proper independence. Likewise, a high-level cadre who becomes rich through influence peddling does not fit the image of the *dahu*, nor would he want to; he is a man of the system, and his power and prestige come from working within, not outside, state structures. By a similar logic, one cannot become a *dahu* through family wealth held jointly: for two brothers both to qualify as *dahu*, each must demonstrate his own economic prowess independent of the other. This was the case of two of my acquaintances on the stock market who made all of their trading decisions separately and scoffed at me when I asked whether they ever pooled their money.

Further, to fit the stereotype of the *dahu*, it is not sufficient that one become rich on one's own. Two of my closest acquaintances, private entrepreneurs who were investing a portion of their savings in the stock market, had enough money at their disposal to be qualified as *dahu*. However, beyond the fact that one of them had received regular remittances from his father who lived in Canada and the other had received the help of her whole family in her business operations, my friends would not be described as *dahu* (or would be described so only jokingly) because they did not act like *dahu*. More precisely, though they were relatively independent in their sources of income, they were constrained in the ways in which they spent this money, as their spending behavior was heavily weighed towards fulfilling family obligations. One was "investing" in a couple of years in Japan for his son, with the clear idea that the family would be able to recoup this investment in the future.[2] The other had inter-mingled the family's money with no efforts made to track individual own-ership over each member's contribution; rather major spending decisions passed through the father, and his wife and children were given sizable allowances for personal use.

We find here an answer to the question left open above as to why women do not fit the image of the *dahu*. As a general rule, women are thought to subordinate their needs to those of their families; in particular, this means that women are held to spend the money they earn on food, household items, and gifts for their children, rather than on themselves or their pro-jects. As is so often the case, this stereotype, which is thought to follow and explain social practice, actually precedes and dictates it. For, despite the commonly held belief that women control the purse-strings in Shanghai families,[3] in most of these families it was expected that the woman spend her salary on the household, while the man could hold onto at least a portion of his earnings for personal use. Thus while a fair number of women may be economically independent when it comes to income, they rarely display the freedom from social constraint in their consumer behav-ior necessary to qualify them as a *dahu*. A woman – and they do exist – who became rich independently, went out to restaurants, and bought herself expensive consumer goods was considered a perfectly adequate *dahu*, though she might not be considered a very good woman.

One important consequence follows from the fact that the *dahu*, as an ideal type, works outside organized institutional channels, and this was the lingering atmosphere of illegality surrounding his wealth. The common perception was that *dahu* earned their money on the various black markets which have sprung up throughout China, primarily since the economic

---

[2] At the time of my fieldwork, many Shanghainese sent their children to Japan to work for short periods of time (one to five years). A sizable network of Chinese and Japanese middlepeople exists to help Chinese find Japanese families willing to sponsor their stays. Typically, the Chinese side pays the middleperson who, after taking his or her cut, trans-fers the greater portion of this money to the Japanese side who would then help the Chinese in applying for a visa. I was told that during the 1980s it was easy and cheap for Chinese to live and work in Japan, but by 1992 this procedure had become quite expensive, and Shanghainese families had to spend as much as 50,000 *yuan* to arrange a stay of one year.

[3] During interviews with Shanghainese and non-Shanghainese alike, my interlocutors almost invariably expressed the belief that Shanghai women are "fierce" (*lihai*) and Shanghai men henpecked, frequently with the comment that becoming aware of this state of affairs was crucial to any real understanding of the city. As it was not my impression that Shanghainese women were particularly "fierce" nor their husbands particularly sub-missive, I suspect that this perception of disorder in Shanghainese sex roles had other sources, specifically, a deflected national uneasiness about Shanghai's unabashed moder-nity and cosmopolitanism.

reforms. These markets ranged from illegal trade in foreign exchange, to ticket scalping, to postage stamp speculation, to the gray market sale of goods (rice, oil, etc.) which were distributed until the late 1980s under a rationing system. As we shall see, by 1992 these generalized perceptions were only half accurate, motivated as much by symbolic structures surrounding wealth and power as by social reality. The fact remains, however, that before large-scale urban reforms in the mid 1980s, illegal activity was the only way of earning money in the cities outside a state or collective sector job.

As urban policy changes began to take on an appearance of stability in the late 1980s, the possibilities for becoming a *dahu* expanded to reach categories of people in the state sector and at its margins, and many of these have proved profitable. While these businesses are legal, and often actively encouraged by local government, they too have been haunted by an aura of immorality, as many students of China's blossoming entrepreneurial sector have remarked (Bruun 1993, Gold 1991). The numerous small stores lining Shanghai's streets, which function for the Western tourist as cheery indications of the hardworking entrepreneurial Chinese spirit, are greeted with very mixed feelings by local residents. A common stereotype was that individual entrepreneurs were people who had spent time in prison and hence could not find jobs in the state sector. Consequently, the sellers of jeans and T-shirts, even restaurant owners and hairdressers were frequently viewed with a mistrust which more than five years of experience has done little to diminish, for, as one businessman put it: "all business is cheating; if you don't cheat, how are you going to make any money?"

If the essence of the *dahu* as an ideal type seems to revolve around a certain freedom from constraint and an ability to control one's destiny outside institutional channels, the ambivalent stereotyping surrounding this character reflects the mixture of fear and excitement which this freedom calls forth. *Dahu* symbolically disrupt the social landscape; in Maussian terms, they respect the obligation neither to receive nor to give. Furthermore, an element of sexual license is frequently associated with the image of the *dahu*.[4] However, it must be emphasized that the immorality dogging the *dahu* image has its foundations in the particular relationship which *dahu* entertain with money, and not in some general hedonism. The

---

[4] And not just with the image. On my first visit to a group of *dahu* regulars at a stock brokerage, I was greeted with the following patter from a young man whom others were quick to qualify as a "hooligan": "Are you married? Doesn't matter. There's always divorce. Don't marry him [pointing to an acquaintance], he's old, he's no good any more (*ta buxing*). But me, I'm young/small (*xiao*) but I'm not bad (*wo hai keyi*)."

best illustration of this is to be found in the numerous and often very rich prostitutes working the international hotel circuit in Shanghai. These women fit only uncomfortably within the category of *dahu*, for while their earning and spending behavior match the image developed thus far, the fact of sexual impropriety (particularly, I suspect, its perceived passivity) runs counter to the proper entrepreneurial spirit, even in the revised moral world of the *dahu*.[5]

If *dahu* have an obligation, it is to earn and to spend their money actively and freely, that is, without regard to the dense network of relations which characterizes economic and social exchange in Shanghai generally. *Dahu* "freedom" is manifest in their identifying markers: motorcycles, which allow for a great degree of geographic mobility; portable phones and beepers, which allow one to contact people without visiting them – the next most efficient method given the relative scarcity of non-portable public or private phones; even gold, which, besides being a clear-cut display of wealth, is popular in China because it allows for a relative freedom from the pressures of inflation. Likewise, morning *dim sum* with a beautiful young woman (another stereotypical *dahu* act) is not only a display of sexual license and prestige but also an expression of freedom from the social constraints usually present at expensive meals: in contrast to the self-interested wining and dining which accompanies the *guanxi* system, and which might be conceptualized as "investing" in social rela-tions,[6] a love-bird breakfast represents an act of pure "consumption," for the woman is not presumed to be of any "use" to the *dahu* in future social relations.[7] And, it now becomes clearer why losing all one's money on the stock market does not diminish one's status as a *dahu*: quite the contrary, it may be the ultimate expression of *dahu* freedom that he may squander his money in this way.

I have been discussing the general stereotype of the *dahu*. It is important to note, however, that the stock market provides a particularly pure example of the context in which *dahu* can flourish, and the image of the *dahu* sits close by the image of the stock market in the popular imagina-tion. A couple of my acquaintances even insisted that the term *dahu* was reintroduced into the post-Mao lexicon through the stock market, where it

---

[5] Of course, a clear-cut sexual double standard is in operation here as well. Male *dahu* may take sexual license where female *dahu* cannot.

[6] I have heard the term "investment in feelings" (*ganqing touzi*) used in the related context of employers taking their employees out to dinner.

[7] Women *dahu* are subjected to a double standard in the area of consumer behavior as well. A woman would not be expected to ask a handsome man out on a date of this sort, nor would she pay for such a meal, no matter how much richer she might be than he.

was heard in late 1991, and spread from there to other areas of activity. Indeed, it is possible that this term re-entered popular vocabulary when state-run brokerages opened *dahu shi* ("big player rooms," commonly translated by Chinese brokerages themselves as "VIP rooms"), suggesting the degree to which actors within the tributary apparatus master and manipulate the counter-hegemonics of *dahu* imagery.

Whatever the precise linguistic history of this term may be, stock market *dahu* (*gupiao dahu*) clearly represent an important manifestation of the cluster of symbols we have found associated with *dahu* in general. Investing in the stock market is frequently referred to, as in English, by the verb "play," in contrast with "work":[8] one "plays" with stocks (*wan gupiao*) (or with women or cats). In Shanghai, the notion of play has particular resonance, for it accords with the commonly evoked image of pre-Revolutionary Shanghai as "an adventurer's playground" (*maoxianjia de leyuan*), and with the term used to refer to the famous gangleader/businessmen of the time, Du Yuesheng, Huang Jinrong and Zhang Xiaolin, who are called, in Shanghainese dialect, the "three play people" (*sege buh'xiangning*). The link between "play" and Shanghai is further intensified by the fact that Shanghainese dialect has a special word for "play" (*buh'xiang*) which, unlike most words in Shanghainese, has no Mandarin equivalent and hence cannot be written without ideographic improvisation.[9] The notion of play, of course, fits well with the image of the *dahu* as frivolous and generally subversive.

More importantly, however, earning one's living on the stock market is one of the "career tracks" now open in contemporary urban China which requires the least possible institutional involvement. True, a stock market is an institution run by the state. But to play it, one needn't be hired; the stock market is in no way a work unit. Nor need one go through the nerve-wracking, time-consuming and expensive procedures necessary to obtain licenses for opening a private business. One needn't cultivate one's official connections, which inevitably means treating well placed individuals to cigarettes, expensive dinners, even video cassette players. Indeed, for the moment, one need not even pay taxes on one's earnings. All one needs to become rich, in the words of one friend, is "a small bag for a pencil and notebook ... and a brain."

---

[8] This parallel between Chinese and English metaphors further justifies translating "*dahu*" by the somewhat vulgar "big player."

[9] In my experience, *buh'xiang* is one of the first words Shanghainese teach non-Shanghainese speakers interested in learning their dialect.

Dahu live in concert

I have been examining the ways in which the *dahu*, and particularly stock market *dahu*, are conceptualized as a cultural category by society at large. We turn now to the social reality of big players on the stock market. The principal locus for stock market *dahu*, and the place where I collected most of my field data on the subject, are the "VIP Rooms" (in Chinese, "big player rooms" [*dahu shi*]) established by stock broking companies throughout the city in 1991. For a monthly fee (which varied with the market from between 200 and 800 *renminbi* in 1992), investors with a minimum amount of money placed in accounts at that brokerage (this amount also varied with the market, from 200,000 to 1,000,000 *renminbi*) were issued a card which gave them access to special rooms in which they could watch market movements on computer terminals directly linked with the Exchange, and place their buy and sell orders directly with brokers assigned to the room. By way of contrast, small investors had to stand in crowded lobbies straining to read prices off a single, distant computer screen or electronic board; they also had to wait hours, sometimes days, to place their orders, and these were often not processed for some time, at least not before all *dahu* orders were processed.

The VIP room was a social place, in which *dahu* could meet every day and in which friendships were made and opinions formed. In the VIP room in which I spent most of my time, the atmosphere was particularly relaxed (some of my Shanghainese friends said "low class"): there were generally a number of card games (with bets) going on at tables around the room, people reading newspapers, napping, eating sunflower seeds, and, of course, drinking tea and smoking. However, not everyone wished to be associated with these activities, and there were a fair number of people who spent the entire day watching the computer screens, exchanging words with only a select number of friends.

For the first part of my stay, I attempted to maintain a cordial distance from everyone so as not to be perceived as anyone's special confidant. While I was able to interact with a broad spectrum of people, I was frequently being warned by various *dahu* not to spend too much time with one person or another as they were untrustworthy in some way, or too uneducated to be speaking with a Ph.D. candidate. Furthermore, many of the more than one hundred investors in the VIP room never exchanged more than formal greetings with me in the five months I was there. Some *dahu* did not talk to me through lack of interest; others because they feared possible complications from talking with a foreigner which would stem from what I published or said, or simply from the fact of being seen with me. Over time, I became more interested in a core of somewhat uneducated, free-spoken men who fit the *dahu* image better than others. I believe the insights this favoritism allowed me to gain were well worth the risk I took that I would alienate other members of the room.

It should be stressed at the outset that the actual people sitting around these VIP rooms did not in their majority resemble the stereotyped image of *dahu* discussed above. This stereotype creates the impression that the market is overrun by *parvenu* toughs. In fact, nothing like a single subculture characterized stock market *dahu*, although, as we shall see below, they were unified by a straightforward desire to make money, by common understandings of how the market worked and by a small number of shared investment strategies. In the VIP room I frequented, the oldest in Shanghai by most accounts, there was a great diversity of background, educational level, age and attitude. To understand this variety of backgrounds, I conducted an entirely voluntary questionnaire survey, with a return rate of approximately 50 percent. If we combine the results of my informal survey with estimates by a particularly well-informed *dahu* who served as a key informant (he himself was interested in the question of sociological background), we obtain the following picture.

In terms of education, we estimated that about one-sixth of the people in the room had higher than high school education; another sixth had less than five years of schooling (this category included a spectrum of individuals: two older women whose children had sent them money from abroad and a younger peasant from a rich family in a neighboring province who had been entrusted family money, etc.). The rest fell somewhere in between. Virtually everyone between the ages of thirty and forty-five had had their schooling disrupted in some way by Mao's anti-educational policies during the Cultural Revolution. In terms of age, over half of the total investors were in this last age group, between thirty and forty-five years of age; of the remaining half, 50 percent were below thirty and the other 50 percent above forty-five. Approximately 10 percent of *dahu* were women.

The most difficult category to trace is occupation. As discussed, in contemporary urban China, the category a person volunteers as his or her "job" tells one little about how this person actually spends his or her time. Most of the people in the *dahu* room were there throughout the Exchange's operating hours, from 8:30 to 11:30 and 1:30 to 4:00 Monday through Friday. However, we estimated that at least half of these investors had maintained formal ties with a state-run work unit, from which they had been granted one of a number of possible "leaves" (see Davis 1992a). The nature of their previous or current work at this work unit varied considerably: about one-sixth of the *dahu* in the room I frequented were currently or had been employed as professionals of one sort or another, corresponding to the sixth with some form of higher education (I knew of one doctor, a number of engineers, and a factory manager); the rest of those who still had a work unit might be workers, clerks, salespeople, even researchers at the Shanghai Academy of Social Sciences, who had managed, through connections with doctors or functionaries in their units, to obtain paid or unpaid leaves of absence.

This leaves another half of our *dahu* with no formal links to a state or collective work unit. Some of these people had officially quit work at their assigned job for one reason or another. A small but culturally significant group of investors were people who had quit their state job to go abroad (usually to Japan) for a couple of years, saved up money and were now returning to play the market. Still others had never been assigned a state job and were "waiting for work," during which time they had generally employed themselves in various forms of business, legal and illegal (see Jefferson and Rawski 1992); still others had quit their state jobs to open their own businesses, many of which they were running simultaneously by hiring people to look after the shop while they played the market. Finally, as in the stereotype, there were those *dahu* who had lost their state jobs after being convicted of crimes or misdemeanors; these people had generally supported themselves on Shanghai's various black markets before turning to stocks.

Needless to say, with this variety in backgrounds, no single set of stereotyped behaviors characterized these investors. Many did not identify as, or did not want to be identified as, *dahu*. This was particularly true for those people who, through their degree of education, qualified as intellectuals. Investors with professional training or a college education exhibited the modesty in discussing questions of money which is considered typical, even required, of the genuine intellectual in China. Others, like the two older women mentioned above, would call themselves *dahu* only jokingly, tacitly acknowledging that they did not fit the stereotype. And among those who did (even proudly) identify as *dahu*, an effort was always made to distinguish real *dahu* from the "hooligans," thereby attempting to distance themselves from the negative imagery associated with the *dahu* stereotype while retaining its positive aspects. This move to distance themselves from the negative side of popular stereotypes was motivated by a number of factors: a sense that being a *dahu* possessed a kind of dignity which deserved respect; the desire to improve the status image of *dahu* generally; and the fear that flaunting one's wealth invited government reprisals. Many of the older *dahu* pointed out to me that they never wore expensive suits or gold because their experience with the government told them that this would be rash; the younger *dahu*, who generally displayed their wealth more freely, dismissed their older colleagues as overly "conservative."

Nor were *dahu* unified in the moral evaluation they had of the stock market and its benefits. Some viewed the stock market as a temporary step in their careers, a place to accumulate the capital necessary to start a "real," that is productive, business which they viewed as both more honorable and more secure. Others condemned the stock market (often with every intention of continuing to play it) because it represented, in their view, a kind of zero-sum game in which the dollar one earned was a dollar someone else had lost. (This closed circle of exchange was generally conceived of in terms of big players earning money off of small players, as will be discussed in detail in chapter 6). Still others defended the stock market in terms reminiscent of the official line; they reasoned that since the stock market was important to China's overall development policy, those pioneer investors who donated their capital to this cause had every reason to be remunerated. A second, more imaginative, positive vision of the market was based on the fact that, as already mentioned, most *dahu* called on virtually all of their time, skill and energy in order to "play." The considerable investment of self required to invest in the stock market was frequently emphasized when people discussed with me the ideological contradictions posed by profiting from capital in a "socialist market economy." In their arguments, this investment of time and energy disproved the Marxist notion that profiting from capital meant exploiting the labor of others. In Shanghai, I was told, one must labor to make one's capital fructify.

Each of these visions of the morality of the stock market, and the many variants on these themes which float about the city of Shanghai (see Gamble 1997), merits analysis in its own right. For our purposes here, however, I wish only to emphasize the futility of coming to a quick synopsis of the "economic culture" of this class of investors. Geertz has observed that "between those [Moroccans] in commerce and those not, there has been, and is, essentially no line save that" (Geertz 1979:141). The same could be said about Chinese investors in general, and those lucky enough to become *dahu* in particular. *Dahu* cannot be clearly distinguished from the population at large in terms of a stereotyped "capitalist" mentality, just as the non-investing public cannot be said to reject the stock market for anything resembling "Marxist" or even "traditional" reasons. If we remain at the level of "attitudes" – the statements, often self-serving, which people provide to describe their "beliefs," generally prompted by the questions of an inquisitive social scientist – we find a great variety of individual responses.[10] To unearth the cultural deep structure of *dahu* attitudes, we must begin with local categories of moral evaluation. These categories operate in the context of actual *dahu* investment practice. And for this analysis to make sense, we must first outline the technical aspects of the market as viewed from the *dahu* point of view.

The market from the *dahu* point of view

While *dahu* generally invest in a number of different stocks (and also bonds) for different periods of time and with different calculi in mind, in principle (and as we shall see, almost as a matter of principle) *dahu* investment is short-term. *Dahu* do not content themselves with a slow, steady increase in the value of their investments over years, sometimes decades, as do many investors in the West. If most *dahu* spend all of their time observing, noting and predicting price movements, it is because they hold any individual stock only briefly, and always with the aim of beating market trends. A year, even a six-month, investment is considered long-term; generally, the only reason *dahu* would leave money tied up in a particular stock for such a period of time is because it has suddenly dropped to a price below that at which they bought it, and rather than cut their losses (*gerou*, literally "cut flesh"), they have decided to remain "caught" (*taozhu*, as in a lasso or noose) – but then this is no longer investing. Average "investment" times run from two days to two weeks, and it is not at all unusual for a *dahu* to buy stock in the morning which he sells during the afternoon of the same day. The commonly employed term for this speculative activity, in the stock market and out, is *chao*.

Chao literally means "to stir-fry," the characteristic cooking technique in Chinese cuisine. It is used in the stock market – but also in the stamp, real estate, antique, goldfish, foreign currency and other markets – to refer to buying and selling within a very short time period, profit being earned through price differentials (*chajia*), rather than "real" increase in value. My

---

[10] One of the surprises of my fieldwork was a dinner with some "Western" stock-brokers working in Hong Kong, during which they roundly condemned the moral and economic barrenness of financial markets: one (an Australian man) wanted to move into direct investment in production, calling the market "fluff"; another (a Malay-Chinese woman educated in England) launched into a full-scale critique of capitalism, based on the fact that women did 70% of the world's labor and owned 1% of the world's total wealth. Naively, I had expected of the Western financial world the same uniformity of attitude which others expect to find in China.

informants always appeared mildly amused by the term, suggesting that its culinary connotations remain close to the surface. When explaining the analogy, informants highlighted rapidity, that is, the fact that the contents of the wok are transformed from raw into cooked food in a very short time. At a second level, the reference to food highlights the fact that one earns one's living (and hence one's eating) through this activity: someone who "stir-fries" stock for a living eats as a result of what he does. Finally, stir-frying involves a quick flip given to the contents of the wok; this flip has its analogy in the somersault (*gentou*) which stocks make when they double in price, and, paradigmatically, it is this quick somersault, as opposed to the steady climb of long-term investments, on which the *dahu* nourishes himself.

The apparent simplicity of this imagery masks a complicated practice. It is all very well to follow the proverbial stock market advice "buy low and sell high"; the trick, of course, is knowing when a given stock is "low" and when it will become "high." *Dahu*, like all investors large and small, look to a variety of indicators in predicting market movements (to be discussed in greater detail in chapter 6). But beyond the passive relation to the market which prediction involves, *dahu* often work together to force the market to move in one direction or another by buying to raise prices or selling to make them crash. In the following section, I describe these cornering and cartelizing devices, keeping in mind that levels of cooperation and independent decision-making varied continuously among *dahu*. While lending of stock and money between *dahu* was quite common, the primary mode of action among *dahu* was that of every-man-for-himself. At no time did there emerge cooperative groups to which individual *dahu* subordinated their investment decisions in any long-term way. Likewise, what I will call "active" investment strategies were always accompanied by "passive," that is predictive, investment techniques. Ideally, the two merged to the point that they were indistinguishable.

Predicting price movements involves following three indicators, the relative importance of which varied over the course of my fieldwork. The first was government policy (*zhengce*). Local government regulations concerning the stock market changed frequently, and could have significant effects on price (indeed, this was often the regulators' express intent). During the first three months of my stay, various forms of price controls (ceilings, minimum trading amounts) were in place to keep price movements within what were thought to be reasonable bounds. Different regulations were made public almost every week, and it was crucial to be among the first to know of these new policies. In late May, when price control measures were lifted, another form of government policy became important: this consisted in decisions about when new stocks were going to come on the market, and in what quantity. Those who learned of these changes late in the day found themselves behind the wave's crest, unable to buy when prices were rising, and unable to sell when prices were falling. Thus, to learn of policy changes as quickly as possible was a necessity for all investors, and much time after closing hours – during evenings and weekends, and over lunch – was spent reading and analyzing news reports, and collecting and sharing gossip about possible future policy decisions.

The second element to good market predicting was being able to read the popular mood (*renqi* or *shiqi*, literally "popular" or "market energy"). "Energy" manifests itself in sudden spurts of interest or disinterest in a given stock or in the market in general – what Western analysts would place under the label of mass psychology. Investors attempted to second-guess "market energy" in two ways: first, by circulating among various groups of investors (on the streets, at stock *salons*, etc. – these will be discussed in detail in chapter 6); second, by trying to discern buying and selling patterns from the record of market activities reported on computer screens in the VIP rooms.

The third element – and one which became increasingly important over the course of my stay – was "the relation between supply and demand" (*gongqiu guanxi*). Looking at supply and demand involved attempting to look objectively at prices, the range of stocks which were available, and the amount of liquid capital in society to determine how prices would move independently of what government regulators may have wanted or the mass of investors may have been feeling. This meant constant observation, charting and analysis of buying and selling as reported on the computer screens that played so central a role in the VIP rooms.

Two types of information were commonly displayed on these screens. The basic screen provided a list of all stocks on the market (this number mushroomed over the course of my stay, from eight to more than fifty), total trading in each stock for that trading period, and the stock's highest offer, lowest sale price and closing price for the previous day. This screen was of general aid, and it was available for reference throughout trading hours. Most stock brokerages also had analytic software at their disposal, which would chart price movements of single stocks over time, against volume, with high–low–close averagings, etc., but these programs were generally used, if at all, only after trading hours. The main center of action was around a second display. This display reported each successful transaction in the market, the time of trading, the price, and the amount. As every brokerage house in the city was assigned a number – and, more importantly, as every individual VIP room received a separate number indicating trading orders placed by brokers directly servicing that room – *dahu* could read on this display which other *dahu* were buying and selling what at any moment.

Here, then, amidst the anonymous operations of thousands of small investors, lay the possibility for individuation – and, along with it, the code of unspoken rules governing reputation. Through the numbering system, a small group of VIP rooms gained individual reputations. Over the ten months of my stay in Shanghai, the number of VIP rooms mushroomed, from about twenty in early February to almost 100 in December, and of course not every VIP room could sustain an identity. There were, however, a select few that managed – among which two of the rooms I spent time in, and another one that I received reports on through one of its *dahu*. And, within these VIP rooms, while people would not generally be known by name, certain key personalities would gain city-wide reputations.

Reputation (*mingqi*) on the market worked as follows: *dahu* tracking trades on the computer screens would notice a particularly "beautiful" (*piaoliang*) maneuver. The *dahu*'s relation to "*piaoliang*" is much like the logician's relation to parsimony. A move is "beautiful" when it brings in the maximum of money with the minimum of effort. A maximum of money is calculated along entirely neo-classical lines, in terms of marginal efficiency and opportunity costs. It is not a lot of money, but rather the best possible return on one's investment at any given moment.[11] Money not earning money is money losing money. In its extreme form, a beautiful maneuver predicts the market so closely that it appears to make the market do its bidding, as illustrated by an anecdote I was told by a *dahu* acquaintance who modestly qualified himself as one of the three best on the market. While my acquaintance came from a rich family, for a complex of reasons he had very little money at his disposal when he decided to "set out to sea" and play the market. As a result, he worked first as an agent for a "very rich man" who needed an assistant.

He came to the brokerage and asked if there were any capable people below (*xiamian you shemma ren*), so they came and found me. At the time, I didn't feel like accepting his offer because the three people who had worked for him before had all gone broke. Then, he asked me out to dinner to talk things over and start establishing a basis for a friendship (*jianli ganqing jichu*) because he didn't trust me

---

[11] This neo-classical perspective on efficiency is striking only because it is in stark contrast to the way in which companies are ranked in the state sector, the emphasis there being on size.

and I didn't trust him. Then, he set up a test for me. We were sitting in the main lobby, not in the VIP room, smoking cigarettes, and I was looking at the screen, and I was pretty sure that when Shenhua's turnover for the day reached 20,000, the price would jump. I smoked my cigarette and looked at the screen, and when I saw that Shenhua had reached 18,000 I turned to him and said, "Do you have any cash on you, because if you do, go buy 140,000 *yuan* worth of Shenhua." "Why 140,000 *yuan*?" he asked, and I said, "If you trust me, then buy." I lit another cigarette. Before I had finished smoking it, the price of Shenhua doubled.

Reputation is of central importance to virtually everyone who identifies as a *dahu* (leaving to one side, then, those people "sitting" in VIP rooms who, while rich, do not consider themselves and are not considered "real" *dahu*). Reputation is a tricky commodity, for one of its components is modesty. Hence, one cannot be seen to want to have a good reputation; it must be granted by others without one's striving for it. People regularly introduce each other to new friends or among groups of investors by flattering each other's reputations, acclaiming the other's skill as an investor and downplaying their own. This is a way of playing the reputation game by simultaneously displaying one's own modesty and indebting the person one is praising through one's praise.

The many facets of reputation are best explored through the commonly heard epithet of *suzhi* (literally "quality"). Individual *dahu* or whole VIP rooms are said to have or lack "quality." What is meant by this is a mixture of material and moral characteristics. As with being a *dahu*, one cannot be a *dahu* of "quality" without being wealthy in comparison with other *dahu*. However, this is not because money in and of itself conveys "quality" (to the contrary) but rather because if one has the other qualities which make up "quality," money cannot help but follow. These other qualities cluster along two seemingly opposite poles. On the one hand, "quality" involves intelligence, even wiliness, or at least better than average skill at out-smarting others and, ultimately, the market. On the other, it involves honesty and integrity, particularly in one's public predictions about what the market will do. Somewhere in between come virtues such as "culture" (*wenhua*) (a concept which includes manners), education and some kind of "class" – although how this "class" is defined depends greatly on where in the class/status system the speaker places himself. The tension in this definition of "quality" stems from the fact that, from the *dahu* point of view, the market is organized by two kinds of competition: competition among *dahu*, and competition by *dahu* as a group (at least conceptually) against small players and the state. Furthermore, these two types of competition are in constant interaction.

Dahu relations are structured by competition, sometimes friendly, at other times outright hostile. *Dahu* earn the respect and loyalty of their colleagues by performing particularly well on the market, and to this end they regularly exchange information about how much money they have, what they have recently earned and what they are buying and selling. Of course, this practice is of a highly delicate nature, and some *dahu* never exchange personal information with others, although they will certainly be marginalized as a consequence. Openness about one's wealth is viewed as a virtue, the sign of a lack of selfishness, the assumption being that if one is openly wealthy, others are entitled to ask one for favors, favors which can easily become a financial burden. However, openness about one's wealth is also a purely self-serving act, for it is crucial to the building of reputation. Furthermore, exaggerated claims about one's wealth are viewed in a poor light, though most investors agree that they are more than common.

As reputations get built up around individual *dahu*, these people begin to accumulate a certain following (both of other *dahu* and smaller investors) who will tend to copy the investment decisions of their informal leader. Often, a critical mass of investors in a single VIP room can be seen investing together, and the reputation of the room forms around how these joint investment decisions pan out. Needless to say, a *dahu* of "quality" is never a follower and commonly a leader in these arrangements. We see, therefore, why lying about one's investment decisions becomes a critical infringement of the "quality" code. Just as one can use one's reputation and intelligence to guide lesser investors towards profitable decisions, one can also consciously deceive them in order to earn money off them, and stories of such deception make up a significant part of *dahu* gossip.

But the problem of reputation is even more complicated than this, for as groups of investors following a single leader gain in size, they gain the capacity actually to affect market movements. As word gets out that such-and-such a *dahu* has bought such-and-such a stock, others will assume that the entire VIP room will follow him, driving the price of this stock upward. Not wanting to miss out on riding the wave, these observers may well begin to buy, and in the bootstrapping fashion typical of stock markets, price actually does rise. Of course, interest in when so-and-so *dahu* or VIP room sells such-and-such stock will be just as intense, and the effects precisely reversed. Unscrupulous *dahu* can work with these forces in the opposite way: spreading the news that they are planning to sell such-and-such stock, they precipitate a selling spree; once the price has dropped as far as it can go (needless to say, a great deal of skill goes into identifying this point), they secretly buy up at lower prices, often through intermediaries so that their actions will not be observable on the computer display. To get in on this action at the proper moment is to earn a very good living; to get caught in its wake can be disastrous.

"Cornering" the market

While *dahu* come from many backgrounds and have differing views of the market, a certain form of ideal-typical *dahu* activity can be discerned, centering around a particularly "active" understanding of *chao*. For our purposes, we can translate the active form of *chao* with the English term "cornering" a market, though the connotations of these two terms are rather different. With these active "cornering" techniques, the imagery of stir-frying takes on a further degree of complexity: when *dahu* talk about a fellow *dahu* who "stir-fried the price of such-and-such share up to 200" ("*ba X gu chao dao liangbai kuai*") the imagery is of a master chef "stirring up" the public to a pitch of such excitement that they do exactly what he wants, at which point he "eats" them. "Big players eat scattered players" (*dahu chi sanhu*) is a common metaphorical observation in stock market discourse, suggesting that the contents of the wok may be not shares but other investors.

"Cornering" in China takes place in many markets: stamps, ticket scalping, real estate, goldfish, crickets, and antiques are other examples. By contrast, one cannot "corner" sweaters, bedspreads, bicycles – in fact, all those objects, whether sold by private business people or the state, for which supply is, theoretically at least, elastic. What characterizes cornerable markets is that "artificially" created demand may be whipped up to raise price. When the price is judged high enough, a sudden sell-out brings the market crashing down, and the cycle begins again. Successful cornering thus depends on gaining control over a limited market. Here, socialist planned economies have proved very helpful, as state monopolies provide fertile ground for the kind of control over supply which makes for profitable manipulation. And, of course, scarcity of economic opportunities creates the conditions for an excited and manipulatable public.[12]

The cleanest example of this interaction between *dahu* cornering, state monopolies and the public can be found in the speculative market for stamps. Since about 1986, a market of stamp speculators has arisen in urban China with links to similar markets in the Chinese diaspora:

---

[12] I believe a more complicated semantic code underlies the distinction between cornerable and non-cornerable commodities, but I have not been able to figure it out. What is clear is that "natural" scarcity is not enough, as "cornering" frequently involves manufacturing the conditions of scarcity.

Taiwan, Singapore, Malaysia, etc. Stamp prices rise and fall, with cities specializing in a given stamp: Shanghai in the "little panda," Beijing in the "peony," etc. According to one well-placed acquaintance, the market in stamps is controlled by four large stamp cartels located in Beijing, Chengdu, Shanghai and Guangzhou, each of which controls a certain territory. More to the point, each of these cartels controls – that is, buys off – those post office officials in their areas responsible for the release and distribution of stamps. In this way, cartels maintain complete control over the supply of stamps onto the market.[13]

Practically speaking, stamp cartels make their money in the following manner. Setting up shop in a hotel near the main stamp trading centers, cartel leaders send their employees into the market to begin buying up a certain stamp. Let us say that they have in their possession 10,000 sheets of this stamp which they purchased at a face value (plus the costs of kickbacks) of 20 *yuan* a sheet.[14] Buyers on the market soon perceive that there is a run on this stamp, and want to get in on the action. Slowly, the cartel releases its supply of this stamp by sending its agents to sell some portion (let us say half) of this supply, bidding the price higher and higher. When it is estimated to have reached its upper limit (let us say 40 *yuan* a sheet), it then floods the market with its remaining 5,000 sheets, gradually bringing the price back down to 20 *yuan*/sheet. Those who have purchased at higher than 20 *yuan* will now be in a hurry to sell, accepting even 25 *yuan* as higher than the market norm. The cartel agents proceed to buy back their 5,000 sheets at 25 *yuan*. The cartel has made 25,000 *yuan* in a couple of days and still has its initial investment for use in creating future bubbles.

Of course, in the stock market, cornering can never have the purity of form which we find in the stamp market. *Dahu* cannot control the source of stocks in the same way they can control the postmaster of the regional post office. If they want a position of market dominance in a given stock (*konggu quan*, literally "the power to control a stock"), they must, with few exceptions, purchase this stock on the market like everyone else. Barring the use of *guanxi* by officials in very high places, it is impossible to buy large quantities of stock at "face value" directly from the issuer.

---

[13] There is every reason to believe that this account is somewhat exaggerated. As the world observed with OPEC, cartels are difficult to maintain over long periods of time. Hence, it is unlikely that four cartels with clearly defined territories could completely dominate the stamp market in the way described to me by my acquaintance. This in no way undermines the point I am trying to make, which is that markets are conceived and practiced in terms of control over supply.

[14] In the speculative market, the smallest unit one can purchase is a sheet (*ban*), and traders usually deal in tens or hundreds of these sheets.

Furthermore, stocks are never issued from one source, but rather from a number of brokers throughout the city. Thus, one cannot buy up the majority of shares on the market in one move. However, on the other side of the coin, stock markets also provide richer terrain for the spreading of rumors and mass manipulation, as stocks, unlike stamps, have "real" value, that is, they are related to the productive economy, and through the judicious spreading of rumors these relations can and are used to fuel price movements. It is difficult to measure how much cornering actually goes on among *dahu* and even more difficult to know how much of this cornering actually works. However, it is safe to say that cornering – that is, gaining control over the market in a given stock – represents the ideal form of *dahu* participation in the market.

It might be objected that this "investment technique" is by no means unique to Shanghai. During the financial boom of the 1980s, many investment houses in the United States became very rich by inventing new financial instruments (junk bonds, mortgage bonds, etc.) the market for which they then cornered, at least for the time it took competitors to figure out how to enter. The acute journalistic portrayal of a New York brokerage in *Liar's Poker* (M. Lewis 1989) describes the ways in which brokers sold mortgage bonds back and forth to each other, forcing prices to rise. The logic of *chao* appears to have universal appeal. But, at least two factors distinguish the Shanghai *chao* from the New York corner. First is the fact that New York financiers manage – overall – to maintain their image of openness, honesty and integrity despite the activities of *dahu* such as can be found in *Liar's Poker*. In China, popular faith in financial magnates does not extend this far. Thus, "cornering" in China and in the West differ in intensity because the discourses and institutions surrounding them differ – and this brings us to our second point. In China, the presumption up until very recently was that all markets are and should be controlled. If the state is not controlling them, then someone else is. Innumerable articles in stock magazines and newspapers were devoted to analyzing just this question: who (big players, dispersed players or state) is controlling market movements? In actual practice, the state often wittingly or unwittingly maintains the conditions which allow the "corner" to continue, by restricting competition in various ways. Thus, beyond the "natural" tendency to cartelize, found in both East and West, institutional and cultural structures determine the significance of this behavior for society as a whole.

We see now why virtually all of my *dahu* informants told me, generally during our very first interviews, that one could not study economics in China without studying politics. Money is made not through appealing to the public with the quality of one's goods but through "market power," a term which in China sheds its "natural" economic connotations. Money is earned by manipulating supply and demand, when possible by building on the distributional monopolies of the state tributary bureaucracy. If *dahu* play as powerful a role as they do in the social imaginary, this is because their ideal-typical activity acts as a counter-hegemonic mirror of state control over the economy.

Dahu as a collectivity

If it is clear that *dahu* can be treated as a collectivity, it is much less clear in what, precisely, their collective nature lies. Blinded by the glitter of new *dahu* wealth, some observers have succumbed to the temptation to treat *dahu* as the new Chinese bourgeoisie. If this chapter demonstrates anything, it is that this interpretation of the *dahu* phenomenon is mistaken. *Dahu* demonstrate none of the rationalizing, ascetic relation to productive investment that, in Weberian terms, characterizes the capitalist spirit in general and the bourgeois/capitalist classes in particular. Furthermore, in the terms of the Marxist analysis of class, *dahu* are most emphatically not in a particular relation to the "means of production." They make no attempt to use their capital to gain control over corporate decision-making, nor would such an attempt be permitted under the current state of "corporate democracy" regulations. Rather, ideal-typically they view their portfolios purely as vehicles for speculation, in which single shares are, of necessity, held but temporarily in order to facilitate effective "cornering."

Even in its broadest sense – that which associates the "bourgeoisie" or "capitalist classes" with a certain level of education, breeding, high culture, tastes, professional activities and, most generally, "life style" – the notion of "class" is inappropriate. If we start from the social stereotype described at the beginning of this chapter, then *dahu* as a "class" appear to lack all of those attributes that make up the Western bourgeoisie: they lack education, culture and taste, they operate on the fringes of the legal economy, and they squander their ill-gotten wealth in ostentatious acts of libidinous and/or vaguely subversive consumption. Leaving behind this social stereotype and turning to the actual people crowding the VIP rooms I frequented, the notion of "the bourgeoisie" becomes equally inapposite to describe a group of investors who hail, as we have seen, from a variety of educational, cultural and professional backgrounds, and demonstrate a variety of cultural/moral interpretations of what the stock market is and why they play it.

Indeed, a "class" analysis of *dahu* leads us to the conclusion that "big players" are in precisely the same relation to the means of production as "small" or "scattered players." They are simply luckier, more risk prone or slightly more knowledgeable about the workings of the market.[15] This is why the *dahu* phenomenon has met with such a powerfully ambivalent reaction on the part of "ordinary people" (*laobaixing*), in Shanghai and elsewhere in urban China. The mixture of admiration and resentment which the stereotype of the *dahu* inspires stems from the fact that, in the urban economy in general but in the stock market in particular, nothing but luck distinguishes the wealthy from the poor. *Dahu* wealth is both admired and despised because it should be within reach of all and yet, in the zero-sum game which is the stock market, it is not.

Following Gates' (1996) analysis, investors, "big" and "scattered," are, first and foremost, more or less fortunate members of the "commoner" class functioning within the state tributary mode of production. Their implications within the petty capitalist mode of production – and the various secondary class distinctions to which this economy gives rise – are not what divide them into two categories. Rather, *dahu* are a category because of the particular (largely imaginary) relation to the market that they enact. Big players are imagined as manipulating the market, while small players are imagined as being manipulated by it. Here, we must modify somewhat the image of *dahu* with which this chapter began. I stated that to qualify as a *dahu* one must operate independently of the dual structures of family and state which define China's economy. We can see now with more precision that *dahu* reverse the power relations within these structures; they operate not outside of them but from a position of dominance within them. In the case of the state, the more important of the two poles ideologically, the ideal-typical *dahu* leads the life of a powerful parasite, coopting state tributary structures without succumbing to the state tributary logic of loyalty and obedience. In the process, the *dahu* shows the tributary system up for what, in contemporary Chinese counter-hegemonics, it is: a closed circuit of production and exchange that manipulates the "commoner" class in order to satisfy the prestige demands of an extractive, parasitical "official" class.

This explains another paradox of Shanghai stock market discourse, the

---

[15] An intermediary category of "mid-sized players" (*zhonghu*) came into usage in about June 1992. The coining of this term reflects the fact that "big" and "small" did not cover the size of the investments of everybody in the market. During the time of my fieldwork, *zhonghu* did not have a clear-cut social profile or cultural significance. According to Gamble (1997:190–191), this category has taken on an importance of its own since then.

fact that, from the *dahu* point of view, it is "the State" and not the "scattered players" that are the adversary. True, money earned through successful "cornering" is conceived of as coming from the pockets of the less fortunate "dispersed" or "small players"; "small players" are the sheep which are herded into the corral for slaughter. However, this is viewed as a necessary evil, and because the dice are loaded in the *dahu*'s favor little honor accrues from "winning" against the small player. By the same logic, "winning" against the stronger party, in this case the state, is unambivalently good. In the next two chapters, we consider what this morality tale looks like from the point of view of the other two collective players on the market.

6

The dispersed players (*sanhu*)

The opposite of a big player is a "small player" (*xiaohu*) or, in the more commonly employed phrase, a "dispersed player" (*sanhu*). The category of *sanhu* includes all those investors, the overwhelming majority, who do not own shares in quantities sufficient to qualify as *dahu*, and thus cuts across the entire spectrum of class/status distinctions within urban Chinese society. As opposed to *dahu*, *sanhu* are not represented by a social stereotype; indeed, the notion of *sanhu* is not really applicable outside the stock market (and perhaps a few other speculative markets such as the postage stamp market discussed in chapter 5). However, *sanhu* are to the stock market what "the People," "the public," "the masses" or even "the market" are to other spheres of urban Chinese life. By examining *sanhu* we are thus indirectly examining the structure and dynamics of these larger, more historically charged categories of Shanghai social history.

The "*san*" in *sanhu* literally means loose, scattered, random or unorganized. The word features in a famous and troubling aphorism in which Sun Yat-sen described "the Chinese people" as "a sheet of loose sand" ("*yi pian san sha*"). It is worth lingering for a moment over this appellation, for it suggests that a "small" investor is not merely small; he or she lacks coherence, togetherness, a group. If the *dahu* is stereotypically a lone hero/anti-hero – the cowboy of the Shanghai stock market – the *sanhu* is a crowd *manqué*.

Compensating for this lack of togetherness is the primary activity of the "dispersed player." Few investors in this category operate in a context which one could call individual. Rather, these dispersed individuals draw upon all of the forms of networking, group formation and collusive action which urban Chinese have developed over centuries to glean reliable information from a tight-lipped and deceptive state. During the Maoist period, particularly during the "ten years of chaos" as the Cultural Revolution is commonly called, urban livelihood crucially depended on using these institutions of Chinese "civil society" to follow the twists and turns of official policy, both political – during the many and often mysterious shifts in political "winds" – and economic – when access to goods and services could turn on the size and position of one's information network.[1] These "revolutionary" forms of social organization transferred smoothly to the area of stock market practice, where accurate and rapid access to information is the *sine qua non* of competent investing.

In this chapter, I analyze these popular group formations, their unofficial character and counter-hegemonic potential. In the first five sections, I describe the different types of group and network on which *sanhu* depend for their market information, putting special emphasis on the rules of sociality which governed these groups. In the last two sections I, like the Shanghainese, take *sanhu* as a collectivity, examining the particular methods they adopt for playing the market, and their mass effect on this market. In so doing, I try to tease out of these groups and associations the social organizational logics (principally tributary and petty capitalist, but also "revolutionary") that govern them, on the Shanghai stock market and beyond.

If information-gathering is the primary purpose of the various social clusters and clubs I will be examining here, then the general connotations of the Chinese terms for "information" merit a brief detour. Perhaps the most neutral word for information is *xinxi*, used in the compound "information science" (*xinxixue*). Investors will sometimes use this word to denote what it is they collect in order to make investment decisions. *Xinxi* certainly includes information read in the newspaper (also called "news" [*xinwen*]) and may also designate information gathered by word of mouth. However, the colloquial word for information is *xiaoxi*, which refers principally to information gathered by word of mouth and not to "official" information. The term *xiaoxi* shares a character with the word *xiaofei*, meaning "to consume." *Xiao* alone means to disappear, to eliminate or to pass time is a leisurely way. For our purposes, it is important to note that both information gathering and consumerism – two socio-economic practices which have become indispensable under conditions of state-led economic reforms – connote a kind of dissipation, a concern with

---

[1] For a fine discussion of the circulation of and access to information before the reforms, see Whyte and Parish 1984:290–295, 300.

unproductive "society" events at the expense of more productive endeavors. Thus, a tacit face-off between state "policy" and popular "strategy" lies bubbling beneath the surface of the very petty-capitalist reforms on which the tributary system depends for survival and self-renewal.

In 1992, all investors, large and dispersed, could avail themselves of what we in the West would consider normal sources of information on the stock market. Indeed, an avalanche of information crashed down around them. The single most important of these sources, for all Shanghai investors, was the official *Shanghai Securities Weekly* (*Shanghai Zhengquan*) published by the Shanghai Securities Exchange.[2] This weekly newspaper contained tables of high, low and closing prices for all stocks and bonds on the market, published explanations and editorials about new regulatory policy, was the official locus for announcements of new share and bond offerings, and ran "society" pieces in which the "psychology" (*xinli*) of "stock people" (*gumin*) was discussed and analyzed.

Beyond this specialized paper, Shanghai's principal newspapers (the *Liberation Daily* [*Jiefang Ribao*], the *Wen Hui Bao*, and the *New People's Evening News* [*Xinmin Wanbao*]) carried frequent if irregular reports of closing prices, as did the local radio and television stations. Furthermore, a number of specialized journals and newsletters were widely available and read: the *CVIC Market Watch Weekly* (*Yizhou Touzi*) published by China Venturetech Investment Corporation (Zhongguo Xin Jishu Chuangye Touzi Gongsi) in Shanghai, and the *Securities Market Weekly* (*Zhengquan Shichang Zhoukan*), published by the Stock Exchange Executive Council (Zhongguo Zhengquan Shichang Yanjiu Sheji Zhongxin) in Beijing, were the two with the widest circulation. New books, ranging from sophisticated discussions of Western techniques of market analysis to cartoons depicting the dos and don'ts of smart investing, flooded the bookstores.[3] The Shanghai Municipal Library registered 200 new titles having to do with the securities market in 1992.

The information gleaned from these various sources was necessary, but it was hardly sufficient in the eyes of the Shanghai investing public. It was on the basis of this "news" (*xinxi*) that the real activity of informing oneself began. For it was generally believed that official information,

---

[2] At the time of my arrival, this paper had a circulation of approximately 20,000. In December 1992, its circulation had reached 200,000. In celebration of the second anniversary of the Exchange, the newspaper changed its name to *Shanghai Securities News* and its frequency increased to two editions per week. This was increased again to three times weekly in April 1993, and the paper became a daily on October 1, 1993.

[3] The *Far Eastern Economic Review* reported that Beijing's Xinhua bookstore's best-selling title in 1991 was *Stock and Bond Trading Common Sense* (*FEER* 1991d).

unsupplemented by unofficial verification and interpretation, was not only insufficient but potentially misleading. Equally dangerous, however, were rumor (*yaoyan*) and gossip (*xiaodao xiaoxi*), to be distinguished from *xiaoxi*. Neither rumor nor gossip could be counted on as "information" (*xinxi*). The great difficulty, of course, came in trying to distinguish the former from the latter. For this, more *xiaoxi* was needed in an endless pursuit of reliability. To this end were formed the groups of various sizes, memberships and functions to be examined below. Five principal types of group should be distinguished.

Crowd clusters

The tight circles of people talking about the stock market which gathered night and day in front of the major stock brokerages throughout the year of my fieldwork in Shanghai were one of the most remarkable aspects of "stock fever," and were frequently commented on by Shanghai residents themselves. Inspired by Elias Canetti, I have labeled them "crowd clusters."[4]

The first thing to note about these public manifestations of interest is that, despite the curiosity they provoked on the part of the Shanghai citizenry, gatherings of this type were less new to the Shanghainese than the other, more private groupings to be discussed below. Circles of people gather on Chinese streets frequently: to observe an accident or an argument, to follow a game of cards or chess being played on the sidewalk, or, in the good old days, to stare at a foreign guest. *Sanhu* crowd clusters shared some qualities with these other moments of encircling, but took a more elaborate form. My focus here is not so much on the externally "feverish" appearance of these groupings, but on their internal dynamics. These circles were governed by very particular rules of conduct, rules which were in most ways diametrically opposed to the rules governing the other groupings created in the stock market's wake.

Sanhu crowd clusters were open to anyone, without introduction. They were formed by groups of people, between five and fifty in number, who gathered in front of most brokerage houses in the city throughout the day.

---

[4] Canetti uses the term "crowd crystals" to designate the core of hierarchically ordered devotees who form the nucleus for the creation of a "crowd" – a spontaneous massing of people who free themselves from their individuality (Canetti 1984[1960]:15–75). I have avoided the term "crystal" in Canetti's sense as its connotations lead us in directions we cannot yet go. Likewise, the word "circle" (*quanzi*) as its connotations in Chinese cut against the grain of the point I wish to make. *Quanzi* is frequently used to denote a closed group of like-minded people (friends, artists, politicians). By contrast, these clusters are eminently open, and presuppose no shared opinions or status.

The clusters grew in size when the Exchange closed at 3:30, thinned out at dinner time, and then thickened again at around 8:00 p.m., lasting sometimes until 2:00 or 3:00 in the morning. With crowd clusters, the ratio of ten men for one woman which I found for other groupings connected with the stock market did not apply. I estimated that at most one in twenty persons in these crowd clusters was a woman, probably because women could not legitimately pass their time hanging around on curbsides, a fact which tells us something about the gender symbolism of a certain kind of "public" in urban Chinese culture.

Crowd clusters were amoeba-like, attracting greater or lesser numbers of people depending on the charisma of the principal holders-forth, and on the random ebb and flow of passers-by. However, often a changing core of people remained in essentially one place on the street for hours, and during days of heavy activity one could find die-hard crowds at 2:00 in the morning, standing approximately where one had left them at 3:00 that afternoon. It went without saying that all discussions took place in Shanghainese. As such, crowd clusters were clearly one or two notches more "popular" than the other groupings to be discussed in this chapter. This is not to say that the people in crowd clusters could not have spoken Mandarin if they had wanted to. But several characteristic features of these gatherings – their democratic format, their performance aspects, and their "counter-cultural" tenor – mandated that discussion take place in dialect.

As Canetti has noted, the first characteristic of a crowd is that it is a place in which unknown people come into physical contact – often to a degree which would be considered prohibitively intimate for all but romantic partners – without this contact registering as unpleasant or out of place (Canetti 1984 [1960]:15–16). *Sanhu* crowd clusters were a case in point. Because attention was centered on those at the core of the cluster, the audience listening at the outer rings of the cluster pressed itself insistently but unaggressively against the bodies of those in the center. Individuals on the outside of the circle who wished to talk would either work their way slowly towards the center or begin to talk where they were, creating the core for another cluster. Sometimes these clusters existed in parallel for a while, linked by a band of peripheral listeners now dangerously near the center of the action, but generally the circle either reformed to absorb one center into another or split into two distinct crowd clusters.

The principal rule of these small groups was that no one knew anybody else, and this is the first reason why crowd clusters belong to the category of "the public." When it happened that two or more people did in fact know each other from another setting, they rarely manifested this as long as they were still within the boundaries of the group. All talking that was not going on in the center took place at a discreet distance from the crowd. I attended many of these clusters, often with a Shanghainese friend who would help me to follow the various and rapid dialects being spoken. Whenever my friend found it necessary to explain something to me, he always took me aside, turning his back to the circle to indicate separation.

The "public" nature of these clusters extended beyond their anonymity. In the crowd cluster, one of the most common courtesies of Chinese society was not observed: one smoked one's own cigarettes without offering cigarettes to anyone else. It was this anonymity that marked these circles of discussants off as a "public" and not a "group." Only in gatherings in which the element of mass participation is present – at the cinema, at sports matches – does one find Chinese smoking their own cigarettes. In virtually all other situations, one offers cigarettes to all others present as a gesture of inclusion. Strangers in a railway station waiting room will frequently offer each other cigarettes, even hurling them vast distances across the Stalinist chambers towards others waiting with them. At a restaurant, one offers one's cigarettes to each and every person at the table, and this enthusiasm sometimes spills over onto neighboring tables as well.

Sanhu crowd clusters were further characterized by a kind of mass democratic spirit. There was no *a priori* ranking of participants. Those who wished to speak were free to, the only criterion being that the speaker continue to hold the attention of his audience. Thus, in addition to providing a context in which information could be exchanged and interpretations elaborated, crowd clusters were a form of oratorical contest, in which small "big men" attempted to convince the crowd of the virtues of their predictions, gossip, and analysis. Attention was held and respect won for humor, displays of cynicism towards the government, well-documented rumoring and opinions which cut against the grain. On the other hand, many were there as moderating influences, repeating commonly held opinions about the virtues of this stock or that policy, the probability that a central government leader was currently visiting Shanghai, or that a particular VIP room was currently cornering such-and-such stock.

As a sample of the topics for discussion in a single crowd cluster, I detail here the discussions on which I eavesdropped over the course of half an hour in mid 1992: (1) discussion of fact that the government had lost control over the market; (2) observation that the government must find a way to drive up the price of shares for foreign investors (B shares) or it would lose face at home and abroad; (3) argument over how to interpret the fact that the *Shanghai Securities News* did not print anything about when new shares issues would be approved for trading on the Exchange; (4) speculation over what would happen to the market when Deng Xiaoping died; (5) discussion of the rumor that the Exchange was spreading the rumor that prices would start rising shortly; (6) complaint that the price for shares on the primary market was too high;[5] (7) discussion of the natural rule that the stock market cannot fall without rising again; (8) theoretical discussion of the fact that many factors influence stock movements, never just one. In my experience (I listened in on the discussions of a dozen such groupings), this series of topics was typical of crowd cluster discussions throughout the year of my fieldwork.

Curiously, crowd clusters were the only place in the more than three years which I have spent living in mainland China where the fact of my being foreign went unnoticed. For reasons which I do not entirely understand, I was not once asked to explain what I was doing eavesdropping on a discussion carried out in dialect in the middle of a Shanghai street at night, frequently in the rain. I can only speculate that this represented an extension of the openness and all-inclusiveness of "the public" gathered in the crowd cluster. Just as anyone was free to enter and leave the on-going discussions at whatever moment he pleased, often hopping from one circle to another to find one which suited his interests, so even a foreigner was free to listen in if she wanted.

That I should talk, however, was utterly out of the question. Here again, this situation contrasted with many others in which foreigners of all stripes find themselves when in China. The simple fact of being a foreigner at a gathering of any importance frequently means that one should say a few words. If one knows no Chinese, then one speaks in one's native tongue, and if there is no translator available, then one speaks a few words that few in the audience understand, but this in no way alters the fact that one is duty bound to speak. Here, however I was not duty bound. Furthermore, I would never have dared speak had I been asked. For what I realized with a pounding heart as I contemplated the possibility that I would be asked to give my "expert opinion" during the first evening of observation, was that great quantities of face were at stake in these performances, and that I had neither the courage nor the skill to risk mine.

Note that a particular kind of face was put at risk in these gatherings. If, as we have said, face divides into a public form of reputability (*mianzi*) and a private form of respectability (*lian*) (see Hu 1944, Jankowiak 1993:62),

---

[5] This complaint is mentioned in chapter 2, p. 53 above.

here we had public face at its most public. This was, if I may coin the term, "mass face," the face that comes from "speaking reason" (*jiangde you daoli*), from appealing to public standards of persuasiveness and meeting them. This aspect of face deserves attention because it is so easily overlooked in the general hustle and bustle of urban China.

Urban public space in China is frequently characterized as harsh, aggressive and alienating, and there is much about negotiating daily life in a Chinese city which resonates with this characterization (Chen 1995). Chen cites a Chinese short-story writer discussing the anger, boredom and anomie palpable on a Chinese public bus (Liu 1990), and one can experience gratuitous rudeness and petty aggression in any state-run department store or restaurant in the city. Shanghai streets are frequently blocked by heated and abusive arguments between strangers, sometimes degenerating into fistfights and worse. The content of these arguments is frequently summed up by exchanges of the insult: "You have a defect/you are not normal" ("*Ni you maobing*").[6]

In a fine discussion of public disputes and "civic consciousness" in Huhhot, Inner Mongolia, Jankowiak found in that city a shared public duty to resolve disputes (1993:125–164). My observations suggest that disputes in Shanghai always attracted attention, but mediators rarely stepped forward. Indeed, on three occasions I was so disturbed by the fact that no one had volunteered to mediate that I stepped into the dispute myself, much to the embarrassment of the disputants and the amusement of the bystanders. Rather, to palliate the rigors of the urban public sphere, the general thrust of urban society in Shanghai was to attempt to transform "public" groupings into "private" ones, lending them the qualities of intimacy, politeness and loyalty characteristic of the private sphere. *Sanhu* crowd clusters stand out as an exception to this rule. Unlike many anonymous urban encounters, there was no pent-up aggression apparent in the tone or content of discussions. On the other hand, lacking also were all of the ritualized formulae of politeness and flattery which accompanied more "social" groupings, as we shall see below. Disagreement and agreement were equally open, and those disagreed with did not then spend their time defending their honor, but rather moved on to another topic or another cluster.

Informal groups

Of a quite different order of sociability – perhaps even diametrically opposite – were the informal groups of dispersed players which came together

---

[6] On the question of normality in Chinese culture, see Chen (1994).

in the stock market's wake. What I am calling "informal groups" are groups of friends, all of whom know each other, who get together to discuss the stock market or invest together. These groups draw on the immensely powerful body of tradition regulating relations between friends in Chinese society.[7] Friendship is governed by an ideology of intimacy which contrasts both with the "public" gatherings discussed above and with the "social" gatherings to be discussed below; it operates in what we could call the "private" sphere, and takes many of its norms by analogy with codes of behavior regulating relations between members of the same family and husband and wife.[8]

Friendship implies duties of particular loyalty and allegiance which go beyond the formal civility which makes up the "social" norm. Friends are expected to dispense with all displays of politeness, for politeness signals distance. However, the direct and informal nature of exchange between friends is based on a very different set of premises from the negotiation of "mass face" which governed crowd clusters. In a sense, no room for face was left in the private sphere, the assumption being that everybody knew everybody else so well that nothing was left to hide behind. Thus, friends would, as statements of fact and without malice, make comments to each other which to my ears sounded openly insulting: "you're not as smart as so-and-so," "you're not very pretty," "you're too fat," "you're a fool." By the same logic, it was considered odd, even somewhat hostile, to thank a close friend, a spouse or a child for a service rendered, or to say "please" when asking for a favor. The service was demanded and accepted without any of the padding which softens the blow of these acts of aid and sub-servience in the West. In further contrast to "public" relations, friends were required to share money, time, information and opinions – indeed everything but that element which American culture places at the heart of friendship, "feelings." What we in the West identify as the "sentiments" of intimacy, are, in China, perceived in behavioral terms. Intimacy is that series of acts which are loyal and which represent the pooling of destinies.[9]

These general rules governed the exchange of information, the joint use of money and the discussion of investment strategy in informal investor

---

[7] Friendship is one of the five "basic relations" in Confucian philosophy, the only one which is egalitarian in structure.

[8] We should not think of these "spheres" as entirely distinct entities. Much of the dynamics of the "social" sphere comes about through appropriation of the rhetoric of the "private" sphere for instrumental use. The "public" and the "social" spheres are likewise constantly shading back and forth into each other, as with the stock *shalong* to be discussed below.

[9] For an excellent discussion of "the cultural construction of emotion" in Chinese peasant society see S.H. Potter (1988). Many of her observations apply equally well to the urban setting.

groups. (I note that the only groups of this sort which I witnessed were groups of men. However, I doubt this is a uniquely male form of social gathering, as groups of friends of both sexes are common among Shanghai youth.) Informal groups generally gathered over a meal in a fully private place (at somebody's house), a meal for which no one thanked the host, although many helped in the kitchen. All forms of formality were dispensed with, no one appeared obliged to pay deference to anyone else for reasons of face, and opinions were freely exchanged. A friend who was suspected of withholding information, analysis or opinions would be confronted. Furthermore, each person would feel free to tell his or her friends just how stupid he found their investment behavior and/or analyses. Generally, a hierarchy of competence was openly acknowledged within the group, in which certain individuals were recognized as better investors than others. This inequality in status was compensated by an inequality in "returns" on the gathering. Less talented investors may have had their egos bruised by these meetings, but they acknowledged the benefits of learning from their smarter peers.

By way of illustration, a discussion I participated in at a gathering of friends to which I was invited in late 1992 touched on the following subjects over the course of a three-hour (twelve-course) meal: (1) a long discussion about one member of the group who was called a "sacrificial object" (*xishengpin*) because he had just lost 20,000 *yuan* and expressions of anger over the fact that the government did not do enough "propaganda" (*xuanchuan*) on the risks of bear markets; (2) the fact that stock broking companies were illegally selling short their clients' shares and making a bundle; (3) the incompetence of city leaders administering the stock market; (4) the general corruption on the market; (5) an article in that week's *Shanghai Securities News* which misleadingly suggested that this was a good moment for long- and middle-term investing; (6) last Friday's rise, the "correctness" of which was demonstrated through "technical analysis"; (7) the poor "technical analysis" performed by the Shandong VIP room (number 111) which cost them 79,000,000 *yuan*; (8) the five stages through which a young stock market must go in order to "mature"; (9) how government "interference" (*ganyu*) was bringing the market down; (10) the grave problems of social unrest which the government would face if the Shanghai index dropped below 400; (11) the basic flaws in the stock lottery system; (12) recent gossip about a pronouncement by the Chairman of the Shanghai Securities Exchange (on this topic, the original source of the gossip was identified so that the other members of the group could judge its reliability for themselves); (13) the fact that three principal papers in Shanghai had stopped printing market news, the reason (gathered through gossip channels) being that each had been coopted by one of the big government brokerages which was using the paper for its own purposes, forcing the Municipality to intervene; (14) a recent visit to Shanghai by the Chairman of the US Securities and Exchange Commission, along with reports that the Mayor of Shanghai had asked him a question which showed that he didn't understand anything about stock markets.

Informal clubs

Slightly more formal but no more official were the numerous "clubs," "meetings" or "associations" (*julebu, hui,* or *xiehui*) which sprang up throughout the city in the wake of "stock fever." Unlike groups of friends, these clubs gathered people who would not otherwise have come together, although there were numerous relations of friendship or collegiality which linked many of the participants outside the context of the club. While "stock clubs" were new to the Shanghai scene, they were based on a model of social interaction which was hardly new in urban Chinese society. Clubs of amateur lovers of all manner of things exist throughout Shanghai and in other Chinese cities: Beijing opera clubs, bird-raising clubs, martial arts clubs, literary and artistic clubs, calligraphy clubs, etc. Like the other gatherings examined here, these clubs were governed by distinct rules of conduct.

I sat in on the meetings of two such clubs which had the following form. Between fifteen and thirty people were present, and membership was selective (by introduction through a member of the club). The clubs met in a semi-public space, one in an empty schoolroom on Saturday afternoons, the other in a tea house on Monday mornings, and this regular meeting time was set and respected. While attendance was not mandatory, a repeated absence was noticed, and the offending member would be asked whether he or she was still interested in participating. Sometimes these clubs engaged in a certain amount of paraphernalia creation: membership cards, xeroxed charts, etc., but generally they were meant to be informal discussion groups in which each member shared his or her view on recent market developments. Women were again present in the 10 percent proportions noted as a general rule.

The rules of participation in these clubs were different from those of crowd clusters. Here, many of the forms of what I am calling "the social sphere" were observed, like, for example, the mandatory flattery of older, richer or more educated members which opened each presentation. This praise could be genuine, in the case of individuals recognized as being particularly well educated or intelligent, or it could be hypocritical, in the case of individuals who were flattered simply because they thought highly of themselves. (In the terms of Jankowiak, in one case one is giving "admiration," in the other "respect" [1993:61–63]). The speaker then made self-deprecatory remarks about how he or she had not prepared anything to say, was not an expert, was new to the club, etc. As with crowd clusters, it was the practice to recognize public speaking according to standards of persuasiveness and oratorical delivery, with the occasional burst of applause for a particularly good speech. However, in this setting, food was always shared, tea was always poured for those around one before oneself, and cigarettes were distributed within a large radius before the distributor lit up himself.

A sample of the topics of discussion during one two-hour afternoon meeting which I observed in early 1992 runs as follows. I was introduced to the club as an "American expert on the stock market." Then the agenda was announced by the principal organizer as first, a general exchange of information; second, the results of participants' market research; third, the situation in Shenzhen; other topics. This agenda was promptly ignored and instead each member of the club was invited in turn to tell the others what they had bought and sold that week and why. Members also gave their opinions or asked questions as follows: (1) discussion of what had been happening recently with the shares of X company, speculation that government was taking "measures" (*shouduan*) in relation to it, further speculation that a *dahu* from Zhejiang was cornering this stock; (2) discussion of an article in the *Wen Hui Bao* on new policies concerning "state" and "legal person" shares; (3) rumors of new trading ceilings, and discussion of the reliability of the rumors; (4) news of a leak from a *dahu* about new government attitudes towards the proper prices for the market; (5) rumor that a certain *dahu* would try to corner shares in Y company; (6) discussion about the dividing line between *dahu* and *sanhu*: if one has 30,000 *yuan* is one a big or small player?

The interest of these clubs lies in the way in which they navigated between the codes of "mass face" described for crowd clusters, and the loyalty code described for informal groups. For behind the sharing of tea and cigarettes lay an underlying tension: would each individual share with the others her real opinion and full sources of information, or would she keep some portion of this precious analysis for herself? The tacit understanding when one became a member of such a club was that one was joining one's fortunes with it. While club members rarely acted in concert, members being expected to come to their own decisions about what and when to buy and sell, these individual decisions were taken on the basis of what was presumed to be a shared pool of facts. Participants' small speeches were thus littered with rhetorical gestures such as "frankly speaking" (*tanshuai de shuo*), or "to tell the truth" (*shuo shihua*). Whereas with crowd clusters, the understanding was that anyone could take from the discussion without giving back to it, in informal clubs one was held to a responsibility to give and to give honestly and fully. In other words, while the ideology of quality (*suzhi*) formulated by big players was not articulated as such,[10] a tacit adhesion to this honor code was expected.

Likewise, one was held to a responsibility to express one's disagreements with others' opinions openly. These disagreements were couched in flattering and appeasing rhetoric, suggesting that the speaker ran the risk of being disagreeable as well as disagreeing. He (and here the "he" is appropriate, as it was mainly differences of opinion among men that ruffled feathers and posed the risk of degenerating into conflict) would typically turn towards the person he disagreed with and say "I don't want you to get angry" (*ni buyao shengqi*), in what was designed to be a demonstration of fear which, because of its publicness, obliged the other to behave magnanimously in return. In these exchanges, the face stakes ran rather high, while the club as a whole tried to benefit from the maximum of frankness in the expression of competing views, without allowing personal enmities or competition to disrupt the smooth functioning of the group. Whether or not the atmosphere remained productive depended on the diplomatic skills of the club organizers.

Adult-education classes

For those not lucky enough to have a group of friends or a club to belong to, another group activity formed around the stock market were the night and weekend classes on stock market investing offered throughout the city. These classes were held in public buildings, and necessarily had a sponsor with some degree of officiality. I attended one such course organized by Industry University (Gongye Daxue) which met weekly over a period of months. Another which I attended a number of times was organized by professors at the Shanghai Academy of Social Sciences. These courses tended to be announced in the newspapers or through wall posters. Entrance fees ranged between five and fifteen *yuan* a session, and no beverages were provided.

---

[10] See chapter 5, p. 144 above.

The lecturers at these courses varied tremendously in quality and background. Some were university professors in economics or finance, eager to earn a little money to supplement their low salaries. Others were officers of companies on the market or officers in state-run brokerage houses who took these occasions to promote their own business. Finally, particularly successful *dahu* were often invited to give talks on their techniques for analyzing the market, thereby enhancing their reputation with and arousing the jealousy of other *dahu*. One investor who made it a practice to attend these courses categorized the speakers into three schools: the "market school" (*shichangpai*), the "academic school" (*xueyuanpai*), and the "company school" (*gongsipai*). While this scheme probably attributed too much coherence to the generally rambling presentations of all speakers, two examples of classes I sat in on should demonstrate the great variety in style and quality which one could encounter.

In one case, the lecturer was a senior researcher in economics. His lecture was one of a five-part series in which he was responsible for discussing the Shenzhen market. He reviewed the history of the market, touching on key policy interventions and large price movements. He outlined the structure of the Shenzhen Exchange, which is slightly different from Shanghai, and analyzed some of the major problems in the Shenzhen market. Finally, he gave his predictions about future developments.

By contrast, the following subjects made up a *dahu*'s presentation in a class I attended at Industry University: (1) the *dahu*'s belief that the tone of recent issues of *Shanghai Securities News* suggested that the government was not worried if the Exchange index fell below 400; (2) the prediction that the bear market would last six months, but would decline in small steps, not one steady fall; (3) the conclusion that short-term investing was the only possibility; (4) an anecdote about a careless neighbor who did not pay close enough attention to the market and lost his shirt; (5) the recommendation that investors prepare themselves mentally (*sixiang zhunbei*) for the possibility that they might have to skip work; (6) a prediction that the government was going to intervene continually in the market over the following few weeks as it prepared for the Fourteenth Party Congress; (7) the conclusion that this was why the newspapers were pretending that the market was looking up; (8) a statement of general applicability: if the Exchange itself suggests that it's time to buy, don't buy.

Despite the improvised nature of this second "class" I observed, taken overall adult-education classes were rather more academic in nature than the other groupings around the stock market. Basic principles of stock ownership were explained, the workings of new regulations were discussed, and techniques for analysis and "manipulation" (*caozuo*) were outlined. Not infrequently, however, specific companies were named, bits of gossip were exchanged, explanations were ventured for the market's movements, and so forth. While classes frequently began in Mandarin, responding to the notion that public education should take place in "ordinary language" (*putong hua*), half an hour into the presentation the speaker was generally speaking mostly Shanghainese without realizing it, and by the end all discussion was taking place in Shanghainese.

These courses were attended by people of principally "worker" or low-level "cadre" background, as well as by students. Many people came alone or with a friend or two, and while casual conversations were struck up, there was no presumption that interests were shared. The audience participated by asking questions, most often written on slips of paper to avoid the pressures of public speaking. These questions often pressed the speaker for more concrete predictions, even instructions on how to proceed, and were the butt of much laughter from the audience who recognized in the naivety of the question, even if it were their own, a fundamental clumsiness, a violation of the rules of a game which they were just beginning to learn.

Stock *salons* (*gupiao shalong*)

Somewhere in between informal clubs and adult-education classes was the *shalong*, a Chinese word borrowed from the French "*salon.*" *Salons* are a common feature of contemporary urban life in China. This form of gathering came into being in the mid-1980s, and was originally equivalent to the informal clubs discussed above. The first *salons* were mainly artistic and political in focus: new forms of painting, literature and film, newly translated Western theorists, and recent political events were discussed in an atmosphere of energetic openness, indeed, with the kind of energy which only exists in societies where the opportunity for open discussions cannot be taken for granted.

In Shanghai in 1992, stock *salons* (*gupiao shalong*) had taken on a distinctly commercial character. Organized by stock broking companies or semi-governmental associations,[11] *shalong* took place in tea houses or public halls throughout the city. They attracted an attendance of between 40 and 150 people, and were scheduled for a two- to three-hour period, usually in the evenings or on weekend afternoons. An admission fee of up

---

[11] Such as, for example, the Shanghai Gufenzhi Qiye (Gongsi) Xiehui (the Shanghai Joint-stock Enterprise [Company] Association) established, with government backing, by an association of professors and enterprise managers.

to 15 *yuan* was charged, and tea served. In late 1992, there were seven well-known *shalong*,[12] and new ones were constantly being formed. I got my first indication that I had finally reached a sort of proficiency in stock market discourse when, during an interview with a famous *dahu*, I listed all of these *shalong*, and received an admiring "you're one of us" response. This is an indication that *shalong* represented a kind of insider institution for "stock folk" (*gumin*).

In stock *shalong*, a variety of speakers took the floor, usually four or more in one session. Generally a guest speaker was featured – a successful *dahu*, an employee at a stock-broking office, an officer of one of the joint-stock companies on the market, or an agent responsible for processing buy and sell orders on the floor of the Exchange ("red jackets"). After the guest speaker or speakers, other organizing members of the *shalong* or invited personalities delivered further prepared speeches. The audience, made up principally of regulars, was then given the opportunity to ask questions, frequently in writing. One tea-house *shalong* which I attended featured as a typical afternoon's program a "red jacket" from one of the larger brokerages. His talk started out rather "official," but soon degenerated into the spreading of rumors about particular stocks and predictions about future policy moves by the government. Questions from the floor read as follows: (1) Can "legal persons" (*faren*) buy "individual shares" (*gerengu*)? (2) How long will the shares of Z company continue to fall? (3) What was happening with a Shenzhen company which had recently been suspended from trading on the Shenzhen Exchange? (4) What of the rumor that such-and-such company's bonds would be converted into stock? In a concluding portion of the meeting, the speaker asked the audience what their "psychological price" (*xinli jia*) for a particular share was, and what shares they thought would be hot (*redian*) in the next few weeks.

Needless to say, with 50 to 100 people in the average audience, many people in *shalong* were strangers to each other. Some people attended numerous *shalong* throughout the city, but there was a tendency against *shalong*-hopping, as one of the attractions of the *shalong* was the chance to meet and develop friendships and information sources, and this required a certain regularity of attendance. *Shalong* did not take the anonymous form of crowd clusters or evening classes. Generally everyone in the audience knew a number of others through friends. Furthermore, *shalong* were in some sense the "highest class" of stock grouping, and

---

[12] At the Workers' Club, at a restaurant in the Changning district, at the Yuanmingyuan restaurant, at the Lantian Hotel, at the Bailemen tea house, at the Peace Hotel, and at the Shipping Association offices.

attracted well-known figures on the market. A number of *dahu* had reputations large enough to be known by a good number of *sanhu*. Certain officials, professors and company managers became familiar faces as well, and there followed the building of reputation which goes with familiarity. As a general rule, a regular participant would know how to locate socially almost everyone in the room, even if he had never spoken with the majority of them.

These *shalong* were also a place where the *dahu* and *sanhu* communities could come into contact. "Friendships" would be struck between disciple *sanhu* and a master *dahu*. The implications of such friendship, of being "good with" such-and-such a *dahu* (*he ta hao*), extended beyond the fact of a friendly relation between the two individuals. The presumption was that these two individuals might begin to look out for each other's interests and to act concertedly against the interests of others, for, as we have seen, the anonymity of *sanhu* was a valuable asset to *dahu*, just as the expertise and connections of the *dahu* could come in handy for a *sanhu*. This was a "special relationship" which could and frequently did lead to cartelizing and cornering activities.

The relation between a *dahu* and his *sanhu* was hierarchical, characterized by the traditional phrase "to honor someone as a master" (*bai ta wei shi*). The *sanhu* became the *dahu*'s "helper" (*zhu shou* or *xia shou*). Helpers acted for their "boss" (*tou*) by appearing in public and taking actions which he directed, thus shielding him from public appearances. These special relations might be kept secret, so as better to protect the *dahu* from public scrutiny. Furthermore, it was also frequent for helpers to cheat on their bosses, for there was no reason an ambitious *sanhu* would choose to remain a helper for very long. This gave rise to another form of speculation among *sanhu*, for they had to be alert to the possibility that such-and-such a *sanhu* might be acting as the agent for a *dahu*, might be pretending to act as his agent in order to borrow his power, or might be acting behind the back of his boss.

The market from the *sanhu* point of view

All of the formal and informal groupings examined above concentrated their efforts on "market analysis" (*shichang fenxi*). When explaining what this analysis consisted in, investors generally contrasted the methods appropriate to Shanghai with methods used in "the West." Westerners, I was repeatedly informed, look at three elements in order to predict market movements: basic indicators on the financial health of companies (fundamental analysis or *jiben fenxi*), patterned movements in market and individual stock prices (technical analysis or *jishu fenxi*), and the political environment (political analysis or *zhengzhi fenxi*). In the West, I was further told, fundamental and technical analyses are the most important, political analysis less so. In China things are otherwise, they continued. Most important to analyzing the stock market in China is "something you don't even have in the West": "policy analysis" (*zhengce fenxi*). Political analysis, technical analysis and fundamental analysis come next, in descending order of importance.

Whether this description of the state of the art of financial analysis in the West was accurate is not important for our purposes. Rather, it indicates both the tenor of market analysis in China, and the ways in which this analysis was perceived as "particularly Chinese." Investors were unanimous in the belief that fundamental analysis meant little in the Chinese context because reliable information about companies' financial conditions was almost impossible to come by. Furthermore, with most investors operating in the purely speculative, short-term mode, even if one had access to this information, it would not help one predict short- or even medium-range prospects. All of the informal groups thus divided their time equally between "political" and "policy" analysis, information-sharing and gossip, and technical analysis.[13]

The distinction between "political analysis" and "policy analysis" requires elucidation. Political analyses consisted of those discussions – which Chinese have developed into a high art – of what direction central and municipal leaders were leaning in, as individuals and as cliques, and of the jockeying for power currently taking place among these leaders. In Beijing, where much of the population followed the political profiles of important central leaders, extreme attention was paid to hints in newspapers and photographs which shed light on power plays among these figures. In Shanghai, fewer central authorities were known by name, and minute-by-minute changes of favor were followed less attentively. Central leaders were more likely to be referred to as a group (*zhongyang lingdao*) motivated by a single decision-making center, than as competing political forces. However, leaders from Shanghai (Jiang Zemin, Zhu Rongji, Chen Yun) would be individuated, key events in the state's calendar noted (the coming of meetings of the National People's Congress, of the Communist

---

[13] A nuance is necessary for adult-education courses. The more serious speakers at these classes generally tried to convey a certain amount of expert knowledge of Western varieties, but this information was frequently dismissed as "academic" by the audience, and these discussions as well often degenerated into the sharing of gossip and personal predictions.

Party's Central Committee), and the media combed for signs of changing political winds.

In a sense, this political analysis is much like that which goes on in the West before or after major political events. Before the 1992 US elections, the general line in the securities investment community was that a Clinton victory would provoke a fall in the New York Stock Exchange, as investors were thought to be generally unfavorable to his economic leanings.[14] The Gulf War, the Mexican debt crisis, tensions in US–China relations all might have had repercussions on the New York Stock Exchange which were not directly linked to concrete effects on particular companies or industry sectors but rather to general investor "jitters." Likewise in China, changes in the Central Committee of the Communist Party are presumed to have an effect on the stock market, and one could expect investors to react in consequence. However, an important distinction should be noted at once. If the New York Stock Market reacts to Clinton's election, it is because investors, particularly large institutional investors, make judgments about the future of the American and world economy, and react in consequence. If the Shanghai stock market reacts to the Fourteenth Party Congress, it is because investors know that a change in leadership could lead to direct and immediate intervention – unmediated by law or by the presence of the "private sector" – in the workings of the market itself.

The second factor which Chinese investors look to is "policy analysis," a "Chinese characteristic." Policy analysis involves discussing and attempting to interpret the numerous small and large policy announcements aimed directly at the stock market which the Shanghai Securities Exchange, the People's Bank of China (Shanghai Branch), the Municipal Securities Commission, one vice-mayor or another, or the Central People's Bank of China promulgate with alarming frequency, as discussed in chapter 2. Again, these policy changes and the analysis they necessitate have an analogy in the moves which the US Federal Reserve takes to monitor inflation and guide investment through changes in the interbank lending interest rate and monetary supply. But again, a crucial difference exists. As discussed in chapter 2, the Chinese government did not avail itself of these indirect incentives to guide investor behavior on the stock market.[15]

---

[14] This prediction was wrong.

[15] Chinese economic reformers, particularly at the national level, are well aware that macroeconomic regulation is more effective and less destabilizing than direct intervention in the economy, and they have been working, in cooperation with the World Bank and others, to create the conditions necessary for full use of interest rate policies (see generally Xia, Lin and Grub 1992). However, at the time of my study interest rate movements had relatively little effect on the behavior of even large institutional investors, and still less on the calculations of individual investors.

Rather, it attempted to intervene directly in the movements of the stock market through the tributary state apparatus in place. This difference has implications not only for the economic behavior elicited by market participants but, more importantly perhaps, for the political tenor of the "policy analysis" it called forth. In contrast to the objective calculation of indirect consequences which a change in the US interest rates requires, what investors in China performed was not really "analysis" at all but the mere sharing of gossip in an attempt to penetrate the often obscure and sometimes deliberately secret moves taken by the various agencies responsible for the market. These gossip-sharing sessions, because they tried to shed light on what the government preferred to keep dark, were necessarily surrounded by a slightly subversive aura. It is not surprising, then, that the most successful of these new *sanhu* groups, the stock *shalong*, were formally forbidden shortly after I left Shanghai in December of 1992.

Technical analysis occupied third place in the list of topics discussed in *sanhu* gatherings. Technical analysis included a wide range of approaches, some rather intuitive, others highly sophisticated. The most basic technique was to follow the day or week's market movements closely, to know which stocks were actively traded, which rose and which fell. Most *dahu* charted these movements every day as part of their nightly homework, and a certain number of *sanhu* did as well. The truly devoted memorized the high, low and closing prices for all stocks on the market for a single day, or even a week. A fair number of *sanhu* had also read up on Western techniques for charting stock movements. High-low charts (*Hi-Lo tu*) and K-waves (*K-xian tu*) were included in some specialized magazines on stock investing. Other theories which were mentioned to me included average fluctuations charts, Elliot waves, and the CANSLIM theory. The CANSLIM theory, for example, was actually not a theory at all but a mnemonic device for remembering a series of fundamental and technical factors one must examine for each stock: "C" = current quarterly earnings per share; "A" = annual percentage increase; "N" = new products, new management, new stock highs; "S" = shares of common stock outstanding; "L" = leader or laggard; "I" = institutional sponsorship; "M" = market direction. Most people who read up on these techniques were perfectly aware that they could not be applied to the Shanghai market directly, and sometimes could not be applied at all. Nevertheless, many were fascinated by these simulacra of Western expertise.

Fundamental analysis, when it was brought up, generally took two forms. On the one hand, invited speakers at adult-education classes or *shalong* might promote the shares of a particular stock on the market by discussing its excellent financial health and the prospects for its industry sectors. These speakers were generally officers of the very company under discussion, or outside "experts" with connections to this company. *Dahu* and *sanhu* analysis of fundamentals, on the other hand, generally focused on the company's short-range development plans, and on its links with the municipal bureaucratic system. Dividend announcements and stock splitting also formed part of the information exchanged under the rubric of fundamental analysis.

Absent from this list are analytic techniques considered non-rational, in China as in the West. In none of the formal or informal gatherings which I witnessed did investors make reference to throws of the *bagua*, or readings of hands, facial features or the *Yijing* which I knew, from individual interviews, were competing analytic techniques for at least some portion of the investing public. Unfortunately, I cannot estimate what portion of this public made use of these forms of esoteric knowledge. Techniques of this sort were intensely personal, and were not the subject of much open discussion. Of the dozen investors whom I knew intimately enough to raise these issues, only one reacted with any enthusiasm.[16] As in the West,[17] some investors used what they would qualify as rational and non-rational predicting techniques simultaneously. However, unlike the techniques used by investors in the West – where prediction focuses on the market *per se* – Chinese "non-rational" investment techniques generally link market movements to patterns of individual "fate" (*mingyun*).[18] The question was not whether the market would rise at a given moment, but whether one's luck (*yunqi*) was good. Reference to personal *yunqi* also provided a way of justifying losses (more than gains) retrospectively, for it could always be that one had lost money not because one had performed the wrong forms of analysis but because one's luck was bad.

Sanhu as a collectivity

As should be clear, *sanhu* represent an even larger slice of the Shanghai population than *dahu* and are unified by fewer shared norms of behavior and belief. The forms of social organization by which *sanhu* participate in

[16] More research on the important question of the mounting interest in what the Chinese government classifies as "superstitious practices" is clearly called for. However, this is a general phenomenon in China today, and has, I believe, no unique link with the particular evolution of stock market practice and ideology which this book traces.

[17] Maturi mentions the following "irrational" investment techniques found on US markets: astrological readings, magnetic field theories, tarot cards, presidential elections (the patterning of Democratic versus Republic terms, etc.), Super Bowl results, hemlines, the Fibonacci series and sunspots (1993:179–193).

[18] See the discussion of personal fate in chapter 3 at p. 90 n. 27.

the market vary enormously, and each of these forms creates a slightly different relation to what the market is all about.

If I treat *sanhu* as a collectivity, it is only because the dominant discourse did so. *Sanhu* were routinely referred to as a sort of collective actor, most often as victim of the manipulations of the two other collective players on the marketplace, the *dahu* and the state. Furthermore, *sanhu* were distinguished by the unequal treatment which they received as a group in comparison to *dahu*.

Sanhu were not unaware of this unequal treatment. Indeed, early in my stay, a gathering of small investors had protested in front of the Municipal government, claiming the city was not doing enough to protect and promote the interests of the "common people" (*laobaixing*). Perhaps as a result of this demonstration, perhaps out of its own sense of fairness, in May 1992 the city moved to set up a trading point where *sanhu* could buy and sell without waiting in lines and without having their orders subordinated to those of *dahu*. This trading point was the "Cultural Palace" (Wenhua Guangchang), a large amphitheater which had figured prominently in Cultural Revolution mass denunciations and which was now used for various cultural activities. This enormous hangar was quickly equipped with desks and telephones for each of the city's brokerage houses. Thousands of *sanhu* could gather there without crowding; market prices were announced over the loudspeaker every fifteen minutes; lines were short; and orders were processed promptly.

It was with the creation of the Cultural Palace trading point that *sanhu* took on a genuinely collective force of their own. With thousands of individual investors spending their entire day following the market, gossiping and panic trading began to take on astounding proportions. Both the government and *dahu* tried to tap into this source of energy by spreading rumors which they believed advantageous to their particular positions. However, the Cultural Palace had a mass dynamic of its own, which set in motion the 80 percent drop which the market was to experience in the second half of 1992. To understand these dynamics, we must turn now to the third actor in this drama, the super-player (*chaoji dahu*), largest *hu* of them all – the state.

7

Guojia: The rise and fall of a super-player

The allegory of the Chinese stock market in 1992 begins and ends with "the State." In chapter 2, we examined the structural position of the state tributary system in the formation and regulation of the market for shares in Shanghai. In this chapter, we examine "the State" in action – the ways in which it used this tributary power during the speculative cycle of 1992 – and ask what this examination tells us about how "the State" conceives of itself and how it is conceived of by "the People." The best picture of the state as social actor can be given through a blow-by-blow description of the market's rises and falls over the course of 1992, a description which pays special attention to the language – both official and "counter-cultural" – in which this cycle was articulated.

As usual, a note of caution is necessary at the outset. I have translated "*guojia*" simply as "State," as is the standard practice. However, the connotations of the Chinese use of the term "*guojia*" merit a study in their own right. "*Guojia*" – literally "the national family" – has a standard translation in "country, state, nation" (The Commercial Press, *A Chinese–English Dictionary*). In the discourse surrounding the stock market, however, *guojia* refers to the Party/State and its leaders, or at least all of those leaders in Beijing or Shanghai with authority to make policy decisions. Thus, the "imagined community" of *guojia* is in no sense "the nation" – the collection of people within a given territory sharing a common culture and language – but rather the organs of government ruling this collection of people. The notion of representation inherent in the Western concept of "nation" is absent; indeed, the entire thrust of what has come so far should demonstrate that, because the dominant mode of production, ideological and socio-economic, is tributary, *guojia* is conceived of as external to, even opposed to, "the People," or as Gates calls them, "the commoners," in popular discourse and in actual practice.

An interventionist cycle

1991 had been a listless year for the Shanghai stock market. Unsure of the direction of "political winds," Shanghai regulators set tight controls on price movements[1] and approved no new shares. The shares of eight companies circulated within the limits of the possibilities set for them by these price controls, frequently among *dahu*. The *dahu*, for their part, entertained themselves by buying and selling shares amongst themselves to reach the turnover limits necessary to kick the price of shares up 1 percent a day. To this, stock market officials responded with menacing statements about the need to fight against *dahu* manipulation, issuing temporary rules forbidding rigged trades (*duibi jiaohuan*) within a single brokerage. These rules were easily circumvented, however, by simply rigging sales amongst VIP rooms in different brokerages, to which stock market officials responded with more menacing statements.

With Deng's Southern Tour and the political opportunities it created, Shanghai officials became bolder. Price movements on two shares on the market were freed on February 18, and five new shares came onto the market on March 23. As a consequence, of course, *dahu* also had more room for maneuver, and they honed their cornering and cartelizing skills, much to the consternation of officials who again issued menacing pronouncements on March 16 that all share-holders would be required to register officially with the city government before trading. (For the record, this threat was never acted upon.) The results of these three months of government regulation and popular reaction are depicted in graph 1.

The principal effect of this game of cat-and-mouse between *dahu* and state regulators was to exaggerate, both in their own minds and among the general public, the power which these *dahu* really possessed. At its most flamboyant, *dahu* discourse evoked the "good old days" of Republican Shanghai when the KMT government was forced into an unsavory cooperation with Shanghai underground gangs who represented important sources of wealth and power through their control over opium, prostitution and gambling rings. "You see," said one of my most ambitious *dahu* friends, "the State needs us more than we need it." In April of 1992, he estimated, the combined share-holdings of big players in the VIP room where he worked were greater than the share-holdings which most brokerages had at their disposal on their own accounts. "*Dahu* have the power to

---

[1] 1% movement/day on those shares which recorded a turnover for that same day of 3/1000 of total shares issued. Needless to say, under these conditions the prices of shares in most state-run companies and in companies with a very large share-base simply did not move at all.

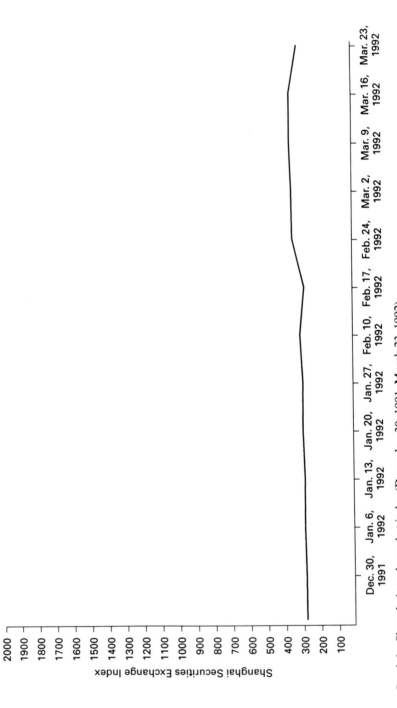

Graph 1   Shanghai stock market index (December 30, 1991–March 23, 1992)

control prices (*konggu quan*)," he boasted, adding "You talk about a 'sinister plot' (*heimu*), well this is it."

This "sinister plot", important as it was in the minds of market participants and government officials, was never to materialize. The second three months of 1992 were taken up with the progressive liberalization of price ceilings. On March 27, the price ceilings for five new shares (*xingu*) which had just come on to the market were eliminated. Then on April 13, three "old shares" (*laogu*) were allowed to fluctuate within a 5 percent rather than a 1 percent margin. This brief period in which three different regimes governed stock price movements was jokingly called "one country, three systems," parodying the slogan "one country, two systems" (*yi guo, liang zhi*), used to describe Hong Kong's July 1997 transfer to Chinese sovereignty. Then, on May 11, all shares not fluctuating freely were shifted to a 5 percent margin, and finally, on May 21, the prices of all shares on the Shanghai market were freed.

Just as officials feared, there followed an immediate and enormous jump in the Shanghai Stock Index, bringing it to its historical high-water mark of 1953. Frightened by this extreme reaction – and jealous, many said, of the new wealth it was creating – the Vice-mayor of Shanghai responsible for the stock market issued a public pronouncement on June 2, in which he intimated that *dahu* were cornering the "four little dragons" (*si xiao long*). This appellation is an ironic reference to the four Asian countries (Hong Kong, Singapore, Taiwan and South Korea) which have registered spectacular growth rates in recent times. The "four little dragons" on the Shanghai market were the four collectives first transformed into joint-stock companies. Because their share based included no state-owned shares, *dahu* could buy up controlling majorities in these companies.

As can be seen from graph 2, the reaction to this declaration was immediate: the Shanghai Stock Index dropped more than 900 points to 1,103 in three days.

This event marks what most investors consider the turning point of the 1992 market. For the next three months, share prices made a steady dive of 400 points. This decline, after months of stock market euphoria, was at first met with utter disbelief. After all, said investors only half jokingly, the "special characteristic" of stock markets in socialist countries is that one can make money and but one can never lose it. In the pained words of one investor – a sales clerk in a state-run department store without a lot of capital or savvy at her disposal – "The State called upon me to lend it money and I did. It's not going to let me lose all of that money, is it?" Even the most cynical *dahu* who at other moments readily admitted to making

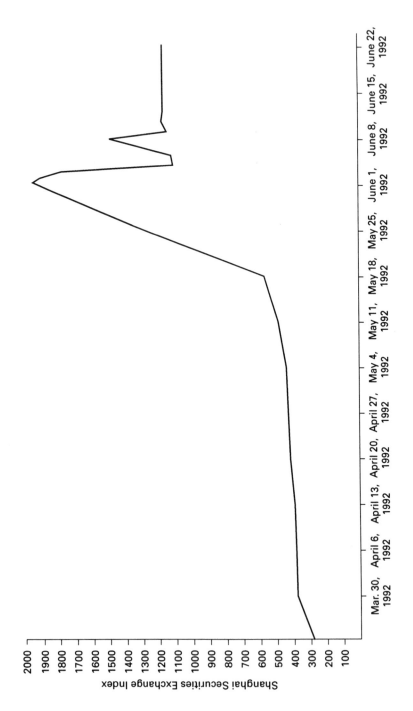

Graph 2 Shanghai stock market index (March 23, 1992–June 22, 1992)

their money out of the gullible little guy, repeatedly told me how "cruel" (*can*) it would be of the State to let these people lose what little savings they had accumulated over years of hard work.

As the market continued to decline over the course of the summer, this disbelief rapidly turned to bitterness. Whatever form government regulation of the market took – even regulations aimed at curbing market manipulation by *dahu* – was generally summed up by investors in a single word: "interference" (*ganshe*). Most investors believed that the long declining market of the second half of 1992 was largely the fault of this "interference." After all, they pointed out, China's economic indices were excellent. She was reaching record-breaking rates of economic growth; there were no objective reasons for the stock market to go down. "From that point on," said one friend, "stock people became pessimistic about the market (*gumin kanhuai le*)." The power of *dahu* to control prices on the market, to the extent that it ever existed, disappeared definitively from the scene. *Dahu* were reduced to trying to corner "old shares," those collective companies first authorized on the Exchange which possessed a very small share base compared with the new state-owned enterprises flooding the market. However, with small investor capital increasingly locked into their losing portfolios, there were no longer any *sanhu* lambs.

In fact, the primary reasons for the bear market in the summer of 1992 had more to do with the market *per se* than with government attempts to manipulate price. The shares of sixteen new companies were approved for trading on the Exchange, absorbing vast amounts of investor capital.[2] However, what is important for our purposes is the general perception – shared by government officials and investors – that political forces could determine the direction of market movements. It was this belief – which we may call a form of state fetishism – which was to be slowly and almost imperceptibly challenged as the bear market ran its course.

That stock people held the State responsible for the losses they suffered over the summer of 1992 was demonstrated by two incidents of great concern to stock market officials. The first, which took place in Shanghai on July 7, was immediately labeled the "July 7 Incident" (*qi-qi shibian*), a joking reference to the famous July 7 Incident of 1937, the opening battle of World War II in Asia. (I note this as a further illustration of the tendency within stock market discourse to assimilate, in parodic form, the market to great moments in Chinese and world history.) This event was barely

---

[2] Seven of these new shares were B shares, sold and traded only among foreigners. These shares do not affect prices on the domestic A share market, as they do not draw on the same sources of capital.

publicized but it was the object of intense gossip throughout the investing community. According to the version I heard, the head of the Industrial and Commercial Bank in Shanghai made public pronouncements about the lottery system being used to distribute shares on the primary market, suggesting that it was going to be discontinued. This lottery system formed the basis for an active black market in lottery tickets which accounted for a good portion of the wealth surrounding the stock market. Infuriated, one hundred or so of the scalpers (*huangniu*) who made lottery tickets their business surrounded the car of the bank head, and threatened his life. The official was hurriedly escorted out of town under police protection, but Shanghai leaders were, from all accounts, greatly shaken.

Not long after this event, on August 10 the Shenzhen share-subscription application riots broke out.[3] Hundreds of thousands of Shenzhen investors, angered by rumors that Shenzhen share subscription coupons were being sold to the friends and relatives of officials instead of the public, rioted for more than twenty-four hours under the eyes of foreign journalists. Rumor on the stock market had it that in the repression that followed, more than a dozen people lost their lives. In Shanghai, the most commonly heard reaction to this event was to point out that if the "apolitical" city of Shenzhen could be whipped up to such a pitch, one need only imagine what kinds of scenarios were possible for Shanghai. The central government took immediate and severe action against Shenzhen officials allegedly involved in this corruption. Needless to say, a generally cautious wind floated through Shanghai at this time. The results of overall investor pessimism, the release of large quantities of new shares, and these two anti-government incidents can be read in graph 3.

During the fourth trimester of 1992, the Shanghai stock market bottomed out and began its route to slow recovery. The events leading to this comeback were again largely linked to the dimensions of the market itself and the rhythm of policy changes associated with it. Over the course of 1992, Shanghai had authorized an increasing number of securities companies from other provinces to set up offices in Shanghai. Shanghai brokerages had also seized upon opportunities provided by the "open" climate of that year to set up branch offices in many of Shanghai's rural counties and even in large cities in other provinces. Late in the year, with share prices dropping to affordable levels and possibilities opening for investors

---

[3] This riot made front-page news in newspapers throughout the world. See *The Boston Globe* 1992, *Le Courrier* (Geneva) 1992, *Jornal do Brasil* 1992, *Le Monde* 1992, *The South China Morning Post* 1992a, 1992b, 1992c, 1992d, 1992e, 1992f, and *The Standard* (Hong Kong) 1992.

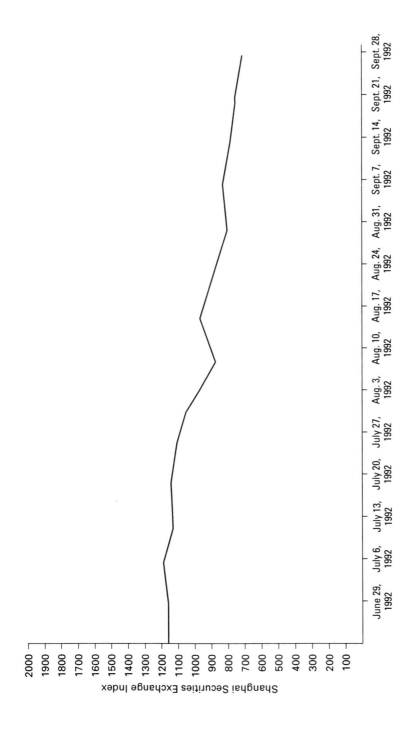

Graph 3 Shanghai stock market index (June 22, 1992–September 28, 1992)

outside the city, new capital began tentatively to enter the market, pushing prices slowly up.

However, while the principal forces behind market movements were, in this sense, purely economic, the principal event of this period was perceived in purely political terms. With the imminent opening of the Fourteenth Communist Party Congress in Beijing on October 10, rumors began to circulate that the central authorities hoped for a healthy stock market in Shanghai – more precisely, an index somewhere between 800 and 1,000 – to mark this solemn occasion. State-run brokerages were ordered to begin massive buying on their own accounts in an attempt to give the market new "breath" (*shiqi*). *Dahu* and *sanhu* positioned before their computer terminals could witness numerous examples of brokerage houses throughout the city spending millions of *yuan* on shares in their attempt to kick off a new wave of investor enthusiasm. However, paralleling and undermining this effort was the fact that eleven new shares had already been approved for trading on the Exchange, putting further downward pressure on prices. In the words of investors, it was the *sanhu* who were controlling the market now, and if the *sanhu* thought the market looked bad (*kan huai shichang*), then the market was bad.

The orchestrated attempt to put a good face on the Shanghai market for the Fourteenth Party Congress was an unmitigated failure. The Shanghai Share Index did interrupt its steady slide briefly on October 9, rising from 643 to 680, and then to 690 on Monday October 12, the next trading day, but it then promptly reversed direction again and continued to plummet until well into November. On November 17, the index bottomed out at 393, thus bringing the market back to the levels at which it had begun its spectacular trajectory in early 1992. The immediate cause for the market turn-around in November was generally identified as a massive buying spree by Caizheng Securities Company (under the central and local Ministries of Finance), but it was the slow but steady entry of new capital from outside Shanghai which brought the necessary energy to maintain the new bull market. For the next month, first organizations, then *dahu* and then finally *sanhu* began buying in again at rising prices, and the market had completed its first speculative cycle, as depicted in graph 4.

"Papa Deng came out for twenty minutes . . ."
The lesson of the Fourteenth Party Congress must have been a difficult one for the State to swallow. It is impossible to know the precise sum which the government threw away over the course of September and October in its efforts to prop up the market, but local estimates ran into the billions of

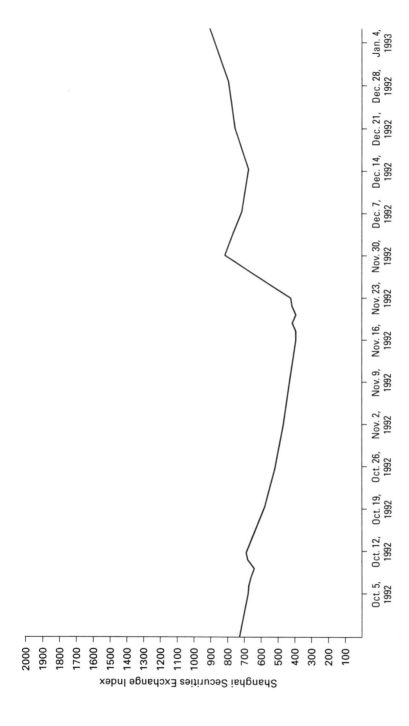

Graph 4 Shanghai stock market index (September 28, 1992–January 4, 1993)

yuan. Perhaps most disturbing of all was the terrible publicness of the entire event. Investors throughout Shanghai had watched spellbound as the government repeatedly failed to manipulate the market to suit its needs.

For Shanghai investors, particularly *dahu* who made the market their career, this was a moment of triumph. Not that they had not suffered terribly with the market collapse of the second half of the year. Many had been reduced to honorary *dahu*, their entire fortunes eaten up in the fall. But the demonstration of state weakness worked as a kind of revelation which offset much of their feelings of despondence. A sardonic comment which circulated around Shanghai at the time of the Fourteenth Party Congress did much to elucidate this new consciousness. During the Congress, the ailing Deng Xiaoping, father and symbolic anchor of the reform policies making the stock market possible, made a brief but well publicized appearance of twenty minutes among Party leaders. All over the city, one could hear investors, tickled pink by their formulation, repeating to each other: "Papa Deng came out for twenty minutes, and the stock market rose for twenty minutes" (*"Deng baba chulai le ershifenzhong, gushi zhang le ershifenzhong"*). This joke worked because it brought to the fore in parody form the previously unconscious fetishization of state power over market movements. Suddenly it was clear, in the words of one illuminated investor, that "the market has its own natural rules" (*"shichang you zishen de guilu"*), and not even Deng Xiaoping could do much about them.

This demonstration of state weakness was to have profound effects on investors and regulators alike. In a sense, it provoked a shift from an ideology of state fetishism to a kind of market fetishism, as participants realized that beyond a certain size, markets can no longer be commanded by "political" forces. Rather, the *sanhu*, left to their own devices, made their own decisions about price, and the cumulative effects of these decisions were beyond the scope of government manipulation. Furthermore, the "natural rules" governing this market were somehow egalitarian, that is, they were equally mysterious and equally regular for everyone who tried to penetrate them. The attempt to predict market movements was thus an activity in which everyone was placed on an equal footing. In the words of one triumphant *dahu* who had accurately predicted the market's continued collapse throughout the Fourteenth Party Congress, "Deng Xiaoping lost to me!" (*"Deng Xiaoping shugei wo le!"*).

The "victory" of the *sanhu* was, finally, the result of the normal workings of "the market." Indeed, the entire story of the stock market's rise and fall might be read as a different morality tale, as the emergence in Shanghai of a more "perfect" market in shares. Clearly, the fact that, by the end of the year, neither big players nor the State had the capital to influence price on the market is an indication of increasing "perfection" in the economic sense. The developments of the market since that time which would confirm or disprove this hypothesis of increased perfection will be examined in detail in chapter 9. For the moment, however, it is important to emphasize the fact that it was not in these terms that Shanghainese investors read the events of that year. While we in the West might view the developments of 1992 as a victory for the market, the Shanghainese viewed them primarily as a defeat for the state. We might better ask, then, why the state – which, in less reified terms, is a frequently intelligent collection of bureaucrats – led itself down the garden path as it did.

The greatest pressures which state regulators experienced over the course of 1992 were internally generated. Once the decision to open stock markets had been taken, reformers were under the obligation to make this opportunity available to everyone, or at least to avoid the perception of favoritism or corruption. Thus, paradoxically, the primary force behind the decision rapidly to increase the supply of shares on the market – which was in turn the primary force behind its spectacular decline – was not free market ideology but state-tributary egalitarianism, underlying which lay the fantasy and fact of popular discontent. This egalitarian imperative also dictated that share prices be maintained at artificially low levels on the primary market, thus increasing rather than decreasing the speculative quality of the secondary market.

External pressures from the international financial system also played their part in determining the shape of the market over the course of the year, but these pressures were, comparatively speaking, minor. Perhaps the greatest of these was China's perceived need to expand the market as rapidly as possible to increase its credibility internationally. Contact with foreign officials and financial service executives also taught Shanghai regulators to replace the language of interference and control with the rhetoric of law and oversight, but this rhetorical shift was principally directed at a foreign audience. Indeed, it would seem that during much of the following period, this shift in language was largely successful in convincing the international community that it was dealing with an "emerging market" like any other. The separation of the domestic and foreign markets through A and B shares further worked to insulate the domestic market from international scrutiny. And, those in the international financial community who were well informed about the A share market[4] rarely took the time to think seriously about its "special characteristics."

Domestic and international pressures aside, in the end it must be admitted that the Chinese state set itself up for its spectacular fall because, as one exasperated Shanghai regulator suggested, some officials simply "didn't understand how markets worked" (*budong shichang*). Put less polemically, Shanghai regulators, particularly at the local level, did not understand – or it took them a few painful months to learn – that once this large public market had been capitalized beyond a certain point, it would take more money than they were willing to spend, maybe even than they had, to control prices as they hoped to do. Thus, "the market," not as ideology but as institution, did exercise real internal pressures which led to the "defeat" of state projects.

It is important, however, to measure the effects of these pressures. Certainly, Shanghai regulators had lost face. But had they really lost "control," as some investors intimated, or had they merely to scale down the nature and direction of their regulatory ambitions? Virtually all of the elements which lent the Shanghai market its "special nature" remained intact: the state share-holdings had been untouched by the market's collapse, for as state shares did not circulate, their value was only indirectly, even speculatively, related to prices on the secondary market. Likewise, the tributary framework which governed the conversion of state-owned enterprises to the share-holding form remained in place, as did the system of bureaucratic control which governed share distribution and set issuing prices on the primary market. Similarly, all of the problems of lack of transparency, inchoate regulatory structure and insider information which made the secondary market an almost purely speculative arena remained, for the "defeat" of the state was in no sense the overthrow of the state-related *guanxi* system which touched upon every aspect of the market's operation, as it touched upon every aspect of Shanghai society at large. In sum, all of the characteristics of the market which articulated with the tripartite bureaucratic, radical egalitarian and connections-based social logics examined in chapter 4 were still very much present.

Viewed from the regulatory point of view, what had changed were the terms in which state action and popular reaction were to be negotiated at the level of the secondary market. On the one hand, the state had to renounce the idea of direct intervention in the market to stabilize price and stave off the possibilities of popular unrest. On the other hand, the

---

[4] The best English-language reporting on the domestic market in Shanghai was undoubtedly the *South China Morning Post*.

long bear market of 1992 had taught state regulators that investors' "psychological ability to accept" (*xinli chengshou nengli*) was sturdier than they had thought. I encountered this phrase everywhere on the stock market, from investors talking about other investors, from government officials talking about "stock people" (*gumin*) and in the society pieces of the official *Shanghai Securities News*. In a Western context, it would best be translated by a technocratic notion such as "risk aversion." If I have chosen here to preserve the direct translation from the Chinese, this is because the phrase "psychological ability to accept" hints at its opposite, a "psychological" inability to accept, that is to say, a psychological ability to revolt.

However, over the course of 1992, the very notion of a "psychological ability to accept" began to look more like a projection of official fears than a reflection of investor "psychology." Shanghai had had its share of suicides and even the beginnings of an "event," but there had been no large-scale demonstrations or rioting despite the often staggering losses which many individual investors had experienced. What the "defeat" of the state as regulatory super-power demonstrated, to those interested in learning from the demonstration, was that perhaps it was not state power which had been keeping order in the first place. Perhaps, "the People" were not an entity to be controlled, but simply a force to be reckoned with.

8

Conclusion: The trading crowd

The story of the Shanghai stock market in 1992 started with a boom and ended with a bust. Over the course of this speculative cycle, the three collective actors I have discussed – big players, dispersed players and the state – were each, at a certain point, attributed the power to move the stock market in their particular way. The dynamics of government regulation and market movement which were played out that year were obvious to all investors; they served as an allegory for the relative strengths of "the State" and "the People," the latter in the dual form of a hyperbolized individual (the big player) and a chaotic collectivity (the dispersed players). In the process, something new – a new dynamic associated with a new kind of collective actor – emerged. I have called this something "the trading crowd."

The speculative cycle of 1992 was kicked off by the big players: in the eyes of investors, the minuscule and highly regulated market of the beginning of the year was governed primarily by the cartelizing techniques of these masters. Next, as the market grew in size over the spring and summer, the state was seen as taking the upper hand. Though "the State" received no credit for the spectacular rise of the market from February to May 1992, the market's decline from May to September of that year was universally blamed, even by state officials themselves, on the decisions and pronouncements of state officials, in short on "state interference" (*guojia ganshe*). By September 1992, however, it was becoming clear to even the most ardent stock market dissidents that the state alone could not account for market movements: rather, the cumulative effects of a million dispersed players were responsible for the market's stubborn refusal to rise upon command.

Rather than an abstract "market," what emerged from "the State's" "defeat" in 1992 was an altered image of "the People," one which sat uncomfortably with the tributary ideology which had made this duality the primary class division in China for the past thousand years. I have tried to encapsulate this tension through a coinage that has no "native" equivalent; indeed, I am not even sure how one would translate "trading crowd" into Chinese (*"jiaoyi (de) qunzhong"*?). However, I believe that the qualities I identify as belonging to the trading crowd were thoroughly perceptible in and through stock market discourse. It seemed and seems to me that if we are to demonstrate what is new about the Shanghai stock market, a new term is in order.

As a social actor, the trading crowd, like big players, dispersed players, and the state, is a collective agent. However, it operates on a different set of premises from those governing the other collective actors present in stock market discourse. In the traditional dialectical opposition between state hegemony and popular counter-hegemony, both "the State" and "the People" are granted intentionality. This intentionality is best demonstrated in that most essential mechanism of policy application in China, the mass mobilization campaign. With mass mobilization, "the State" emits its intentions for reforming the shape of the social landscape and those intentions are acted out by "the People." The moments of counter-hegemonic performance we witnessed with "fevers" mirror this structure, for precisely because they are *counter*-hegemonic, "fevers" remain caught within the framework laid down by the tributary state logic. With mass mobilization and fevers, urban Chinese subordinate their individual wills and "rush as one into mass action." While contemporary urbanites might feel bashful about this "beehive psychology," as they call it, it is the alternatingly creative and destructive potential of these moments of collective belonging that gives modern Chinese history much of its power and poignancy.

The stock market was both a campaign and a fever, both top-down and bottom-up, both hegemonic and counter-hegemonic. Indeed, the struggle between these two poles made up the Shakespearean subplot of the indigenous narrative which I have outlined in this study. Time and time again, the state was attributed powers over and responsibility for the market which it simply could not possess. So too, big players were attributed a kind of unity of purpose, a power to cause the market to do their bidding that, even in their heyday, was more mythical than real. However, when "the trading crowd" finally "won" the discursive contest for control over the market, theirs was a different kind of victory.

With the trading crowd, "the Whole People" does not, in Mao's famous phrase, "stand up"; it goes about its business. And this business is necessarily diverse. The crowd at the heart of the stock market drives a wedge into the fetishized conception of collective actors which structures relations between "the State" and "the People" in urban China. The trading crowd is a community not of intention but of effects. And, it produces these effects not through the mobilization of sameness, but through the realization of difference. It is the differences in the financial situations among investors and their evaluations of different shares which allow for a trade, and it is the accumulation of these differences which allows us to speak as if "the market" is moving in one direction or another. The stock market has – in this sense and in this sense only – provided an occasion for moving contemporary urban ideology beyond an oppositional conception of State–People relations.

In so doing, the stock market sheds light – a very narrow but focused light, I would submit – on a debate that has animated China studies since the fall of the Berlin Wall, the debate around the existence, shape and function of "civil society" in modern Chinese history (*Modern China* 1993, Davis *et al.* 1995). As Elizabeth Perry notes, much of the difficulty in this debate has come from the impossibility of separating a "state" from a "public" from a "private" sphere when examining the details of contemporary urban life (Davis *et al.* 1995:297–301). From student movements (Wasserstrom and Liu 1995) to labor associations (Perry 1995), from legal workers (Sidel 1995) to practitioners of traditional martial arts (Chen 1995), we find officially sanctioned organizations harboring significant "dissident" potential and, conversely, we witness "anti-state" activities practiced by the same people who also engage in active imitation of state-sponsored models of social expression.

The problem with these formulations is that they mirror, with nuances, the precise terms of the State–People dialectic which we have examined throughout this book. It is not in "opposition," "dissidence" and "anti-state" activities that Chinese society can create itself; to the contrary, popular opposition has been a part of the very dialectic that the tributary apparatus has produced and unintentionally nourished for centuries. Rather, discussion of the existence of "civil society" in modern China is appropriate where and to the extent that Chinese "society" is capable, not of opposing the State, but of ignoring it. Like others, I suspect that in contemporary urban China, those social spaces which lie outside the primary opposition between the State and the People are still remarkably few. One of them, however, takes the form of the trading crowd.

9

Afterwords

Financial markets may not be natural but they do abhor a vacuum. The void left by the "defeat" of "the State" over the course of 1992 was quickly filled – by the state. The new actors on the stock market scene since 1992 are "institutions" (*jigou*), a term that is modeled on Western stock markets, hinting at the presence of pensions funds, private insurance companies and the like. To avoid these misleading connotations, I prefer to translate this term by the English "organizations," for if we look at how these organizations are constituted, we find that behind each and every one lies an arm of the central or local bureaucracies which makes up the tributary state apparatus. Given the dimensions of market capitalization in Shanghai – 480 billion *yuan* as of June 1996 – the consensus among the investing public is that "organizations" are the only players with sufficient capital to influence the market.

"Organizations" are state-backed securities firms and state-backed institutional investors. In 1992, these off-shoots of the bureaucratic system were just beginning to get a taste for the kind of money to be made on financial markets. Since then, these organizations have gained increased discretion over the use of funds, especially those funds already raised on the stock market, and have thrown themselves into the game of speculation with a vengeance, drawing on all of the possibilities for official corruption (*guandao*) which this market leaves open. This official speculation is of a different order of magnitude from the practices I followed during the year of my fieldwork. "Organizations" are not individual bureaucrats siphoning off portions of state-allotted "legal person shares" for their own use, or using insider-information to increase the profitability of their "individual shares," although these practices are no doubt still common. Rather, "organizations" work as organizations, that is, they work to enrich the firm or enterprise itself through the same kinds of cornering and cartelizing activities which characterized individual big players' relation to the market in its very earliest stages. In the process, of course, they increase the prestige, power and wealth of the managers and professionals working for the organization. It is these "organizations" which are the main target of "the State's" efforts to regulate the market today. In this game of cops-and-robbers, individual players, big and scattered, are left with the crossfire.

Increasingly, on the stock market as in society at large, "the State" in China is divided. In its guise as regulatory agency, it must rein in other portions of the bureaucratic system which use the new possibilities opened by market reforms to increase their wealth and power. But the state is also the sum total of the bureaucratic hierarchies which structure its relation to society, and it is only through these bureaucratic connections that the organizations playing the market have the power they do. This tension is barely visible in stock market discourse in urban China today: the term "State" (*guojia*) continues to be reserved for those organs of state power whose intervention in the market is justified in terms of the public good. The large institutions and enterprises which work to enrich themselves through the market, while universally recognized as backed by state funds, are not referred to as "the State" or even in terms of their official contacts (*guanfang*) but, rather, simply as "organizations."

Just as the state needed individual big players to get the market off the ground in its initial stages, the state today needs the new organizational big players to maintain liquidity and provide a list of ever more complex services to an ever-growing investing public.[1] The state's dependence on the state – the interpenetration of these instances of state power and control – has resulted in a policy framework and pattern of law enforcement which most investors still qualify as "interference" rather than regulation. Perhaps the best illustration of this dependence is the fact that after seven years of stock market experiments, China still has no capital gains tax on corporate or individual earnings. The explicit reason for this hesitation is the fear that a tax on capital will scare investor money out of the market (*IHT* 1996d). But the main players it would scare away are those with the most to lose, the organizational players that have reaped enormous profits on the roller-coaster rides the market has experienced since 1992.

Over the course of 1992, Shanghai regulators learned that it was impossible for them to intervene directly in the market to control price: try as they might, they could not by fiat stabilize prices on a bull market and even

---

[1] In April 1995 there were a reported 250 firms providing financial services in Shanghai alone (*IHT* 1995c).

less could they slow the tumble of share prices in a bear market. But, though regulators have abandoned efforts to intervene directly in the market to control price, they have not abandoned their penchant for direct rather than indirect controls in other areas of market regulation. The best illustration of this is the on-going battle for control of financial information in the area of the stock market as in other areas of the economy. Already during the year of my fieldwork, local newspapers other than the official *Shanghai Securities News* intermittently stopped printing financial news in response to government worries that these newspapers were being coopted by individuals or institutions with powerful positions in the market. In November 1994, Shanghai officials elaborated on this regulatory stance by issuing "Rules Concerning the Management of Information on the Stock Market," "strictly prohibiting" organizations and individuals from influencing the market by spreading "false information" (*IHT* 1994). What constituted "false information" was not specified, but one of the Rules' first casualties were the stock *salons* examined in chapter 6, Shanghai's most important fora for the sharing of information among the public – and for the spreading of rumors. In November 1995, the authorities suspended a stock consultancy hot-line open to Shanghai investors (*IHT* 1995p), and in January 1996, the State Council ordered all foreign economic news agencies to submit to control by Xinhua (New China) News Agency, the main Party organ governing the mass media in China (*IHT* 1996b; *IHT* 1996a). Finally, in March 1996, Xinhua set up its own Xinhua Financial Information Consultancy Company which provides real-time stock and futures information throughout the country (*IHT* 1996i). These moves are justified as attempts to level the playing field for big and small investors. Following the tributary logic, however, this leveling is accomplished not through increasing the possibilities for competition among service providers, but by tightening state control.

As the market grew in size in the six years after 1992, so did its problems. With its growing integration within the domestic economy, the stock market was affected by shifts in broader macro-economic policy which tended further to increase its volatility. The two principal points at which economic policy interacted with the stock market were in the areas of credit supply and subsidies for inefficient state firms. Official statistics reported that one-third of all state enterprises were currently operating in the red, with another third just breaking even.[2] The government austerity

---

[2] These figures only give half the picture, for as Clarke (1991) and others have pointed out, given state monopolies over certain crucial productive factors such as energy and steel, the prices for which are still largely held below their market price, efficiency and profitability are not necessarily related.

program undertaken in July 1993 put these enterprises under new pressures as bank loans became increasingly difficult to obtain. At the same time, central planners felt compelled to limit the possibilities for bankruptcy, layoffs and plant-closings for fear (well founded in my opinion) of the social unrest which would ensue if these pillars of the state tributary system ceased to provide the services urban citizens counted on them to provide. These enterprises increasingly turned to the stock market to raise funds. At the same time, financial market reformers wishing to expand the market were under increased pressures to compromise oversight standards and grant approval for share issuance to poorly managed, over-staffed and technologically inefficient "joint-stock companies."

The poor quality of companies on the market was a fact of general knowledge, though just how badly off many of these companies were was masked by domestic accounting standards. When company worth was calculated according to international accounting practice, enterprises that made a profit under domestic standards frequently turned up with significant losses because of differences in the way debt, depreciation of assets and inventory write-offs were calculated (*IHT* 1996f). Unable to control the quality of companies on the market through law, regulatory agencies in Shanghai were reduced to intervening directly in the market by suspending companies that reported losses (*IHT* 1996g).

If Shanghai regulators could not count on the law to articulate clear standards for issuing companies, this was because the legal framework for China's securities industry had yet to be clarified. After four years of "consultation with relevant parties," a comprehensive securities law was drafted by the State Council, but publication of the law was blocked by a power struggle between two key central agencies, the People's Bank of China and the China Securities Commission, the central regulatory agency created by the State Council in January of 1993 (*IHT* 1996j). Until this dispute was settled, share issuance remained governed by the administrative system in place in 1992, with all of its particular tributary qualities. Indeed, this turf battle was itself a pure reflection of tributary logic at work, for the agencies fighting for administrative jurisdiction over the lucrative securities industries were not fighting over who would do a better job but rather who would control the distribution of the assets and privileges which guarantee state power in China. Precisely the same logic governed the struggle for control over the Shanghai market being waged at the time between Shanghai municipal authorities and officials in Beijing. Repeated pronouncements that Beijing was taking over this or that portion of market regulation only served to emphasize the fact that thus far central authorities had been unable thoroughly to implement the power they had on paper (*IHT* 1995o).

While many of Shanghai's problems had been with the market since its beginnings, others were new and pointed to the shifting nature of stock market practice as investors – individual and institutional – caught on to the new opportunities it provided. One of the most interesting of these was a growing tendency for companies to appropriate state shares for their own purposes, either personal or collective. In a particularly odd incident in 1994, managers of a state-owned wholesale market in Shanxi Province unilaterally transformed the enterprise into a joint-stock company by handing out 2.15 million free shares in the company which they then refused to recall, threatening to defend their control by force if necessary (*IHT* 1995j). This incident demonstrates how one of the perceived benefits of transforming state-enterprises to the share-holding form – facilitating the valuation and transfer of state assets – can be beneficial to people other than the state planners that state planners had in mind. Even more surprising was the purchase by Isuzu Motors and Itochu Corporation of non-negotiable state shares in Beijing Light Bus Company, giving foreign firms a 25 percent stake in the management of the Shanghai listed company. This move prompted an immediate prohibition on foreigner purchases of state shares in October 1995, and then an almost as immediate assurance from the China Securities Regulatory Commission that such a ban was not permanent (*IHT* 1995r). Reports in 1996 that Goodyear Tire was to purchase between 25 and 30 percent of all state-owned shares in Shanghai Tyre and Rubber Company suggested that the temptation to trade state control for international financing would be increasingly difficult to resist (*IHT* 1996k).

As in all areas of economic activity in China today, central authorities are waging an increasingly violent war against corruption amongst stock market bureaucrats (*IHT* 1995i). Individual officials in increasing number were arrested for embezzlement, market manipulation and securities fraud, often with harsh punishments, but the general consensus among investors was that these harsh punishments were more a sign of the enormity of the problem than a solution (see *IHT* 1995k; *IHT* 1995b). By far the biggest problem in the six-year-old market – and the site of the biggest showdown between state regulatory agencies and state-backed brokerages and investment companies – were the repeated scandals in China's futures markets. In late 1992, Shanghai began experimenting with derivatives, financial instruments which take their value from other securities or commodities on the open market. One market in particular, the market for futures in government bonds, grew to enormous and unstable proportions over the course of the two years from 1993 to 1995. Contributing to its volatility was the fact that investors were allowed to trade bond futures on the margin, putting down only a portion of the purchase price at the time of purchase with the promise of reimbursing the total sum out of the profits made from the trade. Furthermore, short-selling[3] was permitted on the futures market. In the area of bond futures, a further element added to the instability of the market in the form of rumors about the imminent payment of supplementary bond coupons indexed to inflation. When these coupons were finally issued, further rumors about changing index rates added to the tendency for enormous fluctuations on this highly leveraged market (*IHT* 1995e, *IHT* 1995a).

In the February 1995 bond futures scandal, Shanghai's largest securities firm, Shanghai International (Wanguo Zhengquan Gongsi), was caught dumping millions of government bond futures on the market in an attempt to bring prices down, allowing them to recoup large positions they had taken in short sales. On February 23, with turnover on the Shanghai Securities Exchange reportedly reaching US $100 billion in one day, officials suspended the last eight minutes of trades, ordered brokerages to clear their positions at newly negotiated prices, and halted bond futures trading for a week. The chairman of Shanghai International was forced to resign, and the president, a pioneer in the Chinese securities industry well respected by foreign and domestic observers alike, was placed under house arrest.

This event sent a chill throughout the securities community in Shanghai, for the unanimous opinion was that Shanghai International had just had the bad luck to get caught at a game which everybody on the market was playing.[4] Indeed, further scandals proved that market manipulation of this sort, though perhaps not of these dimensions, is commonplace in Shanghai.[5] As the question of how it was that firms had been allowed to

---

[3] Short-selling is the practice of borrowing instruments which one sells with the hope that prices on the market will fall, allowing one to return the borrowed instruments at a profit.

[4] Popular consensus has it that the problem of those publicly accused of corrupt practices is not that they have too many connections, but rather that they have too few, as the really well connected can never be called to account.

[5] In May 1995, bond futures trading was again suspended for a day in the wake of another scandal involving a large state-run investment company from Liaoning Province and numerous associated brokerages which had greatly exceeded the official ceiling on bond futures for a single firm. Again, local regulators intervened directly in the market, ordering brokers to reduce their positions in bonds by half or face the possibility that the Shanghai Securities Exchange would reduce them by force (*IHT* 1995h, *IHT* 1995g). Scandals involving plywood futures closed that market in October of the same year. The Shanghai Commodities Exchange also started and then stopped trading in energy futures in June 1994 (*IHT* 1995n).

exceed their positions to such an extent became pressing, the general manager of the Shanghai Securities Exchange, Mr. Wei Wenyuan, was also forced to step down (*IHT* 1995n). But this solution still did not solve the underlying problem which was, in the now familiar words of one broker, that "[the state] is interfering too much." The question remained, why did the state not insist on and enforce higher margin requirements, rather than intervening directly to shut down the market altogether (*IHT* 1995s)?

The solutions to these problems of market manipulation are difficult indeed for, as I have said, Shanghai and central officials are increasingly dependent on the very institutions they try to control for keeping the market alive. This dependence is apparent in the solutions which government regulators called upon to get Shanghai International out of its difficulties in the wake of the scandal. Both central and local authorities were active in negotiating a deal which would minimize Shanghai International's losses and safeguard its presence in the market (*NYT* 1995). Other securities firms were forced to absorb some of the firm's losses by accepting lower prices on the trades canceled during the last eight minutes of trading. In this way, and through forced loans from other securities firms, the damage to Shanghai International was whittled down from an estimated $120 million (twice the 1994 earnings of the firm) to approximately $60 million (*ibid.*). Completing the bail-out, on February 15, 1996, *Shanghai Securities News* announced that Shanghai International would be merged with Shenyin Securities, Shanghai's second largest brokerage, to make the single largest concern in the financial services community (*IHT* 1996e). While this merger was officially justified as an entirely voluntary move towards market rationalization by the two companies, local investors speculated that Shenyin was coaxed into accepting Shanghai International's damaged operations through tax breaks and other privileges.

In the international community, the glow of "the China play" was significantly tarnished (*IHT* 1995q). As B shares repeatedly showed poor performance, interest in the market languished. Fees and commissions for foreign investors remained high, much higher than fees for the same services on the domestic market (*IHT* 1995c). More importantly, foreign analysts began clearly to articulate the fact that "there is an inherent contradiction between the type of control over the economy that [China's] constitution and [...] political system requires, and the way in which capital markets operate" (*IHT* 1995s, citing Baring Securities' analyst Richard Graham). Thus, for example, in 1995 the international financial community discovered the importance of state shares in the Shanghai market structure when state share-holders with controlling majorities in B share companies began insisting that companies pay out large cash dividends, larger than most foreign investors thought wise for the long-range financial health of the companies (*IHT* 1995f). Even more startling, some companies paid out larger dividends to state share-holders than to foreign investors, arguing that the state had invested earlier in the company and thus deserved to reap more of the benefit (*ibid.*).

Further undermining investor confidence was the fact that an estimated 40–60 percent of all B shares were currently owned by local Chinese investors (*IHT* 1995q). To lure foreign investors into the market, rumors were frequently spread that the A and B share markets were to be merged (*IHT* 1995c), but these rumors were contradicted by other government moves such as regulations issued in 1996 directed at stopping the leak of hard currency by enforcing the rule prohibiting domestic investors from purchasing dollar-denominated B shares. Finally, the persistent tendency of Chinese regulators to resort to administrative measures rather than open competition was amply demonstrated with central authorities' moves to control in-coming foreign financial information. Even "H shares," shares in Chinese companies listed on the Hong Kong Stock Exchange which were generally thought to be the cream of the crop of Chinese listings (along with a handful of Chinese companies listed on the New York Exchange), fared poorly since the initial surge of interest in 1993, and many fund managers internationally became leery of further involvement (*IHT* 1995l).

Though the Western press continued to refer to China's experiments with stock markets, and with economic reforms generally, as "capitalism,"[6] it increasingly came to recognize that the Chinese stock market was a market with a difference. In the words of one international analyst, "most companies listed on the Shanghai Exchange still conduct at least part of their business as if they were still part of China's old command economy rather than to make a profit" (*IHT* 1995u). What this analysis misses is what this book sets out to demonstrate: while listed companies may no longer be a part of China's "old command economy," they are still a part of China's even older tributary mode of production. Lacking a way to describe the persistence of the tributary mode in anything other than negative terms, foreign observers can only regard the behavior of Chinese firms as necessarily temporary aberrations.

---

[6] See *IHT* 1996h ("China has decided to 'roll the dice of capitalism' "); *IHT* 1995t, (Deng Xiaoping's market reforms were designed to "remold the country's economy in the image of 'capitalism with Chinese characteristics' ").

But foreign observers are not the only parties to misread the current state of China's economic system, nor to have difficulty predicting the path of future developments. Ironically, it is the Chinese state itself which seems to have the most trouble cracking this thousand-year-old egg. Buffeted by the winds of free-market economics, the state has an increasingly hard time articulating a justifying ideology for the tributary mode of production by which it keeps itself in place. At the heart of this confusion is its losing battle against official corruption. The Chinese state cannot recognize that corruption – the extraction of wealth by virtue of one's position within the state hierarchy – is the negative face of the very structures by which it produces and reproduces itself. Whether Communist China's "old command economy" ever functioned according to the Leninist flow-chart of rational commands is debatable; what is no longer debatable is the fact that this Leninist model of control has ceded its place to the tributary mode of production in its most exploitative form. Furthermore, this system of control and extraction is increasingly forced to compete with that other system of control and extraction which we call markets. Given the abuses to which the tributary mode has lent itself since economic reforms and before, opportunity and exploitation in the marketplace look increasingly attractive to an overtaxed Chinese citizenry.

If the petty capitalist mode of production which is the tributary mode's other face is gaining force in China today, this is also a different renaissance. China's experiments with radical egalitarianism have done much to undermine the dual ideologies of gender- and age-based exploitation which lent petty capitalism its family dimensions throughout imperial times. To a varying degree and at different moments, "the People," particularly the urban "People," have seen through the naturalizing ideologies which justify the exploitation of women by men and the young by the old. But the lifting of these veils only makes all the more invisible that system of extraction and control which is the open market. The market's invisible hand interrupts the closed circuit of state hegemony and popular counter-hegemony which we have examined throughout this work. It transforms "the People," united and willful, into "the trading crowd," multiple and purposeless.

Glossary of Chinese terms

Aishi	爱使 (上海爱使电子设备股份有限公司)	Shanghai Aishi Electronic Appliances Co. Ltd. Inc.
bagua	八卦	the "Eight Diagrams" (divinatory technique)
ban	板	a sheet (of postage stamps)
baofa	爆发	to explode, erupt
baofa	暴发	to burst forth, break out (esp. water)
baofahu	暴发户	upstart, suddenly rich person
baoshou shili	保守势力	conservative forces or powers (people, cliques)
Bingxiang	冰箱 (上海冰箱压缩机股份有限公司)	Shanghai Freezer Packaging Machinery Co. Ltd. Inc.
Cai Shen	财神	God of Wealth
Caizheng (Zhengquan Gongsi)	财政(证券公司)	Caizheng Securities Co.
can	惨	cruel, tragic, savage
canyu (vs. ganshe)	参与 (vs. 干涉)	participate (vs. interfere, intervene)
caozong	操纵	control, rig
caozuo	操作	operate, manipulate
chajia	差价	price differential
changzhang	厂长	factory director, head
chao	炒	speculate (in a market); lit. stir-fry

chaoji dahu	超级大户	"super-player" (the state on the Shanghai stock market)
chengbao	承包	contracting out
chengjiaoliang	成交量	turnover rate
chengshu/bu chengshu	成熟／不成熟	mature/immature
chongzhi chengben fa	重置成本法	cost of replacement method
chu shiqing	出事情	an event, something (bad) coming up, a problem arising
da	大	big; old; important
dahu	大户	big player(s); important person or family
dahu shi	大户室	"VIP room" (at stock brokerages)
dang zhibu shuji	党支部书记	Party branch secretary
danwei	单位	work unit; unit
Dazhong	大众 (上海市大众出租汽车股份有限公司)	Shanghai Dazhong Taxi Co. Ltd. Inc.
Dianzhenkong	电真空 (上海电真空器件股份有限公司)	Shanghai Vacuum Co. Ltd. Inc.
Diyi Qianbi	第一铅笔 (中国第一铅笔股份有限公司)	China First Pencil Co. Ltd. Inc.
Diyi Shipin	第一食品 (上海第一食品商店股份有限公司)	Shanghai Number 1 Provisions Co. Ltd. Inc.
Dongfang Mingzhu	东方明珠 (上海东方明珠股份有限公司)	Shanghai Pearl of the Orient Co. Ltd. Inc.
dongshizhang	董事长	chairman of the board
duibi jiaohuan	对比交换	matched (or rigged) trades
Erfangji	二纺机 (上海二纺机股份有限公司)	Shanghai Number 2 Textile Machinery Co. Ltd. Inc.
fang song	放松	loose; relax (a government policy)
faqirengu	发起人股	initial investor shares

farengu	法人股	shares held by "legal persons," that is, most enterprises and some organizations
Feile Gufen (Da Feile)	飞乐股份 (大飞乐) (上海飞乐股份有限公司)	Feile Co. Ltd. Inc.
Feile Yinxiang (Xiao Feile)	飞乐音响 (小飞乐) (上海飞乐音响股份有限公司)	Feile Acoustics Co. Ltd. Inc.
feiyingli huiyuanzhi	非盈利会员制	not-for-profit membership organization
Fenghua	丰华 (上海丰华圆珠笔股份有限公司)	Shanghai Fenghua Ballpoint Pen Co. Ltd. Inc.
Fenghuang	凤凰 (浙江凤凰化工股份有限公司)	Fenghuang (Phoenix) Chemicals Co. Ltd. Inc.
fengxian yishi	风险意识	risk consciousness
Fuhua	复华 (上海复华实业股份有限公司)	Shanghai Fuhua Enterprises Co. Ltd. Inc.
gan shimao	赶时髦	follow a fashion or fad, keep up with the times
ganqing touzi	感情投资	"investing in feelings"
ganshe	干涉	interfere, intervene
ganyu	干预	interfere, butt in
gaoganzidi	高干子弟	"sons and grandchildren of high cadres" (also daughters)
gentou	跟头	share which doubles in price (lit. somersault)
geren chengfen	个人成分	individual class status
gerengu	个人股	shares held by (mainland) individuals
gerou	割肉	cut one's losses (lit. cut meat or flesh)
getihu	个体户	individual entrepreneur
gexing	个性	personality, individuality
gonggu	公股	publicly owned shares
gongkai faxing	公开发行	primary issue to the public

gongqiu guanxi	供求关系	(relation between) supply and demand
gongsipai	公司派	"company school" (of stock market interpretation)
Gongye Daxue	工业大学	Industry University
guan shang he ban	官商合办	jointly run official–merchant enterprises
guandao	官倒	"official speculation"
guanfang	官方	official
guanxi	关系	relation, connections
guanxigui	关系鬼	connections addict
guanxiwang	关系网	connections web or network
guanxixue	关系学	the art of using connections, of social relations
gufenhua	股份化	transformation to the share-holding form, "stockifica-tion" of a state-owned enterprise
guifan, guifanhua	规范／化	normal, regularize (see explanatory note, p. 36, n. 6)
gumin	股民	lit. "stock people"; investors
guojia	国家	nation, state, country
Guojia Guoyou Zichan Guanli Ju or Guoziju	国家国有资产管理局 国资局	National State Assets Administration Bureau
guojiagu	国家股	shares owned by the state
guojihua	国际化	internationalization
gupiao dahu	股票大户	big players on the stock market
gupiao re	股票热	stock fever
Gupiao Shangye Gonghui	股票商业工会	Stockbrokers' Trade Association
gupiao zhanghu	股票帐户	stock account (opened through brokerage but registered with the SSE)

Guowuyuan Zhengquan Weiyuanhui or Guozhengwei	国务院证券委员会 or 国证委	State Council Securities Policy Committee
Hainiao	海鸟 (上海海鸟电子股份有限公司)	Shanghai Seabird Electronics Co. Ltd. Inc.
Haitong (Zhengquan Gongsi)	海通 (证券公司)	Haitong Securities Co.
Hi-Lo tu	Hi-Lo 图	high-low charts
hong majia	红麻茄	"red jackets," nickname for brokerage agents seated at the Exchange
hu	户	door; family; person who (suffix)
hua	化	transformation, change
Hualian Shangxia	华联商厦 (上海华联商厦股份有限公司)	Shanghai Overseas Chinese Dept. Store Co. Ltd. Inc.
huang majia	黄麻茄	"yellow jackets": nickname for SSE agents
huangniu	黄牛	black marketeer
hui	会	meeting, association
hukoubu	户口簿	household registration booklet
hun	混	make do, muddle through
Jiabao	嘉宝 (上海嘉宝实业股份有限公司)	Shanghai Jiabao Industries Co. Ltd. Inc.
Jiaodai	胶带 (上海胶带股份有限公司)	Shanghai Rubber Belt Co. Ltd. Inc.
Jiafeng	嘉丰 (上海嘉丰股份有限公司)	Shanghai Jiafeng Co. Ltd. Inc.
jiating chushen	家庭出身	family social origin
jiben fenxi	基本分析	fundamental analysis
jiben yitu	基本意图	basic goals or plan
Jiefang Ribao	解放日报	*Liberation Daily*
jigou	机构	institution, organization
jihui	机会	opportunity, chance

Jinling	金陵 (上海金陵股份有限公司)	Shanghai Jinling Co. Ltd. Inc.
Jinqiao	金桥 (上海市金桥出口加工区开发股份有限公司)	Shanghai Jinqiao Export Processing Zone Development Co. Ltd. Inc.
Jinrong Xingzheng Guanli Chu or Jinguanchu	金融行政管理处 or 金管处	Financial Administration and Regulation Office
jishu fenxi	技术分析	technical analysis
jiti farengu	集体法人股	collective legal person shares
julebu	俱乐部	club
K-xian tu	K 线图	K-wave charts
konggu quan	控股权	power to control (the price of) a share
kuang	狂	arrogant, wild, crazy
laobaixing	老百姓	commoners, the man in the street, the folk
laobaixing jupa de xinli	老百姓惧怕的心理	the people's feelings of terror
laogu	老股	"old shares" (first eight shares on Shanghai market)
Lengguang	棱光 (上海棱光实业股份有限公司)	Shanghai Lengguang Enterprises Co. Ltd. Inc.
lian	脸	face
Lianghua	良华 (上海良华实业股份有限公司)	Shanghai Lianghua Industries Co. Ltd. Inc.
Lianhe Fangzhi	联合纺织 (上海联合纺织实业股份有限公司)	Shanghai United Textile Co. Ltd. Inc.
Lianhua Heqian	联华合纤 (上海联华合纤股份有限公司)	Shanghai Lianhua Fiber Co. Ltd. Inc.
Liannong	联农 (上海市联农股份有限公司)	Shanghai Liannong Co. Ltd. Inc.
lihai	利害	fierce, terrible
lingdaogu	领导股	"leader" shares
linghuoxing	灵活性	flexibility, lability
Lingqiao	凌桥 (上海凌桥自来水股份有限公司)	Shanghai Lingqiao Water Co. Ltd. Inc.

liyi tuanti	利益团体	interest groups
longtang	弄堂	lane, alley
Longtou	龙头 (上海龙头股份有限公司)	Shanghai Dragon's Head Co. Ltd. Inc.
luan	乱	chaos, disorder
Lujian	氯碱 (上海氯碱股份有限公司)	Shanghai Lujian Chemicals Co. Ltd. Inc.
Lujiazui Kaifa	陆家嘴开发 (上海市陆家嘴金融贸易区开发股份有限公司)	Shanghai Lujiazui Commercial and Financial District Development Co. Ltd. Inc.
Luntai	轮胎 (上海轮胎橡胶股份有限公司)	Shanghai Tyre and Rubber (Group) Co. Ltd. Inc.
Mao re	毛热	Mao fever
maodun	矛盾	contradiction(s)
maoxianjia de leyuan	冒险家的乐园	adventurer's paradise
mianjia	面价	face value of share
mianzi	面子	face
mingqi	名气	reputation, fame
mingyun	命运	fate, destiny
minjian jigou	民间机构	non-governmental organization; folk, popular association
miqie	密切	intimately connected
Nanshi	南市	Nanshi (southern) district of Shanghai
nanxun	南巡	southern expedition or tour
niu shi	牛市	bull (rising) market
piaoliang	漂亮	beautiful
Pudong	浦东	Pudong district, east of the Huangpu River
Pudong Qiangsheng	浦东强生 (上海浦东强生出租汽车股份有限公司)	Shanghai Pudong Qiangsheng Taxi Co. Ltd. Inc.
putong hua	普通话	"ordinary language" (i.e. Mandarin)

qi-qi shibian	七七事变	July 7 Incident
qian	钱	money
Qinggong Jixie	轻工机械 (上海轻工机械股份有限公司)	Shanghai Light Industry Machinery Co. Ltd. Inc.
qiye neibu gupiao	企业内部股票	enterprise internal shares (sold only to enterprise employees)
quan	权	authority, power; here position
quanzi	圈子	circle, clique
re	热	fever, fad (lit. hot)
redian	热点	hot
rengouzheng	认购证	share-subscription application or lottery ticket
renminbi (= *yuan*)	人民币	Chinese currency (= Chinese dollars)
renminbi tezhong gupiao	人民币特种股票	special *renminbi* shares or "B shares"
renqi	人气	popular mood, general mood
sanbao	三宝	the "three valuables"
sanhu	散户	dispersed or scattered player(s)
shalong	沙龙	*salon*
Shanghai Dianqi	上海电器 (上海电器股份有限公司)	Shanghai Electric Appliances Co. Ltd. Inc.
Shanghai Gufenzhi Qiye (Gongsi) Xiehui	上海股份制企业 (公司) 协会	Shanghai Joint-Stock Enterprise (Company) Association
Shanghai Huashang Zhengquan Jiaoyisuo	上海华商证券交易所	Shanghai Chinese Merchants' Securities Exchange
Shanghai Pingzhun Gupiao Gongsi	上海评准股票公司	Shanghai Standard Stock Company
Shanghai Zhengquan Bao	上海证券报	*Shanghai Securities Weekly*

Shanghai Zhengquan Guanli Weiyuanhui or Zhengguanwei	上海证券管理委员会 or 证管委	Shanghai Securities Regulatory Commission
shangshi	上市	come onto the market (here, receive permission to trade on an exchange)
Shangye Wangdian	商业网点 (上海商业网点发展实业股份有限公司)	Shanghai Commercial Network Development Enterprises Co. Ltd. Inc.
shehui farengu	社会法人股	social legal person shares
shehui gaoluan	社会搞乱	societal disorder, chaos
Shenbao	申报	Chinese newspaper, referred to in English as "Shun Pao"
Shenda	申达 (上海申达纺织服装股份有限公司)	Shanghai Shenda Textiles Co. Ltd. Inc.
Shenhua Shiye	申华实业 (上海申华实业股份有限 公司)	Shanghai Shenhua Industries Co. Ltd. Inc.
Shenyin (Zhengquan Gongsi)	申银 (证券公司)	Shenyin Securities Co.
Shibai Yidian	市百一店 (上海市第一百货商店股份有限公司)	Shanghai Number 1 Dept. Store Co. Ltd. Inc.
shichang fenxi	市场分析	market analysis
shichanghua	市场化	marketization, transformation to a market system
shichangpai	市场派	"market school" (of stock market interpretation)
shikumen	石库门	lit. stone multiple-storied gate; traditional walled Shanghai house
shiqi	市气	market mood
shiyinglü	市盈率	price–earnings ratio
shouduan	手段	measures, tactics

Shuanglü	双鹿 (上海双鹿电器股份有限公司)	Shanghai Twin Dear Electronic Appliances Co. Ltd. Inc.
Shuixian	水仙 (上海水仙电器实业股份有限公司)	Shanghai Water Spirit Electronics Industries Co. Ltd. Inc.
shunkouliu	顺口溜	jingle, doggerel, rhymed saying
si xiao long	四小龙	Four Little Dragons (English, "Tigers")
sixiang zhunbei	思想准备	mental (or thought) preparation (for war, for criticism/self-criticism session, etc.)
suzhi	素质	quality
taiwan tongbao	台湾同胞	Taiwan "compatriots" (see explanatory footnote p. 31, n. 1)
taozhu	套住	caught (when price of shares on market drops below price at which purchased)
teshuxing	特殊性	special nature or particularity
tiaokong	调控	adjustment; guide
tiaolou	跳楼	commit suicide (by jumping from a tall building); sudden drop in share price
tiaozheng jieduan	调整阶段	period of adjustment
tou	头	boss, head
toutougu	头头股	"head" shares
tuoshi	托市	support the market (by buying securities)
Waigaoqiao	外高桥 (上海市外高桥保税区开发股份有限公司)	Shanghai Outer Gaoqiao Free Trade Zone Development Co. Ltd. Inc.
wan gupiao	玩股票	play the stock market

Wanguo (Zhengquan Gongsi)	万国 (证券公司)	Shanghai International Securities Co.
wenhua	文化	civilization, culture
Wenhua Guangchang	文化广场	Cultural Palace
wuzhihua	无纸化	scriptless (trading)
xia fang	下放	transfer (cadres, students) to do manual labor in the countryside or in a factory
xia hai	下海	"set out to sea", that is, leave the work unit system; go into business
xia shou	下手	underling, helper
xiao	小	small; young; unimportant
xiao	消	disappear, eliminate; waste or pass time
xiaodao xiaoxi	小道消息	gossip, news through the grapevine
xiaofei	消费	to consume, to use up
xiaohu	小户	small player(s); unimportant person or family
xiaoxi	消息	news, gossip, informatiom, scoop
xiehui	协会	association
xin jiao fengchao	信交风潮	"tempest of the bourses"
Xin Jinjiang	新锦江 (上海新锦江大酒店股份有限公司)	Shanghai Jin Jiang Tower Co. Ltd. Inc.
Xin Shijie	新世界 (上海新世界贸易股份有限公司)	Shanghai New World Trading Co. Ltd. Inc.
xing she xing zi [expression]	姓社姓资	lit. [wonder whether] the last name is socialism or capitalism; to worry about ideological correctness
Xingye	兴业 (上海兴业房产股份有限公司)	Shanghai Xingye Real Estate Co. Ltd. Inc.
xingzheng guanli	行政管理	administrative regulations or measures

xinli	心理	psychology, state of mind
xinli chengshou nengli	心理承受能力	(psychological) ability to accept or withstand (loss)
xinli jia	心理价	"psychological price" (price to which investor thinks share will rise or fall)
xinwen	新闻	news
xinxi	信息	information, news
xinxixue	信息学	information science
Xinya	新亚 (上海新亚快餐食品股份有限公司)	Shanghai New Asia Foods Co. Ltd. Inc.
xiong shi	熊市	bear (falling) market
xishengpin	牺牲品	sacrificial object
xuanchuan	宣传	propaganda, publicity
xueyuanpai	学院派	"academic school" (of stock market interpretation)
Yanzhong Shiye	延中实业 (上海延中实业股份有限公司)	Yanzhong Industries Co. Ltd. Inc.
yaoyan	谣言	gossip, rumor
yi hong er shang [a proverb]	一哄而上	rush headlong into mass action
yi guo liang zhi	一国两制	"one country, two systems"
yi pian san sha	一片散砂	"a sheet of loose sand" (Sun Yat-sen)
yihua	异化	alienation
yijia	益价	"premium rate", that is, price at which shares are offered to the public
Yijing	易经	the "Book of Changes", used in divinatory rituals
yiwofeng	一窝蜂	psychology of the beehive, group think
Yixing	异型钢管 (上海异型钢管股份有限公司)	Shanghai Special-Shaped Steel Tubing Co. Ltd. Inc.
Yizhou Touzi	一周投资	*CVIC Market Watch Weekly*
Yongsheng	永生 (上海永生制笔股份有限公司)	Shanghai Wingsun Pen Manufacturing Co. Ltd. Inc.

yuan (= *renminbi*)	元 (= 人民币)	Chinese dollars (= Chinese currency)
yundong (*yuan*)	运动 (员)	movement, campaign; (athlete, political opportunist)
yunqi	运气	luck, personal fate
Yuyuan (Shangcheng)	豫园商城 (上海豫园旅游商城股份有限公司)	Shanghai Yu Gardens Tourist Shopping Center Co. Ltd. Inc.
zhejia rugu	折价入股	convert value into stocks, transform assets into share form
zhengce	政策	policy (esp. government)
zhengce fenxi	政策分析	policy analysis
zhengquan jigou	证券机构	"securities organization," generally brokerage
Zhengquan Shichang Zhoukan	证券市场周刊	*Securities Market Weekly*
zhengzhi fenxi	政治分析	political analysis
zhiduhua	制度化	systemization
zhigong neibu gupiao	职工内部股票	employee/staff internal shares
Zhongcheng	众城 (上海众城实业股份有限公司)	Shanghai Zhongcheng Enterprises Co. Ltd. Inc.
Zhongfangji	中纺机 (中国纺织机械股份有限公司)	China Textile Machinery Co. Ltd. Inc.
Zhongguo Xin Jishu Chuangye Touzi Gongsi	中国新技术创业投资公司	China Venturetech Investment Corp.
Zhongguo Zhengquan Jiandu Guanli Weiyuanhui or Zhengjianhui	中国证券监督管理委员会 or 证监会	China Securities Regulatory Commission

Zhongguo Zhengquan Shichang Yanjiu Sheji Zhongxin	中国证券市场研究设计中心	Stock Exchange Executive Council
zhonghu	中户	mid-sized players
zhongyang lingdao	中央领导	central leaders
zhuguan bumen	主管部门	administrative superior
zhushou	助手	assistant, aide
zichan pinggu	资产评估	assets assessment or appraisal
ziyouhua	自由化	liberalization (implicitly, perhaps, privatization)
zong jingli	总经理	chief executive officer, general manager

Bibliography

Editors' note on Chinese personal names. These are traditionally given with the surname first, and most appear as such – without a separating comma – in the following bibliography. However, some Chinese authors choose to conform to the European ordering of names, reversing the traditional order, so that their names appear in the bibliography with a separating comma to indicate this.

Adler, Patricia A. and Peter Adler, 1984a. (Eds.) *The Social Dynamics of Financial Markets.* Greenwich, CT: JAI Press.
    1984b. "Introduction," in (P.A. Adler and P. Adler, eds.), *The Social Dynamics of Financial Markets,* 1–15. Greenwich, CT: JAI Press.
Amorim, Marilia, 1996. *Dialogisme et altérite dans les sciences sociales.* Paris: L'Harmattan.
Anderson, Benedict, 1983. *Imagined Communities. Reflections on the Origin and Spread of Nationalism.* London: Verso Press.
Appadurai, Arjun, 1986. "Introduction: Commodities and the politics of value," in (A. Appadurai, ed.), *The Social Life of Things: Commodities in Cultural Perspective,* 3–63. Cambridge: Cambridge University Press.
    1992. "Putting hierarchy in its place," in (G. Marcus, ed.), *Rereading Cultural Anthropology,* 34–47. Durham, NC and London: Duke University Press.
Arnold, Thurman W., 1937. *The Folklore of Capitalism.* New Haven, CT: Yale University Press.
Baker, Hugh D. R., 1977. "Extended kinship in the traditional city," in (G. W. Skinner, ed.), *The City in Late Imperial China,* 499–518. Stanford: Stanford University Press.
Balazs, Etienne, 1964 [1957]. "China as a permanently bureaucratic society," in (A.F. Wright, ed.), *Chinese Civilization and Bureaucracy,* 13–27. New Haven, CT: Yale University Press.
Baltimore Sun (Associated Press), 1992. "Stock market puts China under a capitalist spell." June 26, p. 3C.
Banerjee, Tridib, 1993. "Transitional urbanism reconsidered: Post-colonial development of Calcutta and Shanghai," in (G. Guldin and A. Southall, eds.), *Urban Anthropology in China,* 76–100. London and Leiden: E. J. Brill.

Barth, Frederick, 1969. "Introduction," in (F. Barth, ed.), *Ethnic Groups and Boundaries: The Social Organization of Cultural Difference*, 9–38. Boston: Little Brown and Co.

1992. "Towards a greater naturalism in conceptualizing societies," in (A. Kuper, ed.), *Conceptualizing Society*, 17–32. London: Routledge.

Bastide, Roger, 1968. "La Connaissance de l'événement," in (G. Balandier, R. Bastide, J. Berque and P. George, eds.), *Perspectives de la sociologie contemporaine. Hommage à Georges Gurvitch*, 159–168. Paris: Presses Universitaires Françaises.

Basu, Ellen Oxfeld, 1991. "Profit, loss, and fate: The entrepreneurial ethic and the practice of gambling in an overseas Chinese community." *Modern China* 17(2):227–259.

Baudrillard, Jean, 1981. *For a Critique of the Political Economy of the Sign*. St. Louis, MO: Telos Press.

Baum, Richard, 1986. "Modernization and legal reform in post-Mao China: The rebirth of socialist legality." *Studies in Comparative Communism* 19(2):69–104.

Benedict, Ruth, 1934. *Patterns of Culture*. Boston: Houghton Mifflin.

Bennett, Gordon, 1976. *Yundong: Mass Campaigns in Chinese Communist Leadership*. Berkeley: University of California Press.

Berger, Mark T., 1996. "Yellow mythologies: The East Asian miracle and post-cold war capitalism." *Positions* 4(1):90–126.

Bergère, Marie-Claire, 1964. *Une crise financière à Shanghai à la fin de l'Ancien Régime*. Paris and The Hague: Mouton.

1981. "'The other China': Shanghai from 1919 to 1949," in (C. Howe, ed.), *Shanghai. Revolution and Development in an Asian Metropolis*, 1–34. Cambridge: Cambridge University Press.

1986. *L'Age d'or de la bourgeoisie chinoise*. Paris: Flammarion.

Bernstein, Thomas P., 1977. *Up to the Mountains and Down to the Villages*. New Haven, CT: Yale University Press.

Billeter, Jean-François, 1985. "The system of class status," in (S. Schram, ed.), *The Scope of State Power in China*, 127–169. London and Hong Kong: School of Oriental and African Studies, Chinese University Press and St. Martin's Press.

Bloch, Maurice and Jonathan Parry, 1989. "Introduction: Money and the morality of exchange," in (J. Parry and M. Bloch, eds.), *Money and the Morality of Exchange*, 1–32. Cambridge: Cambridge University Press.

Bornstein, Morris, 1985. *Comparative Economic Systems* (fifth edn.). Homewood, IL: Irwin Press.

Boston Globe (Associated Press), 1992. "Chinese police fire tear gas at rampaging stock investors." August 11.

Bourdieu, Pierre, 1980. "Le Nord et le midi. Contribution à une analyse de l'effet Montesquieu." *Actes des recherches en sciences sociales* 35:21–25.

Bowles, Paul, 1990. "Inflation and economic reform in China." *International Journal of Development Banking* 8(2):1–16.

Bowles, Paul and Gordon White, 1992. "The dilemmas of market socialism: Capital market reform in China." *Journal of Development Studies* 28(3):363–385 (Part I), 28(4):575–594 (Part II).

Bruun, Ole, 1993. *Business and Bureaucracy in a Chinese City: An Ethnography of Private Business Households in Contemporary China.* Berkeley: Institute of East Asian Studies, University of California at Berkeley. China Research Monographs, no. 43.

Burling, Robbins, 1962. "Maximization theories and the study of economic anthropology." *American Anthropologist* 64:802–81.

Cancelliere, Vito Mariano, 1996. "Logique réticulaire et risque concurrentiel dans les marchés financiers." *Tsantsa* 1:96–101.

Canetti, Elias, 1984 [1960]. *Crowds and Power.* New York: Farrar Straus Giroux.

Carnegie, Dale, 1981 [1936]. *How to Win Friends and Influence People.* New York: Pocket Books.

Cell, Charles P., 1977. *Revolution at Work: Mobilization Campaigns in China.* New York: Academic Press.

Chamberlain, Heath B., 1987. "Party–management relations in Chinese industries: Some political dimensions of economic reform." *China Quarterly* 112:631–661.

Chang, Parris, 1981. "Shanghai and Chinese politics: Before and after the Cultural Revolution," in (C. Howe, ed.), *Shanghai. Revolution and Development in an Asian Metropolis,* 66–90. Cambridge: Cambridge University Press.

Chao Gu Zui Jia Xuanze: Shanghshi Gupiao Fenxi Bijiao [The Best Choices for Playing the Stock Market: A Comparative Analysis of Stocks on the Secondary Market], 1992. Beijing: China Economic Press.

Chen, Nancy Nu-Chun, 1994. "Possession and the State: Deviation and mental health in the People's Republic of China," Ph.D. Dissertation, University of California, Berkeley (Anthropology).

    1995. "Urban spaces and experiences of *qigong*," in (D. Davis, R. Krauss, B. Naughton and E. Perry, eds.), *Urban Spaces in Contemporary China: The Potential for Autonomy and Community in Post-Mao China,* 347–361. Cambridge, New York and Washington, DC: Woodrow Wilson Center Press/Cambridge University Press.

Cheng, Nien, 1986. *Life and Death in Shanghai.* London: Grafton Books.

Chinese Communist Party Central Committee Documentary Research Office, 1979/1987 (Eds.). *Shiyi jie san zhong quan hui yilai zhongyao wenxian xuandu* (Selected Readings in Important Documents Since the Third Plenum of the Eleventh Central Committee), vol. I. Beijing. (Partial translation in "Quarterly Documentation." *China Quarterly* 77 (March 1979) 168.)

Chossudovsky, Michel, 1986. *Towards Capitalist Restoration? Chinese Socialism after Mao.* New York: St. Martin's Press.

Clammer, John, 1987. (Ed.) *Beyond the New Economic Anthropology.* London: MacMillan.

Clarke, Donald C., 1991. "What's law got to do with it? Legal institutions and economic reform in China." *UCLA Pacific Basin Law Journal* 10(1):1–76.

Clarke, Donald C. and Feinerman, James, 1996. "Antagonistic contradictions: Criminal law and human rights in China," in (S. Lubman, ed.), *China's Legal Reforms,* 135–154. Oxford: Clarendon/Oxford University Press.

Coble, Parks M., Jr., 1980. *The Shanghai Capitalists and the Nationalist Government, 1927–1937.* Cambridge, MA: Harvard University Press.

Cochran, Sherman, 1980. *Big Business in China: Sino-Foreign Rivalry in the Cigarette Industry, 1890–1930*. Cambridge, MA: Harvard University Press.

Codere, Helen, 1950. *Fighting with Property: A Study of Kwakiutl Potlatching and Warfare, 1792–1930*. Seattle: University of Washington Press.

Cohen, Myron L., 1976. *House United, House Divided: The Chinese Family in Taiwan*. New York: Columbia University Press.

Cook, Scott, 1966. "The obsolete 'anti-market' mentality: A critique of the substantive approach to economic anthropology." *American Anthropologist* 63:1–25.

1969. "The 'anti-market' mentality re-examined: A further critique of the substantive approach to economic anthropology." *Southwestern Journal of Anthropology* 25(4):378–406.

Croll, Elizabeth, 1984. "Marriage choice and status groups in contemporary China," in (J. Watson, ed.), *Class and Social Stratification in Post-Revolutionary China*, 175–197. Cambridge: Cambridge University Press.

Dakhlia, Jocelyn. 1995. "Le Terrain de la vérité," *Enquête* 1:141–152.

Dalton, George, 1961. "Economic theory and primitive society." *American Anthropologist* 63:1–25.

Davis, Deborah, 1992a. "Job mobility in post-Mao cities: Increases on the margins." *China Quarterly* 132:1063–1085.

1992b. "'Skidding.' Downward mobility among the children of the Maoist middle class." *Modern China* 18(4):410–437.

Davis, D., R. Kraus, B. Naughton and E. Perry, 1995. (Eds.) *Urban Spaces in Contemporary China. The Potential for Autonomy and Community in Post-Mao China*. Cambridge, New York and Washington, DC: Woodrow Wilson Center Press/Cambridge University Press.

de Certeau, Michel, 1984. *The Practice of Everyday Life*. Berkeley: University of California Press.

de Glopper, Donald R., 1972. "Doing business in Lukang," in (W. E. Willmott, ed.), *Economic Organization in Chinese Society*, 297–326. Stanford: Stanford University Press.

Dicks, Anthony, 1989. "The Chinese legal system: Reforms in the balance." *China Quarterly* 119:540–576.

Dilley, Roy, 1992. "Contesting markets: A general introduction to market ideology, imagery and discourse," in (R. Dilley, ed.), *Contesting Markets. Analyses of Ideology, Discourse and Practice*, 1–34. Edinburgh: Edinburgh University Press.

Dirlik, Arif, 1996. "Critical reflections on 'Chinese capitalism' as paradigm," in (L. M. Douw and P. Post, eds.), *South China: State, Culture and Social Change during the 20th Century*, 3–17. North-Holland and Amsterdam: Royal Netherlands Academy of Arts and Sciences.

Dittmer, Lowell, 1989. "The origins of China's post-Mao reforms," in (V. Falkenheim, ed.), *Chinese Politics from Mao to Deng*, 41–65. New York: Professors World Peace Academy.

Donnithorne, Audrey, 1972. "China's cellular economy: Some economic trends since the Cultural Revolution." *China Quarterly* 52:605–619.

Douglas, Mary, and Baron Isherwood, 1979. *The World of Goods: Towards an Anthropology of Consumption*. London: Allen Lane.

Dumont, Louis, 1977. *From Mandeville to Marx. The Genesis and Triumph of Economic Ideology*. Chicago: University of Chicago Press.

    1986 [1983]. *Essays on Individualism: Modern Ideology in Anthropological Perspective*. Chicago and London: University of Chicago Press.

Dutton, Michael, 1992. "Disciplinary projects and carceral spread: Foucauldian theory and Chinese practice." *Economy and Society* 21(3):276–294 (August).

Ebrey, Patricia and James L. Watson, 1986. (Eds.) *Kinship Organization in Late Imperial China, 1000–1940*. Berkeley: University of California Press.

Elvin, Mark, 1974. "The administration of Shanghai, 1904–1914," in (M. Elvin and W. G. Skinner, eds.), *The Chinese City Between Two Worlds*, 239–62. Stanford: Stanford University Press.

    1977. "Market towns and waterways. The county of Shanghai from 1480–1910," in (W. G. Skinner, ed.), *The City in Late Imperial China*, 441–473. Stanford: Stanford University Press.

Elvin, Mark and G. William Skinner, 1974. (Eds.) *The Chinese City Between Two Worlds*. Stanford: Stanford University Press.

Esherick, Joseph W. and Jeffrey N. Wasserstrom, 1990. "Acting out democracy: Political theater in modern China," *Journal of Asian Studies* 49(4):835–865.

Far Eastern Economic Review, 1991a. "Battle of the bourses." April 4, p. 29 (Ed Paisley).

    1991b. "Coy capitalists: Peking inches closer to reform of financial system." May 9, pp. 42–43 (Tai-ming Cheung).

    1991c. "Good luck charm." August 15, p. 19 (Tai-ming Cheung).

    1991d. "Future Schlock." December 26, p. 23 (Lincoln Kaye).

    1992. "Leaning to the Right. Politburo warns of dangers from leftist deviation." March 26, p. 10 (Lincoln Kaye).

    1993a. "Ge Xiaoguang: Painter whose job it is to recreate Mao." April 15, p. 74 (Dierdre Nickerson).

    1993b. "Mao fever enriches his home town." June 10, p. 32 (Paul Mooney).

    1993c. "Rotten to the core: Monopoly of power leads to rampant corruption." September 16, pp. 16–17 (Lincoln Kaye).

    1993–1994. "Marking Mao's 100th birthday." December 30 and January 6, p. 74 (Frank Ching).

    1994a. "Bursting at the seams. Rural migrants flout urban registration system." March 10, p. 27 (Anthony Kuhn and Lincoln Kaye).

    1994b. "Intelligence. Stillborn watchdog." March 10, p. 14.

    1994c. "China. Point of order." March 17, p. 60 (Henry Sender).

    1996. "A China that can say no." Cover story, October 3 (Matt Forney, Yu Wong, Bruce Gilley).

Fardon, Richard, 1995. "Introduction: Counterworks," in (R. Fardon, ed.), *Counterworks*, 1–22. London: Routledge.

Fei Xiaotong, 1992. *From the Soil: The Foundations of Chinese Society. A Translation of Fei Xiaotong's* Xiangtu Zhougguo, trans. G. Hamilton and Wang Z. Berkeley: University of California Press.

Fewsmith, Joseph, 1985. *Party, State, and Local Elites in Republican China.*

Merchant Organization and Politics in Shanghai, 1890–1930. Honolulu: University of Hawaii Press.

Fortes, Meyer and E.E. Evans-Pritchard, 1940 (Eds.) *African Political Systems*. London and New York: Oxford University Press.

Foucault, Michel, 1979. "Governmentality." *Ideology and Consciousness* 6:5–21 (Autumn).

Freedman, Maurice, 1958. *Lineage Organization in Southeastern China*. London: Athlone Press.

1966. *Chinese Lineage and Society: Fukien and Kwangtung*. London: Athlone Press.

1970. *Family and Kinship in Chinese Society*. Stanford: Stanford University Press.

1979 [1959]. "The handling of money. A note on the background to the economic sophistication of overseas Chinese," in (G. W. Skinner, ed.), *The Study of Chinese Society. Essays by Maurice Freedman*, 22–26. Stanford: Stanford University Press.

1979 [1974]. "The politics of an old state: A view from the Chinese lineage," in (G. W. Skinner, ed.), *The Study of Chinese Society. Essays by Maurice Freedman*, 334–350. Stanford: Stanford University Press.

Fried, Morton, 1953. *The Fabric of Chinese Society*. New York: Praeger.

Friedman, Edward, Paul G. Pickowicz and Mark Selden, 1991. *Chinese Village, Socialist State*. New Haven: Yale University Press.

Frisby, David, 1986. *Fragments of Modernity. Theories of Modernity in the Work of Simmel, Kracauer and Benjamin*. Cambridge, MA: MIT Press.

Fung, Ka-iu, 1981. "The spatial development of Shanghai," in (C. Howe, ed.), *Shanghai. Revolution and Development in an Asian Metropolis*, 269–300. Cambridge: Cambridge University Press.

Gamble, Jocelyn, 1997. "Stir-fried stocks: Share dealers, trading places, and new options in contemporary Shanghai." *Modern China* 23(2):181–213.

Gardner, John, 1969. "The *Wufan* campaign in Shanghai: A study in the consolidation of urban control," in (A. Doak Barnett, ed.), *Chinese Communist Politics in Action*, 477–539. Seattle: University of Washington Press.

1981. "*Study and criticism*: The voice of Shanghai radicalism," in (C. Howe, ed.), *Shanghai. Revolution and Development in an Asian Metropolis*, 326–347. Cambridge: Cambridge University Press.

Gates, Hill, 1987. "Money for the Gods." *Modern China* 13(3):259–277.

1996. *China's Motor. A Thousand Years of Petty Capitalism*. Ithaca and London: Cornell University Press.

Gaulton, Richard, 1981. "Political mobilization in Shanghai, 1949–1951," in (C. Howe, ed.), *Shanghai. Revolution and Development in an Asian Metropolis*, 35–65. Cambridge: Cambridge University Press.

Geertz, Clifford, 1973. *The Interpretation of Cultures*. New York: Basic Books.

1976. "From the 'native' point of view: On the nature of anthropological understanding," in (K. Basso and H. Selby, eds.), *Approaches to Symbolic Anthropology*, 221–237. Albuquerque, NM: University of New Mexico Press.

1979. "Suq. The bazaar economy in Sefrou," in (C. Geertz, H. Geertz and L.

Rosen, eds.), *Meaning and Order in Moroccan Society*, 123–244. Cambridge: Cambridge University Press.

1983. *Local Knowledge*. New York: Basic Books

Glick, I. O., 1957. "A social psychological study of futures trading," Ph.D. Dissertation, University of Chicago (Sociology).

Godelier, Maurice, 1972. *Rationality and Irrationality in Economics*. London: New Left Books.

1977. *Perspectives in Marxist Anthropology*. Cambridge: Cambridge University Press.

1995. *L'Enigme du don*. Paris: Fayard.

Godement, François, 1993. *La Renaissance de l'Asie*. Paris: Editions Odile Jacob.

Gold, Thomas B., 1985. "After comradeship: Personal relations in China since the Cultural Revolution." *China Quarterly* 104:657–675.

1991. "Urban private business and China's reforms," in (R. Baum, ed.), *Reform and Reaction in Post-Mao China: The Road through Tiananmen*, 84–103. New York: Routledge.

Golde, Peggy, 1986 [1970]. *Women in the Field. Anthropological Experiences*. Berkeley: University of California Press.

Goodman, David S. G., 1981. "The Shanghai connection: Shanghai's role in national politics during the 1970s," in (C. Howe, ed.), *Shanghai. Revolution and Development in an Asian Metropolis*, 125–152. Cambridge: Cambridge University Press.

Gregory, C. A., and J. C. Altman, 1989. (Eds.) *Observing the Economy*. London: Routledge.

Gu Xiaorong, 1994. (Ed.) *Zhengquan Guanli yu Zhengquan Weigui Weifa*. [Securities Regulation and Securities Violations.] Fuzhou: Fujian People's Press.

Guan Jinsheng and Wu Zhenbiao, 1992. (Eds.) *Zhongguo Gushi Zonglan* [An Overview of the Chinese Stock Market]. Shanghai: Wenhui Press.

Gudeman, Stephen, 1986. *Economics as Culture: Models and Metaphors of Livelihood*. London:Routledge and Kegan Paul.

Guldin, Gregory and Aidan Southall, 1993. (Eds.) *Urban Anthropology in China*. Leiden and London: E.J. Brill.

Guojia Guoyou Zichan Guanli Ju Jiaoyu Chu [Education Office of the National State Assets Administration Bureau], 1991. *Xinxing Guoyou Zichan Guanli Tizhi Tansuo* [Exploring the New System of State Assets Management]. Beijing: Economic Sciences Press.

Guojia Guoyou Zichan Guanli Ju Zichan Pinggu Zhongxin [Assets Assessment Center of the National State Assets Administration Bureau], 1992. *Zichan Pinggu Gailun* [An Introduction to Assets Assessment]. Beijing: Economic Sciences Press.

Guojia Guoyou Zichan Guanli Ju Zonghe Si [National State Assets Administration Bureau General Office], 1992. (Ed.) *Guoyou Zichan Chanquan Dengji Fagui Zhidu Huibian* [Compilation of Laws and Regulations Governing the Registration of Rights to State-Owned Property]. Beijing: Economic Sciences Press.

Hao, Yen-p'ing, 1970. *The Comprador in Nineteenth Century China. Bridge Between East and West*. Cambridge, MA: Harvard University Press.

Harding, Harry, 1981. *Organizing China. The Problem of Bureaucracy, 1949–1976.* Stanford: Stanford University Press.

Harrell, Stevan, 1987. "The concept of fate in Chinese folk ideology." *Modern China* 13(1):90–109.

Hart, Keith, 1992. "Market and state after the Cold War. The informal economy reconsidered," in (R. Dilley, ed.), *Contesting Markets. Analyses of Ideology, Discourse and Practice*, 214–217. Edinburgh: Edinburgh University Press.

Hartford, Kathleen, 1985. "Socialist agriculture is dead; long live socialist agriculture! Organizational transformations in rural China," in (E. Perry and C. Wong, eds.), *The Political Economy of Reform in Post-Mao China*, 31–61. Cambridge, MA: The Council on East Asian Studies, Harvard University Press.

Henderson, Gail E., 1982. "Danwei: The Chinese Work Unit." Ph.D. Dissertation. University of Michigan (Sociology).

Henderson, Gail E. and Myron S. Cohen, 1984. *The Chinese Hospital. A Socialist Work Unit.* New Haven and London: Yale University Press.

Henriot, Christian, 1991. *Shanghai 1927–1937. Elites locales et modernisation dans la Chine nationaliste.* Paris: Editions de l'Ecole des hautes études en sciences sociales.

Heppner, Ernest G., 1993. *Shanghai Refuge. A Memoire of the World War II Jewish Ghetto.* Lincoln and London: University of Nebraska Press.

Hertz, Ellen, 1994. "Review of Hu Yebi, *China's Capital Market.*" *China Review International* 1(1):147–149.

  1996a. "The Shenzhen and Shanghai stock markets compared: A window onto changing strategies of reform," in (L. M. Douw and P. Post, eds.), *South China: State, Culture and Social Change during the 20th Century*, 85–90. Amsterdam: Royal Netherlands Academy of Arts and Sciences.

  1996b. "The Shanghai stock market: An institutional overview," in (R. Brown, ed.), *Chinese Business Enterprise* (4 vols.), vol. II: 116–132. London: Routledge.

Hodous, Lewis, 1929. *Folkways in China.* London: Probsthain.

Honig, Emily, 1992. *Creating Chinese Identity: Subei People In Shanghai, 1850–1980.* New Haven, CT: Yale University Press.

Howe, Christopher, 1968. "The supply and administration of housing in mainland China: the case of Shanghai." *China Quarterly* 10:73–97.

  1981a. (Ed.) *Shanghai. Revolution and Development in an Asian Metropolis.* Cambridge: Cambridge University Press.

  1981b. "Industrialization under conditions of long-run population stability: Shanghai's achievement and prospect," in (C. Howe, ed.), *Shanghai. Revolution and Development in an Asian Metropolis*, 153–187. Cambridge: Cambridge University Press.

Hsu, Immanuel C.Y., 1982. *China Without Mao: The Search for a New Order.* Oxford: Oxford University Press.

Hsu, Robert C., 1991. *Economic Theories in China, 1979–1988.* Cambridge: Cambridge University Press.

Hu, Hsien-chin, 1944. "The Chinese concept of 'face.'" *American Anthropologist* 46(1):45–64 (Jan.–March).

Hu, Yebi, 1993. *China's Capital Market*. Hong Kong: Chinese University Press.

Huang Wenzhi, 1989. *Gushi Xianxiang Guancha* [Observing the Stock Market Phenomenon]. Taibei: Jingji yu Shenghuo Chuban Gongsi [Economics and Life Publishing Co.] (Tianxia Ren Licai Xilie (Popular Money Management Series)).

Hwang, K., 1987. "Face and favor: The Chinese power game." *American Journal of Sociology* 92(4):944–74.

International Herald Tribune, 1992a. "For Mao, Chinese sainthood of a sort." June 3, p. 1 (Nicholas Kristof).

    1992b. "Deng's pattern takes shape: Hybrid 'capitalist totalitarianism' for China." October 20, p. 1 (Nicholas Kristof).

    1994. "Shanghai moves to crack down on speculation," Nov. 4.

    1995a. "China firm to cover loss." March 11–12.

    1995b. "China punishes 11 bankers for violating rules." March 22.

    1995c. "Would-be investor's journey into Shanghai maze." April 25 (Seth Faison).

    1995d. "*Yuan*'s rise hints that Central Bank has shifted policy." April 27.

    1995e. "Brokers quit in China." April 27.

    1995f. "China's dividend habit saps firms." May 13–14.

    1995g. "New scandal halts Shanghai bond-futures trades." May 13–14.

    1995h. "Shanghai fines firms over bond trades." May 16.

    1995i. "China issues rules to keep state firms 'clean and honest.'" May 30.

    1995j. "China version of hostile takeover." July 20.

    1995k. "Very briefly." Sept. 1.

    1995l. "China's bursting bubble." Sept. 1.

    1995m. "Traders skeptical on energy-futures plans." Sept. 22.

    1995g. "China cites bond culprits." Sept. 22.

    1995o. "Very briefly." Oct. 10.

    1995p. "Stock firm suspended." Nov. 4–5.

    1995q. "Investors like China but not Chinese stocks." Nov. 7.

    1995r. "China to ease foreigner ban." Dec. 12.

    1995s. "China can't seem to stop worrying and love its markets." Dec. 19.

    1995t. "The great Shanghai shakedown: Growing pains of a new market." Dec. 22.

    1995u. "'The great Shanghai shakedown: 'Capitalism with Chinese characteristics.'" Dec. 22.

    1996a. "Beijing imposes strict controls on economic news." Jan. 17 (Steven Mufson).

    1996b. "China affirms curbs on market wires." Jan. 19.

    1996c. "Government edging towards capitalism," Jan. 20–22.

    1996d. "Very briefly." March 6.

    1996e. "Merger finally weds leading Shanghai securities houses." April 25 (Seth Faison).

    1996f. "Chinese results stump investors." May 4–5.

    1996g. "Very briefly." May 7.

    1996h. "Lacking rules, China plays difficult market game." May 28 (Kevin Murphy).

    1996i. "China wires up finance data." June 24.

    1996j. "Turf battle delays law on Chinese securities." Sept. 18.

1996k. "Goodyear holds talks on buying 20% stake in Chinese tiremaker." Nov. 16–17.

Ivory, Paul E. and William R. Lavely, 1977. "Rustication, demographic changes and development in Shanghai." *Asian Survey* 17:445.

Jacobs, Bruce, 1979. "A preliminary model of particularistic ties in Chinese political alliances: kan-ch'ing and kuan-hsi in a rural Taiwanese township." *China Quarterly* 78:237–273.

Jankowiak, William R., 1993. *Sex, Death and Hierarchy in a Chinese City. An Anthropological Account.* New York: Columbia University Press.

Jefferson, Gary H. and Thomas G. Rawski, 1992. "Unemployment, underemployment, and employment policy in China's cities." *Modern China* 19(1):42–71.

Jiang Lemin, Li Xianpei and Li Shaodan, 1991. (Eds.) *Guoyou Zichan Guanli Tonglun* [A General Survey of State Assets Administration]. Beijing: Economics Press.

Jin Jiandong, Xiao Zhouji and Xu Shuxin, 1991. (Eds.) *Zhongguo Zhengquan Shichang* [China's Securities Market]. Beijing: China Economic Press.

Jones, Susan, 1974. "The *Ningpo Pang* and financial power in Shanghai," in (M. Elvin and W. G. Skinner, eds.), *The Chinese City Between Two Worlds*, 73–96. Stanford: Stanford University Press.

Jornal do Brasil (Agence France Presse), 1992. "China reprime 'revolta dos investidores.'" August 12, p. 13.

Journal of Asian Studies, 1995. "Coping with Shanghai: Means to survival and success in the early twentieth century – A symposium." *Journal of Asian Studies* 54(1):3–123.

Kallgren, Joyce K., 1969. "Social welfare and China's industrial workers," in (A. Doak Barnett, ed.), *Chinese Communist Politics in Action*, 540–573. Seattle: University of Washington Press.

Keith, Ronald C., 1991. "Chinese politics and the new theory of 'rule of law.'" *China Quarterly* 125:109–118.

Kilani, Mondher, 1983. *Les Cultes du cargo mélanésiens: Mythe et rationalité en anthropologie.* Lausanne, Switzerland: Editions d'en bas.

Kim, Ipyong J., 1969. "Mass mobilization policies and techniques developed in the period of the Chinese Soviet Republic," in (A. Doak Barnett, ed.), *Chinese Communist Politics in Action*, 78–98. Seattle: University of Washington Press.

Kindleberger, Charles P., 1989 [1978]. *Manias, Panics, and Crashes: A History of Financial Crises.* New York: Basic Books.

King, Ambrose Yeo-chi, 1991. "*Kuan-hsi* and network building: A sociological interpretation," in *The Living Tree: The Changing Meanings of Being Chinese Today. Daedalus* 120(2):63–84.

Klausner, Michael, 1984. "Sociological theory and the behavior of financial markets," in (P.A. Adler and P. Adler, eds.), *The Social Dynamics of Financial Markets*, 57–81. Greenwich, CT: JAI Press.

Kornai, Janos, 1980. *Economics of Shortage.* Amsterdam and New York: North Holland Publishing Company.

Kraus, Richard C., 1982. *Class Conflict in Chinese Socialism.* New York: Columbia University Press.

Kuhn, Philip A., 1984. "Chinese concepts of class," in (J. Watson, ed.), *Class and Social Stratification in Post-Revolutionary China*. Cambridge: Cambridge University Press.

1990. *Soulstealers: The Chinese Sorcery Scare of 1768*. Cambridge, MA: Harvard University Press.

Kung, James Kaising, 1992. "Food and agriculture in post-reform China: The marketed surplus problem revisited." *Modern China* 18(2):138–170.

Lampton, David, 1987. (Ed.) *Policy Implementation in Post-Mao China*. Berkeley: University of California Press.

Lardy, Nicholas R., 1992. *Foreign Trade and Economic Reform in China, 1978–1990*. Cambridge: Cambridge University Press.

Larson, Wendy, 1989. "Realism, modernism, and the anti-'Spiritual Pollution' campaign in China." *Modern China* 15(1):37–71.

Latour, Bruno, 1991. *Nous n'avons jamais été modernes: Essai d'anthropologie symétrique*. Paris: La Découverte.

Le Courrier (Associated Press), 1992. "Des émeutes à la suite de vente d'actions." August 11.

Le Monde, 1992. "Contradictions chinoises. Les troubles de Shenzhen illustrent la coupure entre le pouvoir et la société." August 14, p. 1 (Francis Déron).

LeBon, Gustave, 1895. [1960]. *The Crowd: A Study of the Popular Mind*. New York: Viking Press.

LeClair, Edward E., Jr., 1962. "Economic theory and economic anthropology." *American Anthropologist* 64:1179–1203.

Lee, Edmond, 1991. "A bourgeois alternative? The Shanghai arguments for a Chinese capitalism: the 1920s and the 1980s," in (B. Womack, ed.), *Contemporary Chinese Politics in Historical Perspective*, 90–126. Cambridge: Cambridge University Press.

Lejeune, Robert, 1984. "False security: Deviance and the stock market," in (P.A. Adler and P. Adler, eds.), *The Social Dynamics of Financial Markets*, 173–194. Greenwich, CT: JAI Press.

Leng, Shao-chuan, 1989. "Legal reform in post-Mao China: A tentative assessment," in (Victor C. Falkenheim, ed.), *Chinese Politics from Mao to Deng*, 203–235. New York: Paragon House.

Levenson, Joseph R., 1967. "The province, the nation, and the world: The problem of Chinese identity," in (A. Feuerwerker, R. Murphey and M. Wrights, eds.), *Approaches to Modern Chinese History*, 268–288. Berkeley: University of California Press.

1971. *Revolution and Cosmopolitanism: The Western Stage and the Chinese Stages*. Berkeley: University of California Press.

Lewis, John Wilson, 1971. (Ed.) *The City in Communist China*. Stanford: Stanford University Press.

Lewis, Michael, 1989. *Liar's Poker. Rising through the Wreckage on Wall Street*. New York: Penguin Books.

Li, Bin, 1993. "*Danwei* culture as urban culture in modern China: The base of Beijing from 1949–1979," in (G. Guldin and A. Southall, eds.), *Urban Anthropology in China*, 345–52. Leiden and London: E. J. Brill.

Li Xianpei and Li Shaodan, 1991. "Woguo Guoyou Zichan Guanli Xin Tizhi de Chubu Tansuo" ["A preliminary exploration of the new system of state assets management in our country"], in *Xinxing Guoyou Zichang Guanli Tizhi Tansuo* [Exploring the New System of State Assets Management], 22–35. Beijing: Economics Press.

Li Yining, 1986. "Woguo suoyouzhi gaigede shexiang" ["A tentative outline of ownership reforms for China."] *Renmin Ribao* (*People's Daily*), Sept. 26, 1986. Translated in *Chinese Economic Studies* 22(2): 72–81 (Winter 1988–89) (S. Rosen and G. Zou, eds.).

Libération, 1992. "La Chine adopte le capitalisme rouge." Oct. 19, p. 2 (Caroline Puel).

Lieberthal, Kenneth, 1995. *Governing China: From Revolution through Reform.* New York: W.W. Norton.

Link, Perry, Richard Madsen and Paul G. Pickowicz, 1989. (Eds.) *Unofficial China: Popular Culture and Thought in the People's Republic.* Boulder, CO: Westview Press.

Liu Xinwu, 1990. "Bus Aria," in *Black Walls and Other Stories.* D. Cohn, trans. Hong Kong: Rendition Paperbacks.

Lu Feng, 1989. "Danwei: Yizhong teshude shehui zuzhi xingshi" ["The work unit: a particular form of social organization"]. *Zhongguo Shehui Kexue* [Chinese Social Science] 55:71–88.

Lu, Hanlong, 1992. "On the intellectual environment for theory building in Chinese sociology," in *SASS Papers* (4): 431–442. Shanghai: Shanghai Academy of Social Sciences Publishing House.

Lubasz, Heinz, 1992. "Adam Smith and the Invisible Hand – of the Market?," in (R. Dilley, ed.), *Contesting Markets. Analyses of Ideology, Discourse and Practice*, 37–56. Edinburgh: Edinburgh University Press.

Lubman, Stanley B., 1994. "Introduction," in (P. Potter, ed.), *Domestic Law Reforms in Post-Mao China*, 3–16. Armonk, NY: M.E. Sharpe.

1996. (Ed.) *China's Legal Reforms.* Oxford: Clarendon/Oxford University Press.

Mac Elderry, Andrea L., 1976. *Shanghai Old-Style Banks (*Ch'ien-chuang*), 1880–1935. A Traditional Institution in a Changing Society.* Ann Arbor: Michigan Papers in Chinese Studies (no. 25).

Mackay, Charles, 1980 [1841]. *Extraordinary Popular Delusions and the Madness of Crowds.* New York: Crown Trade Paperbacks.

Mair, Lucy, 1948. *Australia in New Guinea.* London: Christophers.

Malinowski, Bronislaw, 1961 [1922]. *Argonauts of the Western Pacific.* New York: E. P. Dutton and Co.

1926. *Crime and Custom in Savage Society.* London: Kegan Paul, Trench, Trubner and Co. Ltd.

Mandeville, Bernard, 1924 [1714]. *The Fable of the Bees.* Oxford: Clarendon Press.

Manion, Melanie, 1992. "Politics and policy in post-Mao cadre retirement." *China Quarterly* 129:1–25.

Marcus, George E., 1990. "Imagining the whole. Ethnography's contemporary efforts to situate itself." *Critique of Anthropology* 9(3): 7–30.

Maturi, Richard J., 1993. *Stock Picking. The 11 Best Tactics for Beating the Market.* New York: McGraw-Hill.

Mauss, Marcel, 1967 [1923–1924]. *The Gift. Forms and Functions of Exchange in Archaic Societies.* New York: W.W. Norton.

Mayer, Martin, 1988. *Markets.* New York and London: W. W. Norton and Co.

Meaney, Constance S., 1989. "Market reform in a Leninist system: Some trends in the distribution of power, status, and money in urban China." *Studies in Comparative Communism* 22:203–220.

Meisner, Maurice. 1977. *Mao's China. A History of the People's Republic.* New York: The Free Press.

Modern China, 1992. Symposium: "Institutional boundaries, structural change, and economic reform in China." L. Putterman, guest ed. *Modern China* 18(1):3–93 (Part 1), 18(2):138–227 (Part 2).

   1993. Symposium: "Public sphere/civil society in China? Paradigmatic issues in Chinese studies III." *Modern China* 19(2):107–240 (April).

Moore, R. L., 1988. "Face and networks in urban Hong Kong." *City and Society* 2:50–59.

Murphey, Rhoads, 1953. *Shanghai, Key to Modern China.* Cambridge, Cambridge University Press.

   1970. *The Treaty Ports and China's Modernization. What Went Wrong?* Ann Arbor: Michigan Papers in Chinese Studies (no. 7).

   1977. *The Outsiders. The Western Experience in India and China.* Ann Arbor: University of Michigan Press.

Nader, Laura, 1969. "Up the anthropologist – Perspectives gained from studying up," in (D. Hymes, ed.), *Reinventing Anthropology*, 284–311. New York: Vintage Books.

   1978. "Taxation in other societies." Courses by newspaper, sponsored by the California Tax Reform Association Foundation and the California Council for the Humanities in Public Policy, pp. 26–27.

   1986. "Enforcement strategies and the catch they yield at the SEC. Review of Shapiro: *Wayward Capitalists – Target of the Securities and Exchange Commission.*" *Harvard Law Review* 99(6):1362–1373 (April).

   1990. "Orientalism, occidentalism and the control of women." *Cultural Dynamics* 2(3):149–159.

Nathan, Andrew, 1985. *Chinese Democracy.* Berkeley: University of California Press.

   1993. "Is Chinese culture distinctive? – A review article." *Journal of Asian Studies* 52(4): 923–936.

Nation, The, 1992. "Capitalist leap: China plays the market." Dec. 14, pp. 727–743 (Orville Schell and Todd Lappin).

Naughton, Barry, 1985. "False starts and second wind: Financial reforms in China's industrial system," in (E. Perry and C. Wong, eds.), *The Political Economy of Reform in Post-Mao China*, 223–252. Cambridge, MA: The Council on East Asian Studies, Harvard University Press.

   1991. "Why has economic reform led to inflation?" *American Economic Review, Papers and Proceedings*, 81(2):207–11.

   1992. "Implications of the state monopoly over industry and its relaxation." *Modern China* 18(1):14–41.

New York Times, 1995. "President of Shanghai firm quits after trading scandal." April 27 (Seth Faison).

Oi, Jean C., 1986. "Peasant households between plan and market. Cadre control over agricultural inputs." *Modern China* 12(2):230–251.

Orwell, George, 1949. *1984*. New York: Plume Books, Harcourt Brace Jovanovich.

Palmer, Michael, 1996. "The re-emergence of family law in post-Mao China: Marriage, divorce and reproduction," in (S. Lubman, ed), *China's Legal Reforms*, 110–134. Oxford: Clarendon/Oxford University Press.

Parry, Jonathan, and Maurice Bloch, 1989. (Eds.) *Money and the Morality of Exchange*. Cambridge: Cambridge University Press.

Pearson, Margaret M., 1991. *Joint Ventures in the People's Republic of China. The Control of Foreign Direct Investment Under Socialism*. Princeton, NJ: Princeton University Press.

Pellow, Deborah, 1993. "No place to live, no place to love: Coping in Shanghai," in (G. Guldin and A. Southall, eds.), *Urban Anthropology in China*, 396–424. Leiden and London: E. J. Brill.

Perry, Elizabeth, 1993. *Shanghai On Strike*. Stanford, CA: Stanford University Press.

1995. "Labor's battle for political space: The role of worker associations in contemporary China," in (D. Davis, R. Kraus, B. Naughton and E. Perry, eds.), *Urban Spaces in Contemporary China. The Potential for Autonomy and Community in Post-Mao China*, 302–325. Cambridge, New York and Washington, DC: Woodrow Wilson Center Press/Cambridge University Press.

Perry, Elizabeth J. and Li Xun, 1997. *Proletarian Power. Shanghai in the Cultural Revolution*. Boulder, CO: Westview Press.

Perry, Elizabeth J. and Christine Wong, 1985a. "The political economy of reform in post-Mao China: Causes, content, and consequences," in (E. Perry and C. Wong, eds.), *The Political Economy of Reform in Post-Mao China*, 1–27. Cambridge, MA: The Council on East Asian Studies, Harvard University Press.

1985b. (Eds.) *The Political Economy of Reform in Post-Mao China*. Cambridge, MA: The Council on East Asian Studies, Harvard University Press.

Phelps, Edmund S., 1985. *Political Economy. An Introductory Text*. New York: W.W. Norton.

Pieke, Frank, 1996. *The Ordinary and the Extraordinary: An Anthropological Study of Chinese Reform and the 1989 People's Movement in Beijing*. London and New York: Kegan Paul International.

Pigg, Stacy Leigh, 1996. "The credible and the credulous: The question of 'villagers' beliefs' in Nepal." *Current Anthropology* 11(2): 160–201.

Polanyi, Karl, 1944. *The Great Transformation*. New York: Rinehart.

1947. "Our obsolete market mentality." *Commentary* 3:109–117.

1957. "The economy as instituted process," in (K. Polanyi, C.W. Arensburg and H.W. Pearson, eds.), *Trade and Market in Early Empires*. New York: Free Press.

Potter, Jack M., 1968. *Capitalism and the Chinese Peasant: Social and Economic Change in a Hong Kong Village*. Berkeley: University of California Press.

1970. "Wind, water, bones, and souls: The religious life of the Cantonese peasant." *Journal of Oriental Studies* 3(1): 139–153.

Potter, Pitman B., 1992. "The legal framework for securities markets in China: The challenge of maintaining state control and inducing investor confidence." *China Law Reporter* 7(2):61–94.

Potter, Sulamith Heins, 1983. "The position of peasants in modern China's social order." *Modern China* 9:464–99.

   1987. "Birth planning in rural China: A cultural account," in (N. Scheper-Hughes, ed.), *Child Survival: Anthropological Perspectives on the Treatment and Maltreatment of Children*. Dordrecht: D. Reidel.

   1988. "The cultural construction of emotions in rural Chinese social life." *Ethos* 16(2):181–208.

Potter, Sulamith Heins and Jack M. Potter, 1990. *China's Peasants: The Anthropology of a Revolution*. New York and Cambridge: Cambridge University Press.

Putterman, Louis, 1992. "Institutional boundaries, structural change, and economic reform in China. An Introduction," *Modern China* 18(1):3–13.

Pye, Lucian W., 1981. "Foreword." in (C. Howe, ed.), *Shanghai. Revolution and Development in an Asian Metropolis*, xi–xvi. Cambridge: Cambridge University Press.

   1992. *The Spirit of Chinese Politics*. Cambridge, MA: Harvard University Press.

Rabinow, Paul, 1977. *Reflections on Fieldwork in Morocco*. Berkeley: University of California Press.

Ragvald, Lars, 1981. "The emergence of 'worker-writers' in Shanghai," in (C. Howe, ed.), *Shanghai. Revolution and Development in an Asian Metropolis*, 301–325. Cambridge: Cambridge University Press.

Rankin, Mary Backus, 1971. *Early Chinese Revolutionaries: Radical Intellectuals in Shanghai and Chekiang, 1902–1911*. Cambridge, MA: Harvard University Press.

Redding, S. Gordon, 1990. *The Spirit of Chinese Capitalism*. Berlin and New York: Walter de Gruyter.

Reynolds, Bruce L., 1981. "Changes in the standard of living of Shanghai industrial workers, 1930–1973," in (C. Howe, ed.), *Shanghai. Revolution and Development in an Asian Metropolis*, 222–240. Cambridge: Cambridge University Press.

Riskin, Carl, 1987. *China's Political Economy: The Quest for Development since 1949*. Oxford: Oxford University Press.

Rocca, Jean-Louis, 1992. "Corruption and its shadow: An anthropological view of corruption in China," *China Quarterly* 130:402–416.

   1996. "L'Entreprise, l'entrepreneur et le cadre. Une approche de l'économie chinoise." *Les Etudes du CERI*, no. 14. Paris: Centre d'études et de recherches internationales, Fondation nationale des sciences politiques.

Rong Wenzuo, 1986. "Establishing socialist joint stock companies." *Jingji Yanjiu* [Economic Research], January, pp. 11–16. Translated in *Chinese Economic Studies* 20(3) (Spring 1987).

Rose, A. M., 1951. "Rumor in the stock market." *Public Opinion Quarterly* 15:461–486.

   1966. "A social psychological approach to the stock market." *Kyklos* 19:267–287.

Sahlins, Marshall, 1969. "Economic anthropology and anthropological economics," *Social Science Information* 8(5):13–33.

   1976. *Culture and Practical Reason*. Chicago and London: University of Chicago Press.

Said, Edward W., 1978. *Orientalism*. New York: Vintage Books.

Sanford, James C., 1976. "Chinese commercial organization and behavior in Shanghai of the late nineteenth and early twentieth centuries," Ph.D. dissertation, Harvard University (History).

Schein, Louisa, 1993. "Popular culture and the production of difference: The Miao and China," Ph.D. dissertation, University of California, Berkeley (Anthropology).

Schram, Stuart R., 1984. "Classes, old and new, in Mao Zedong's thought, 1949–1976," in (J. L. Watson, ed.), *Class and Social Stratification in Post-Revolution China*, 29–55. Cambridge: Cambridge University Press.

Schurmann, Franz, 1968 [1966]. *Ideology and Organization in Communist China*. Berkeley: University of California Press.

Schwartz, Benjamin, 1985. *China's Cultural Values*. Occasional Paper no. 18, Center for Asian Studies, Arizona State University, Tempe, AZ.

Shanghai Jingji Nianjian [*Shanghai Economic Year Book*], 1992. Shanghai: Shanghai Academy of Social Sciences.

Shanghai Zhengquan [*Shanghai Securities Weekly*], 1992a. "Shanghai zengjia gupiao nian faxingliang" [Shanghai increases its yearly rate of share issuing]. March 16 (no. 36), p. 1.

1992b. "Shanghai zhengjiaosuo meiri gushi hangqing" [Shanghai Securities Exchange daily stock market report]. June 8 (no. 50), p. 3.

1993a. "Editorial." Dec. 31, p. 1.

1993b. "Shanghai zhengjiaosuo zhaiquan hangqing ribao" [Shanghai Securities Exchange daily bond market report]. Dec. 31, p. 3.

Shanghai Zhengquan Nianjian [*Shanghai Securities Year Book*], 1992. Shanghai: Renmin Chubanshe [People's Press].

1993. Shanghai: Renmin Chubanshe [People's Press].

Shirk, Susan L., 1984. "The decline of virtuocracy in China," in (J. L. Watson, ed.), *Class and Social Stratification in Post-Revolution China*, 56–83. Cambridge: Cambridge University Press.

Shue, Vivienne, 1988. *The Reach of the State. Sketches of the Chinese Body Politic*. Stanford, CA: Stanford University Press.

Sidel, Mark, 1995. "Dissident and liberal legal scholars and organizations in Beijing and the Chinese state in the 1980s," in (D. Davis, R. Kraus, B. Naughton and E. Perry, eds.), *Urban Spaces in Contemporary China. The Potential for Autonomy and Community in Post-Mao China*, 326–346. Cambridge, New York and Washington, DC: Woodrow Wilson Center Press/Cambridge University Press.

Silin, Robert, 1972. "Marketing and credit in a Hong Kong wholesale market," in (W. Willmott, ed.), *Economic Organization in Chinese Society*, 327–353. Stanford: Stanford University Press.

Simmel, Georg, 1990 [1907]. *The Philosophy of Money*. London: Routledge.

Siu, Helen, 1989a. *Agents and Victims in South China. Accomplices in Rural Revolution*. New Haven and London: Yale University Press.

1989b. "Socialist peddlers and princes in a Chinese market town," *American Ethnologist* 16(2):195–212.

Smart, Alan, 1993. "Gifts, bribes and *guanxi* – a reconsideration of Bourdieu's social capital." *Cultural Anthropology* 8(3):388–408.

Smith, Adam, 1976 [1759]. *The Theory of Moral Sentiments*. Oxford: Oxford University Press.
1980 [1776]. *An Inquiry into the Nature and Causes of the Wealth of Nations*. London and New York: Penguin Classics.
Smith, Arthur H., 1894. *Chinese Characteristics*. New York and Chicago: F. H. Revell.
Solinger, Dorothy J., 1983. "Marxism and the market in socialist China: The reforms of 1979–1980 in context," in (V. Nee and D. Mozingo, eds.), *State and Society in Contemporary China*, 194–219. Ithaca, NY: Cornell University Press.
1984a. *Chinese Business Under Socialism. The Politics of Domestic Commerce, 1949–1980*. Berkeley: University of California Press.
1984b. (Ed.) *Three Visions of Chinese Socialism*. Boulder, CO: Westview Press.
1993. *China's Transition from Socialism: State Legacies and Market Reforms, 1980–1990*. Armonk, NJ: M.E. Sharpe.
South China Morning Post, 1992a. "Inquiry on Shenzhen chaos." August 12, p. 1.
1992b. "Pledge to reopen exchange." August 12.
1992c. "Pledge to end stocks corruption." August 13, p. 1.
1992d. "Shenzhen chaos may help speed reforms." August 13, *Business Post*, p. 2 (John Kohut).
1992e. "A fair share of greed." August 14, *Saturday Review*, p. 1 (Christine McGee and Kent Chen).
1992f. "Making money out of mayhem." August 16, *Sunday Money*, p. 2.
Southall, Aidan, 1993a. "Introduction: Transcending the urban–rural dichotomy," in (G. Guldin and A. Southall, eds.), *Urban Anthropology in China*, 17–18. Leiden and London: E. J. Brill.
1993b. "Urban theory and the Chinese city," in (G. Guldin and A. Southall, eds.), *Urban Anthropology in China*, 19–40. Leiden and London: E. J. Brill.
1993c. "Introduction: Social, economic and institutional life in city hierarchies and networks," in (G. Guldin and A. Southall, eds.), *Urban Anthropology in China*, 341–344. Leiden and London: E. J. Brill.
Spence, Jonathan D., 1966. *Ts'ao Yin and the K'ang-hsi Emperor. Bondservant and Master*. New Haven and London: Yale University Press.
1990. *The Search for Modern China*. New York and London: W.W. Norton.
Stacey, Judith, 1983. *Patriarchy and Socialist Revolution in China*. Berkeley: University of California Press.
Standard, The, 1992. "Police open fire as mobs rampage." August 11, p. 1 (Kin Yu).
Stearns, Linda Brewster, 1990. "Capital market effects on external control of corporations," in (S. Zukin and P. DiMaggio, eds.), *Structures of Capital*, 175–201. Cambridge: Cambridge University Press.
Stockman, Norman, 1992. "Market, plan and structured social inequality in China," in (R. Dilley, ed.), *Contesting Markets. Analyses of Ideology, Discourse and Practice*, 260–276. Edinburgh: Edinburgh University Press.
Strathern, Marilyn, 1988. (Ed.) *The Gender of the Gift: Problems with Women and Problems with Society in Melanesia*. Berkeley: University of California Press.
Tan Sen and Dun Li, 1993. "Urban development and crime in China," in (G.

Guldin and A. Southall, eds.), *Urban Anthropology in China*, 353–357. Leiden and London: E. J. Brill.

Tang Gongzhao and Gu Peidong, 1988. "The contract system will be turning into a shareholding system." *Zhongguo Jingji Tizhi Gaige [China Economic System Reform]* 12:27–29. Translated in JPRS-CAR-89–016:9–12, Feb. 27, 1989.

Tarascio, Vincent, 1984. "Economic theories of the market: Random or non-random walk?," in (P.A. Adler and P. Adler, eds.) *The Social Dynamics of Financial Markets*, 41–55. Greenwich, CT: JAI Press.

ter Haar, Barend, 1993. "Guan Yu as a demon queller." Presentation at the Second Annual Meeting of the European China Anthropology Network, Zurich, Dec. 7–10.

Thorton, Robert J., 1992. "The rhetoric of ethnographic holism," in (G. Marcus, ed.), *Rereading Cultural Anthropology*, 15–33. Durham, NC: Duke University Press.

Tu Wei-Ming, 1991. (Ed.) "The living tree. The changing meaning of being Chinese today." *Daedalus* (Spring) 28.

van Maanen, Jon, 1988. *Tales of the Field. On Writing Ethnography*. Chicago and London: University of Chicago Press.

von Senger, Harro, 1985. "Recent developments in the relations between State and Party norms in the People's Republic of China," in (S. R. Schram, ed.), *The Scope of State Power in China*, 171–207. London and Hong Kong: The Chinese University Press and St. Martin's Press.

1991. *The Book of Stratagems (Tactics for Triumph and Survival)*. New York and London: Viking Penguin.

Vucinic, Verna, 1993. "Ideology and pragmatism in China's urban land reform during the 1980s," in (G. Guldin and A. Southall, eds.), *Urban Anthropology in China*, 216–242. London and Leiden: E. J. Brill.

Wakeman, Frederic, Jr., 1973. *History and Will. Philosophical Perspectives of Mao Tse-Tung's Thought*. Berkeley: University of California Press.

1977. "Rebellion and revolution: The study of popular movements in Chinese history." *Journal of Asian Studies* 36(2):202–237.

1988. "Policing modern Shanghai." *China Quarterly* 115:408–440.

Wakeman, Frederic E., Jr. and Wen-Hsin Yeh, 1992. (Eds.) *Shanghai Sojourners*. China Research Monograph, No. 40. Berkeley: Institute for East Asian Studies.

Walder, Andrew, 1986. *Communist Neo-Traditionalism: Work and Authority in Chinese Industry*. Berkeley: University of California Press.

Wallace, Anthony F.C., 1956. "Revitalization movements." *American Anthropologist* 58:264–281.

Wang, Gungwu, 1991. *The Chineseness of China: Selected Essays*. Hong Kong: Oxford University Press.

Wasserstrom, Jeffrey N. and Liu Xinyong, 1995. "Student associations and mass movements," in (D. Davis, R. Kraus, B. Naughton and E. Perry, eds.), *Urban Spaces in Contemporary China. The Potential for Autonomy and Community in Post-Mao China*, 362–393. Cambridge, New York and Washington, DC: Woodrow Wilson Center Press/Cambridge University Press.

Watson, James L., 1982. "Chinese kinship reconsidered: Anthropological perspectives on historical research." *China Quarterly* 92:589–622.

1984a. "Class and class formation in Chinese society," in (J. L. Watson, ed.), *Class and Social Stratification in Post-Revolutionary China*, 1–15. Cambridge: Cambridge University Press.

1984b. (Ed.) *Class and Social Stratification in Post-Revolutionary China*. Cambridge: Cambridge University Press.

1985. "Standardizing the Gods: The promotion of T'ien Hou ('Empress of Heaven') along the South China coast, 960–1960," in (David Johnson, Andrew J. Nathan and Evelyn S. Rawski, eds.), *Popular Culture in Late Imperial China*, 292–324. Berkeley and Los Angeles: University of California Press.

1987. "From the common pot: Feasting with equals in Chinese society." *Anthropos* 82:389–401.

Watson, Rubie S., 1985. *Inequality Among Brothers: Class and Kinship in South China*. New York: Cambridge University Press.

Wei, Peh-T'i, 1987. *Shanghai: Crucible of Modern China*. Hong Kong: Oxford University Press.

Wei Wenyuan, 1993. "1992 nian shanghai zhengquan jiaoyisuo huigu yu zhan-wang" [The Shanghai Stock Exchange in 1992: Looking back and looking forward], in *Shanghai Zhengquan Nianjian (Shanghai Securities Yearbook)*, 7–10. Shanghai: Shanghai Shehui Kexue Yuan Chubanshe [Shanghai Academy of Social Sciences Press].

Weimer, Calla, 1992. "Price reform and structural change: Distributional impediments to allocative gains." *Modern China* 18(2):171–196.

Wen Hui Bao, 1992a. "Zhiliang gongzuo yao chang-zhua-bu-xie" [We must hold fast to the need for quality work]. April 30.

1992b. "Si le" lun. March 22.

White, Gordon, 1976. *The Politics of Class and Class Origin: The Case of the Cultural Revolution*. Sydney: Australia National University Press.

White, Lynn T. III, 1981. "Shanghai–suburb relations, 1949–1966," in (C. Howe, ed.), *Shanghai. Revolution and Development in an Asian Metropolis*, 241–268. Cambridge: Cambridge University Press.

1984. "Bourgeois radicalism in the 'New Class' of Shanghai, 1949–1969," in (J. L. Watson, ed.), *Class and Social Stratification in Post-Revolutionary China*, 142–174. Cambridge: Cambridge University Press.

Whiting, Susan H., 1993. "The comfort of the collective: The political economy of rural enterprise in Shanghai." Paper presented at the Annual Meetings of the Association for Asian Studies (March).

Whyte, Martin King, 1993. "Adaptation of rural family patterns to urban life in Chengdu," in (G. Guldin and A. Southall, eds.), *Urban Anthropology in China*, 358–386. Leiden and London: E. J. Brill.

Whyte, Martin K. and William L. Parish, 1984. *Urban Life in Contemporary China*. Chicago: University of Chicago Press.

Wilson, Richard W., 1992. *Compliance Ideologies: Rethinking Political Culture*. Cambridge: Cambridge University Press.

Wolf, Arthur P., 1978. "Gods, ghosts, and ancestors," in (Arthur P. Wolf, ed.), *Studies in Chinese Society*, 130–182. Stanford: Stanford University Press.

Wolf, Margery, 1985. *Revolution Postponed: Women in Contemporary China*. Stanford, CA: Stanford University Press.

Wong, Christine P.W., 1985. "Material allocation and decentralization: Impact of the local sector on industrial reform," in (E. Perry and C. Wong, eds.), *The Political Economy of Reform in Post-Mao China*, 252–278. Cambridge, MA: The Council on East Asian Studies, Harvard University Press.

    1992. "Fiscal reform and local industrialization. The problematic sequencing of reform in post-Mao China." *Modern China* 18(2):197–227.

World Bank, 1988. *China. Finance and Investment*. Washington, DC: The World Bank.

    1990. *China. Between Plan and Market*. Washington, DC: The World Bank.

    1992. *China. Reform and the Role of the Plan in the 1990s*. Washington, DC: The World Bank.

Wu Jianbing, 1988. "Guanyu gufenzhi de falu sikao" [Legal reflections on the stock system], *Zhongguo Faxue* [*Law in China*] 2:60–65.

Wu Jiaxing and Jin Lizuo, 1985. "Establishing a stockholding system for enterprise." *Jingji fazhan yu tizhi gaige* [*Economic Development and Structural Reform*] 12. Translated in *Chinese Economic Studies* 23(1) (Fall 1989).

Wylie, Raymond F., 1981. "Shanghai dockers in the Cultural Revolution: the interplay of political and economic issues," in (C. Howe, ed.), *Shanghai. Revolution and Development in an Asian Metropolis*, 91–124. Cambridge: Cambridge University Press.

Xia, Mei, Jianhai Lin and Phillip D. Grub, 1992. *The Re-Emerging Securities Market in China*. Westport, CT: Quorum Books.

Xu Jing'an, 1987. "The stock-share system: A new avenue for China's economic reform," *Journal of Comparative Economics* 11:509–514.

Yan, Yunxiang, 1996. *The Flow of Gifts: Reciprocity and Social Networks in a Chinese Village*. Stanford: Stanford University Press.

Yang, Martin C., 1945. *A Chinese Village: Taitou, Shantung province*. New York: Columbia University Press.

Yang, Mayfair Mei-Hui, 1989. "The gift economy and state power in China." *Comparative Studies in Society and History* 31:25–54.

    1994. *Gifts, Favors and Banquets. The Art of Social Relationships in China*. Ithaca: Cornell University Press.

Zhang, Zhongli (Chang Chung-li), 1956. *The Chinese Gentry. Studies of their Role in Nineteenth Century Chinese Society*. Seattle: University of Washington Press.

    1990. (Ed.) *Jindai shanghai chengshi yanjiu* [Research on Modern Urban Shanghai]. Shanghai: Renmin Chubanshe.

Zhengquan Shichang [*Securities Market*], 1992. Beijing: Stock Exchange Executive Council.

Zhonggong Shenzhen Shiwei Xuanchuanbu [China Shenzhen Bureau of Propaganda], 1992. *Deng Xiaoping yu Shenzhen. Yijiujiuer chun* [Deng Xiaoping and Shenzhen. Spring 1992]. Shenzhen, PRC: Haitian Press.

Zhou, Daming, 1993. "An approach to the problem of population movement and cultural adaptation in the urbanizing Pearl River Delta," in (G. Guldin and A. Southall, eds.), *Urban Anthropology in China*, 205–215. Leiden and London: E. J. Brill.

Zizek, Slavoj, 1989. *The Sublime Object of Ideology*. London and New York: Verso.

Zukin, Sharon and Paul DiMaggio, 1990. (Eds.) *Structures of Capital: The Social Organization of the Economy.* Cambridge: Cambridge University Press.

Zuo Mu, 1986. "An exploration into several problems created by the restructuring of the system of ownership," *Jingji Yanjiu* [*Economic Research*] Jan., 6–10. Translated in *Chinese Economic Studies* 20(3) (Spring 1987).

Index

Cambridge Studies in Social and Cultural Anthropology

*available in paperback